Scottish cinema

MANCHESTER
1824

Manchester University Press

Scottish cinema

Texts and contexts

Christopher Meir

Manchester University Press

The right of Christopher Meir to be identified as the author of this work has been asserted by him in accordance with the Copyright, Designs and Patents Act 1988.

Published by Manchester University Press
Altrincham Street, Manchester M1 7JA
www.manchesteruniversitypress.co.uk

British Library Cataloguing-in-Publication Data
A catalogue record for this book is available from the British Library

Library of Congress Cataloging-in-Publication Data applied for

ISBN   978 0 7190 8635 9   hardback

First published 2015

Typeset in 10/12pt Sabon
by Graphicraft Limited, Hong Kong
Printed in Great Britain
by TJ International Ltd, Padstow

Contents

List of illustrations

Acknowledgements

This book began as a project in the Department of Film and Television Studies at the University of Warwick and I am grateful to the University for supporting this research by awarding me a Postgraduate Research Fellowship as well as a Humanities Centre Research Fellowship. I am also grateful to the Department itself for providing me with the resources to carry out this research, the opportunity to teach some of this material whilst a graduate student and above all else for fostering the richest intellectual and collegial environment that one could hope for as a student. I would also like to thank various members of the department's faculty for commenting on early drafts of the research. Thanks, especially, goes to Charlotte Brunsdon, my PhD supervisor, whose critical eye and patience were equally invaluable in helping me to develop and shape this project. I would also like to acknowledge the contribution made by my doctoral examiners Sarah Street and Martin McLoone to the process of converting this work to a book. Their comments and feedback on my thesis helped me to sharpen my thinking on Scottish cinema and to see the work with fresh eyes. At Warwick, I was also fortunate to have a network of fellow students without whom completing the early version of this project would have been impossible. Special thanks in this regard go to Amy Holdsworth, Malini Guha, Sarah Thomas and Faye Woods.

At the University of the West Indies, I was fortunate to receive funding for this research from the Campus Research and Publication Fund and scholarly leave to complete the writing of the manuscript. I would like to thank the Dean of the Faculty of Humanities, Funso Aiyejina for his support in obtaining each of these. I am also grateful to Yao Ramesar who acted as Coordinator of the Film Programme in my stead during my period of leave. I would also like to thank Mandisa Pantin, who worked as a research assistant on the preparation of the manuscript as well as Dina Poon Chong, who assisted with illustrations.

In carrying out the research itself, I am grateful to those who agreed to be interviewed for this book, including Roger Shannon, Duncan Petrie, Colin McArthur, Rebecca O'Brien, Stefan Mallman, Robyn Slovo and Andrea Calderwood. I am also thankful for the assistance of Anita Cox who helped to facilitate access to funding applications from Scottish Screen as well as the script drafts which were submitted with a number of the applications. The staff of the BFI Library were also vital to my research, particularly those in the Special Collections division. Thanks must also be extended to Matthew Frost and his staff at Manchester University Press.

The writing of this book in various forms has now spanned nine very eventful years of my life, years which have seen several international moves, innumerable scrambles for paying work which morphed into the hard slog of a full-time academic position, the death of a friend and colleague and the birth of my daughter. Besides this project there has been one other constant in my life during this time. For that reason, and so many others, I dedicate this book to Laura Ortiz-Garrett with great love and gratitude.

Introduction: surveying Scottish cinema, 1979–present

From a handful of locally produced documentaries, television pro-grammes and little else in 1979, Scotland has seen unprecedented growth in feature film-making in the last three decades. Beginning with Bill Forsyth's *That Sinking Feeling*, followed in quick succes-sion by the director's *Gregory's Girl* (1981) and a number of films commissioned by the newly formed Channel 4, Scotland in the early 1980s was already seeing an upsurge in film-making without parallel in the nation's history. Those heady days were followed by a period of disconcerting dormancy in the late 1980s with Forsyth departed for America and Channel 4 losing the appetite to support Scottish production on the scale it had earlier in the decade. In the mid-1990s, with the releases of *Shallow Grave* (Danny Boyle, 1994), *Trainspotting* (Danny Boyle, 1996) and the less-heralded but still significant *Small Faces* (Gillies MacKinnon, 1996), a new era of optimism for Scottish film-making was ushered in. When Lynne Ramsay's acclaimed *Ratcatcher* (1999) and Peter Mullan's *Orphans* (1999) were released in the same year that the first Scot-tish Parliament in 292 years was seated, hopes were higher than ever, with some critics declaring the beginning of a 'new Scottish cinema', befitting the historical moment which was seeing Scotland break away from Britain politically. These hopes have since proved to be overstated, both in cinematic and political terms, but the 2000s were, nonetheless, a decade that saw many important Scot-tish films make big splashes in critical and commercial terms, the decade ending with Peter Mullan's acclaimed film *Neds* (2010).

For these reasons, to adapt Satyajit Ray's famous put-down of British cinema, it is now possible to speak of Scottish cinema without first having to prove that such an entity exists. This exist-ence has long since been established by the range of studies of

Scottish cinema that have emerged in the last thirty years. Indeed, the scholarship of Scottish cinema has seen an exponential growth that arguably outstrips that of Scottish film-making during the same period. The field of Scottish cinema studies was more or less born with *Scotch Reels* (1982), a collection of essays edited by Colin McArthur that sought to unearth a history of cinematic representations of Scotland and to argue for the need for more indigenous production. *Scotch Reels* has since been followed by another anthology published in the early 1990s, *From Limelight to Satellite* (1991), after which followed a period of near dormancy in Scottish film scholarship which mirrored the contemporary malaise in filmmaking. This dormancy would end with the scholarship of Duncan Petrie, whose work would become the most influential writing on Scottish cinema to date. His two survey histories *Screening Scotland* (2000a) and *Contemporary Scottish Fictions* (2004) effectively set the agenda for Scottish film historiography and criticism for years to come. Scholars such as Jonathan Murray, David Martin-Jones, Sarah Neely, Ian Goode, Jane Sillars and others have, along with ongoing work from Petrie and some major figures of the *Scotch Reels* moment, such as John Caughie and John Hill, developed the field to the point where there are many areas of consensus and debate on a subject that was long thought not to exist at all. In short, Scottish cinema studies is now a field that is very much alive and vibrant, as evidenced by a recent wave of book-length publications such as the latest anthology on Scottish cinema, *Scottish Cinema Now* (2009), Martin-Jones's study of popular genre cinema and transnationalism *Global Scottish Cinema* (2009) and Murray's auteur study of Forsyth, *Discomfort and Joy* (2011), as well as numerous other publications.

This book seeks to add to this growing tide of scholarship and in so doing assist with the project of subjecting the works of Scottish cinema to sustained close analysis and historicization. Such an impulse has been present in the current wave of Scottish cinema historiography, including work by Martin-Jones and Murray, as well as extended studies of *Trainspotting* and *Ratcatcher* by Murray Smith (2002) and Annette Kuhn (2008) respectively. This shift in methodology from constructing overarching narratives of Scottish cinema to detailed study of individual films is in some senses a sign of the maturity of the field. Now that the larger generalizations have been made – generalizations that were necessary to establish that the object was worthy of discussion – it is time to examine the films themselves more closely to see if those generalizations were adequate or if they are in need of revision and nuancing.

This book argues that much can still be gained from fine-grained analysis of Scottish films and, it is hoped, will to be of use to both new students and established scholars of Scottish cinema. For the former, this text can function as an introduction and orientation to the field, its key debates and the reasoning underpinning the canon formation that has taken place in the last fifteen years or so, while utilizing the films themselves to thoroughly ground those larger issues. For scholars of Scottish cinema, this book seeks at many points to revise our understanding of the many aspects of Scottish film history, particularly national representation, and the equally widely discussed issue of production cultures and the place of Scottish national subsidy programmes therein. Other issues covered include auteurism in Scottish film culture, adaptation of the national literature, the relationship between film and history, the place of Scottish cinema in relation to the field of British film history and numerous others.

That such a range of topics can be addressed in a book such as this is a testament to the richness of Scottish films, but the methods I employ as well as the films I have selected for textual scrutiny require some explication, particularly to appreciate the need to look more closely at such seemingly well-known films. I have already indicated some of the rationale for opting for lengthy, detailed scrutiny rather than wide-ranging survey, but this need not mean that my discussion are confined exclusively to the films studied or that my findings are only applicable to these case studies, indeed far from it. Instead, the reasoning here is that studying a series of individual films can allow us a 'bottom-up' view of the field that will hopefully allow distinct patterns to emerge across the selection of films, patterns that can then be reasonably sounded out for their applicability to the period as a whole.

The central context of this book is the production landscape surrounding Scottish cinema over the last thirty years. Development of public funding mechanisms in Scotland since the early 1980s is one aspect of Scottish film history that nearly all commentators agree is significant for understanding the contemporary period. The lack of such funding dedicated to indigenous film-making was one of the major problems identified by *Scotch Reels* and consensus has subsequently emerged within the field that these changes have enabled the upsurge in Scottish film-making that followed *Trainspotting*. This argument is laid out most vividly in Petrie's *Screening Scotland*, which devotes an entire chapter to the institutional landscape of what he influentially termed the 'new Scottish cinema' (2000a, pp. 172–190). This argument is also invoked in *Contemporary Scottish Fictions* (2004, p. 4). Subsequent writers would take up this blanket endorsement of Scottish cultural policy creating the conditions necessary for a national cinema to flourish with little qualification, nuancing or debate. Works in this vein include articles by Martin-Jones (2005a), Murray (2004, 2005b) and John Caughie (2007), as well as books by Martin-Jones (2009) and Steve Blandford (2007), whose survey of theatre and cinema in devolutionary Britain focuses in part on Scotland. While Petrie himself subsequently stepped back from the optimism of his earlier work when it comes to how great an impact subsidy funding has had on Scottish cinema (2009), his views are still very much entrenched within the field.

Crucially, this historiography goes beyond claiming that policy has stimulated an industry. Instead, the argument being made in much writing in the field is one of political economy – that indigenous funding mechanisms have made for 'better' Scottish films than the private sector alone had been providing. Influenced by polemic cultural critic Tom Nairn, *Scotch Reels* critics pointed to the lack of funding for indigenous artists as one of the crucial factors in determining what they saw as a long tradition of ideologically pernicious representations of Scotland in the cinema. Despite key differences between his views and those of the *Scotch Reels* critics, Petrie adopted this basic assumption to argue that the 'new Scottish cinema' was the cinema that Scottish critics hoped for, one which was enabled in this ideological project by virtue of being afforded protection from the free market by policy instruments, calling films and television programmes made in the traditions of tartanry and kailyardism 'market-driven distortions' (2004, p. 209). The works that Petrie's historiography favours in this regard have become a canon of sorts, with only Martin-Jones (2009) attempting a substantial expansion of the films up for discussion, and none willing to explicitly take on the assumptions of political economy, which combined with those discussed previously relating to the stimulation of a national industry, have come to be taken for granted in thinking about Scottish cinema.

This book seeks to challenge many of the assumptions that dominate thinking about Scottish cinema. These include the conception of the international market exerting a deleterious influence on Scottish films; the related conceit that instruments of policy have created the environment necessary for a culturally worthwhile Scottish cinema to flourish; and the idea that the condition of Scottish cinema has mirrored the political situation of the nation itself as it is supposed to be breaking away from the UK and looking to forge international relationships of its own. A structuring assumption on my part will be that the imbrication of Scottish cinema historiography with debates about Scottish nationalism has been misleading and had the unintended consequence of obscuring certain realities about the production and circulation of Scottish films. These realities pertain to the industrial expectations that inform the making of Scottish films, the independence of Scottish film-makers from international markets and indeed the same UK that historians have suggested they were moving away from, and finally the representation of the nation itself, which may have certainly moved on a bit from the patterns identified in *Scotch Reels* but not necessarily in ways that could have been expected.

While the case studies in this book will thus challenge the conventional wisdom of the field in some ways, it is important also to stress that these challenges will not amount to a total revolution. Many of the observations of Scottish cinema historians will actually be upheld in these pages, though crucially, the methodological format will allow for more thoroughgoing exploration of the insights and ideas of my predecessors than they were able to offer in more survey-oriented texts. A case in point in this regard is Petrie's observation in *Screening Scotland* that film producers would be essential to contemporary Scottish cinema (2000a, p. 178). All of the case studies in this volume either explicitly or implicitly attempt to account for precisely this dimension of Scottish film-making, helping to give us a fuller understanding of the interrelated nature of industrial practice and cinematic creativity in the nation while also simply attempting to give due credit to the efforts of these vitally important, but too little understood, film-makers. Besides foregrounding film-makers such as Andrea Calderwood, Rebecca O'Brien and others, in the conclusions of this book I also attempt to assess the significance of the producer to our understanding of Scottish cinema generally.

Methods: texts in contexts

Pursuing a project such as the one I have described will necessarily involve attempting to reconstruct production contexts, attempts which will rely on the persuasive use of archival documents and first-person interviews with key figures involved in the making of films. Such a historiographical enterprise is not without its challenges. Documents such as committee reports and funding applications have complex discursive contexts and it is worth explaining at some length just how I have chosen to approach them. Though she does not analyse the documents which I am specifically concerned with, namely funding applications and decision statements, Sarah Street's general advice to read such materials 'against the grain' could be said to be an overarching methodological guide. Problems of dealing with bureaucratic discourse are also astutely described by Street when discussing the issue of agency in documentary research. Describing this category of consideration, Street suggests the researcher ask: 'Why was [the document] written? What was its purpose?' and reminds us that, 'there is often a "gap" between a document's ostensible purpose and its *real* purpose' (2000, p. 7). Such an approach entails keeping in mind that the descriptions of the projects in question are not necessarily accurate reflections of how the producers were envisaging the project. In all likelihood the applications were written to appeal to the mandate of the funding body, just as any grant writer is trained to do. Likewise, the statements by funding committees explaining why they chose to support any given project do not necessarily reflect the 'actual' reasons a project was supported. But in a sense this is what makes these documents so interesting. Even if members of a committee had an extremely idealistic view of film as art and supported a project simply because they believed in the vision of the artists involved, they would still need to justify that decision in terms of the constraints of the system in which they work. In such a scenario, the decision minutes would thus still reflect some truths about the system that governs subsidy decisions even if it does not reflect the 'actual' reasons a film was granted production subsidies. Similar principles underpin my use of other primary sources such as producers' production files (Chapter 1), bureaucratic policy frameworks (Chapter 2) and interviews with film-makers (all chapters). Good critical practice requires reading such sources 'against the grain' even as we rely on those same sources for information about the films under consideration.

It must also be said at the outset that I do not have access to as much material as would be ideal. As literary historian Robert D. Hume has argued, in addition to being explicit about what evidence a historian is basing their arguments on, 'good historical practice requires us to be blunt about what we lack' (1999, p. 118). Despite my best efforts, I have not been able to obtain all the policy papers or to talk to as many people involved in the production of the films studied in this book as I would have liked. I have not been able to access, for example, Scottish Screen's application or decision minutes pertaining to *The Last King of Scotland* (Kevin Macdonald, 2006) or indeed any of BBC Scotland's documents directly pertaining to the making of *Mrs Brown* (John Madden, 1997). This is a problem inherent in historical research, but what I hope to have done is to assemble sufficient material to make a series of original, supportable arguments about the objects of study and at the same time acknowledge that there is still, and likely always will be, more to be done to account for the entirety of what Barbara Klinger calls a film's 'discursive surround' (1997, pp. 108–109).

For attempting to recreate the contexts of production and circulation, this book can be located within the paradigm of Media Industry Studies, which despite its dramatic announcement as a field in works such as Jennifer Holt and Alisa Perrin's anthology *Media Industry Studies: History, Theory and Method* (2009) and a recent issue of *Cinema Journal* edited by Paul McDonald (2013), is an avenue of inquiry that has been shaping national cinema studies for many years. Such can be seen in the preoccupation with issues of industrial development and political economy in Scottish cinema studies. As discussed previously, closely related to claims about the efficacy of policy in protecting Scottish artists from the vagaries of the market are arguments regarding changes in the representational tendencies of Scottish films. Drawing heavily on reasoning derived from the polemics of *Scotch Reels* generally and a conception of national cinema popularized by John Hill, Petrie's argument has been that 'new Scottish cinema' provides a view of

Scotland and Scottish people which is more authentic, realistic and politically progressive than those films which were subjected to the demands of the marketplace. This reasoning has proven more controversial within the field than claims about the institutional causes behind the emergence of Scottish film-making. Martin-Jones (2009) has been perhaps the most strident critic in arguing that Scottish popular genre film-making, which has often been more dependent on transnational private sector finance than its art cinema counterpart, has a great deal to say about Scottishness. Similarly, Murray has shown that Forsyth's cinema generally and his Scottish films particularly are the works of a serious auteur who was able to express himself through the medium even if he was saddled by the demands of nearly exclusively commercial financing (2011). Moreover, Murray at several junctures shows how Forsyth's films presented complex and interesting representations of Scottishness even if this was only one aspect of the director's work, albeit the one that national cinema criticism has been most eager to discuss.

National representation thus remains central to the field as a whole and to most Scottish films and I will thus be pursuing this theme throughout all of the case studies found in this book. Analysing national representation requires textual analysis regarding what we actually see and hear in the films themselves, but it also requires some attention to reception if we are to measure the impact that films have on national and international film cultures to see how exactly the nation is being perceived through these films. To these ends, I am also concerned with box office statistics, promotional campaigns and reviews and commentaries found in newspapers and other publications. In drawing on such materials, I use something akin to the 'historical materialist' approach to film reception influentially deployed by Janet Staiger (1992). By combining such a study of reception with textual analysis and production research, I hope to carry out the kind of national cinema study described by Tom O'Regan in his seminal study of Australian cinema, a kind of analysis that addresses 'the films, the audience (including the critical audience) for these films, the industry within which they are produced, the local and international markets where they circulate, and the strategic role of government in sustaining domestic productions' (1996, p. 2), but which also brings such a framework to bear on individual films. As John Thornton Caldwell has written regarding the American film and television industries,

'one of the best ways to understand political-economic and industrial practice is to understand the texts and content that the media
industries produce' (2008, p. 238). Like Caldwell, I also believe
that the reverse is true, that those contexts can also help us to
understand the texts themselves better.

Aside from the omnipresent concerns of production, representation and reception, the case studies assembled in this book
also focus heavily on the relationship between Scottish cinema
and Scottish history, the relationship between Scottish cinema and
Scottish literature, the artistic achievements of individual films and
many other topics. Such topics are called for when discussing films
in relation to national culture, in short, as national cinema. Crucially
though, the degree of emphasis placed on any of these subjects vary
from case study to case study depending on the nature of the film
under discussion. In this sense, there is no standard approach for
each chapter. Such a method of examining case study films would
be unduly restrictive and I have chosen instead to respect the unique
qualities of each film and to let each take us in slightly different
directions, though a larger argument and series of generalizations
is articulated across these diverse case studies. Even though there
is thus no one set methodology in this sense which structures every
chapter, larger questions do guide the overall book. Primary among
these is the effect of the national and international market on Scottish film-makers and the related question of the efficacy of public
funding in mitigating the pressures of the marketplace. As we have
seen this has been perhaps the dominant question in the field and
this book seeks to generate fresh insights into this old chestnut by
scrutinizing the films themselves in relation to precisely those pressures and institutions.

From this overarching question spring the more specific questions
that motivate the individual chapters. In the case of Chapter 1, no
public institution is present in the funding scenario, but this makes
Local Hero (Bill Forsyth, 1982) all the more interesting, given that
it has been for so long criticized for its representational content
and dependence on the private finance and international audiences.
A related historiographical problem for *Local Hero* is that it is
often seen as an example in which an indigenous Scottish film-maker
lost his way under the sway of the international market. The subsequent chapters each deal with publicly funded works, most of
which involve some combination of public service broadcaster funding

and lottery subsidies distributed by Scottish Screen. Chapter 2 is concerned specifically with the role played by the devolution of public service broadcasters, particularly BBC Scotland, in shaping Scottish cinema. Chapters 3 and 4 are concerned with the role of subsidy programmes and public service broadcasters in fostering the development of indigenous film-makers, while Chapters 5 and 6 are concerned with the ways in which various policy instruments have facilitated the transnational movement of film-makers to Scotland (Chapter 5), as well as the movement of Scottish film-makers to other countries to make their films (Chapter 6). While each chapter thus has a specific focus, there will be a great deal of overlap between them. Public service broadcasters helped fund *Morvern Callar* (Lynne Ramsay, 2002) as well as *The Last King of Scotland* (Kevin Macdonald, 2006); subsidy bodies helped to protect an indigenous director in the case of *Last King*; all the films being studied are transnational co-productions (even if in the case of *Local Hero*, this arrangement is within the context of the British state), and so on. This overlap can only add to the richness of the critical discussion found here, even if this does present us with some historical 'untidiness'.

Even though one basic question motivates my case studies, each chapter takes us in a different direction and this book is thus about a single topic, namely Scottish film-making, but in treating that subject fully it ends up being about a lot more than *just* Scottish film-making. Instead of seeing this as a lack of focus, I hope readers will appreciate the breadth and scope of this study as it seeks to understand Scottish film-making within a wider set of industrial and cultural formations. After all, to study a national cinema in any other way is to unduly limit the object of study.

Corpus and organization

Any time a limited number of films are held up as speaking for a larger national cinema – even one which itself has not exactly been prolific in terms of the sheer quantity of films produced – there are bound to be questions about the extent to which those films are indeed representative of the larger issues facing that national cinema. At the same time, one must eventually sacrifice some degree of scope in order to provide the kind of detailed analysis required if we are to move beyond the survey format and delve more deeply into Scottish films as aesthetic objects and historical artefacts. The question then naturally arises as to which films to select for discussion. While there were no hard and fast criteria, per se, for inclusion in this volume, there was a conscious attempt to take up some of the most significant Scottish films in critical and popular terms. This means going by some combination of box office performance, journalistic reception and academic reputation within Scottish cinema studies.

This final criterion will allow me to bypass the sometimes unnecessarily fraught question of what exactly constitutes a 'Scottish' film, as much of my concern in these pages is with the narratives of Scottish cinema historiography, probing the values implicit in their arguments and pointing out the limitations of their, until recently, nationalist bent. Invariably for a study of national cinema historiography in this day and age, this will mean scrutinizing the implicit, and sometimes explicit, sense of the 'national' within the field. The rise within Film Studies of transnational film theory has productively complicated our understanding of the relationship between nation and cinema, but the idea that national cinema itself has disappeared and that we now live in a 'post-national' age is an extreme exaggeration. The concept of national cinemas is itself a discursive category that still matters for the critical understanding of cinema as well as national and international film cultures generally. Given the increasing movement of artists and capital in contemporary film culture, there will inevitably be films that raise questions about their national origins, but none of the case studies which follow do so, or at least not in ways that need trouble us here. That does not mean, however, that we should ignore transnational dimensions of their production, reception or aesthetic and representational make-up. Indeed, far from it. All of the case studies assembled here provide insights into the relationships between Scottish film culture and the film cultures of other nations, including the larger UK, Europe, America and Africa among other places and a major task for this book will be to account for these larger relationships.

That said we can return to the tripartite criteria I set out above. Some films selected for discussion here are distinguished in all three areas of popular success, critical acclaim and the attention of the field. These include *Local Hero*, *Mrs Brown* and *Ae Fond Kiss*. When discussing these films the respective chapters, some cases, particularly *Local Hero* and *Mrs Brown*, seek to revise the scholarly reputation of films which have either been misunderstood or unfairly overlooked. The subsequent two films to be discussed were not successful with audiences at large but were critically acclaimed and have been significant to accounts of Scottish cinema. These films, *Morvern Callar* and *Young Adam*, are included here because of their reputation within the field as showcasing the potential for interventions in the industrial landscape of Scottish film-making to help develop Scottish film artists and Scottish cinema more generally. The final two case studies deal in more direct ways with some of the transnational flows that have shaped Scottish cinema in 2000s. In the case of *Ae Fond Kiss*, the least discussed of Ken Loach's films made in Scotland, questions about the role of policy in 'importing' Scottish cinema are discussed alongside the film's view of South Asian migration to Scotland. In the book's final case study, a film that was very popular with audiences and critics but ignored by Scottish cinema studies is examined. As we will see, there can and should be a place for *The Last King of Scotland* within Scottish film historiography, even if it, more than any film from the contemporary period, challenges normative definitions of what a 'Scottish film' is.

Though 'prominence' of one kind or another is at the core of my corpus, some of the most prominent Scottish films of the period are not included as case studies in this collection and this deserves some explication. You will not find here in-depth studies of *Trainspotting* or *Shallow Grave*, the two films most central to the breakthrough of the 'new Scottish cinema', nor will you find high-profile works such as *Ratcatcher*, *Orphans* or *Red Road* (Andrea Arnold, 2006). The reasons for this boil down to their thorough treatment by other writers. Though critical prominence is one of my criteria, these films have all been subjected to detailed study, in the case of *Trainspotting* and *Ratcatcher* book-length study, by a range of authors and there is little new to be gained from their exploration here.[1] This does not mean, however, that they will not be discussed here at all. *Trainspotting* is in many ways a structuring absence in this book and, I later argue, Scottish cinema in general. Many films since Danny Boyle's runaway hit have tried to emulate its multi-faceted success, though without ever really being able to do so. *Ratcatcher* is likewise a very familiar film which casts a long shadow over my discussion of Lynne Ramsay's second feature film *Morvern*

Callar. The funding strategies and artistic practices found in *Red Road* and Mullan's films are also discussed as they relate to a number of case studies in this book as well as the closing observations which conclude the book as a whole. That said, space is always a cruel master and given more, I would have liked to also include significant films such as *Small Faces* (Gillies Mackinnon, 1996), and the recent *Neds* (Peter Mullan, 2011), which draws a great deal on Mackinnon's film, or *Stella Does Tricks* (Coky Giedroyc, 1997) among others. I will instead have to grudgingly leave these and other works to future writers with the exhortation to continue the project of detailed analysis.

1

'Raking over' *Local Hero* again: national cinema, indigenous creativity and the international market

More so than any other film examined in this book, and perhaps more so than any film in the history of Scottish cinema, *Local Hero* is a film whose critical reputation is very familiar, so much so that for a time it was commonplace for writing on Scottish cinema to express the need to talk about something else besides the film. In his *Contemporary Scottish Fictions*, Petrie said films such as *Local Hero* no longer require critical attention because of 'the sheer familiarity' of such analysis, as well as 'a desire to move beyond the apparent obsession with these regressive tropes that have blinded many to the more productive achievements and traditions within Scottish cultural expression' (2004, p. 204). Similarly, Martin-Jones concluded a report on a conference dedicated to contemporary Scottish cinema by remarking that the event featured scholarship on a variety of forms of Scottish film-making and that the field as a whole had 'begun to focus more exclusively on the vibrant present, rather than feeling the need to rake over *Whisky Galore!* and *Local Hero* yet again' (2005b, p. 155).

Petrie and Martin-Jones are here responding to a long and polemical tradition of Scottish film criticism which saw *Local Hero* as a crucial text for illustrating the deleterious effects of the market on a potential Scottish cinema. Writings from the seminal *Scotch Reels* collection to Petrie's study in the mid-2000s have presented the film as a moment in which Forsyth, despite his promise as an emerging indigenous talent, succumbed to the worst kinds of regressive discourses of Scottish cultural representation. For many of these critics, the fact that this project was Forsyth's first intended for an international audience was not a coincidence and the film has become an example par excellence of the necessity of subsidy systems for film production in Scotland. If properly managed, such systems, it has been argued, would shield film-makers from the demands of the marketplace and therefore keep them from following *Local Hero*'s lead and resorting to cultural stereotyping.

Before the film was even released some were voicing concerns over the ways the project would represent Scotland. Writing in his 'The Iniquity of the Fathers' essay in *Scotch Reels*, McArthur articulates some of these fears:

> As this essay is being written a newspaper announces that Bill Forsyth's next project will be a big-budget, international film. One's spirits rise: here is a gifted Scottish film-maker whose two feature films [. . .] have decidedly eschewed Tartanry/Kailyard and deployed discourses which are not maudlin but which relate to aspects of the lived experience of contemporary Scots. However, as one reads on a cold chill begins to come over the heart: the story will be set in the Highlands; it will be about the impact of off-shore oil; and Burt Lancaster will play the president of a multinational oil company. One tries to blot out memories of *The Maggie*, but they will not go away. (1982b, p. 66)

In his article calling for a 'Poor Celtic Cinema', McArthur let it be known that his fears had been well founded. Arguing that the film bowed too much to the marketplace, he called it 'ideologically equivalent' to films like *The Maggie* (Alexander Mackendrick, 1954) and *Brigadoon* (Vincente Minelli, 1954) and goes on to describe the film as the 'locus tragicus' of a native Scottish artist coming 'to live within the discursive categories fashioned by the oppressor' (1994, p. 119). McArthur traces what he sees as Forsyth's usage of culturally denigrating discourses to the specific industrial conditions surrounding *Local Hero*: 'To offer an axiom to Celtic film-makers: the more your films are consciously aimed at an international market, the more their conditions of intelligibility will be bound up with regressive discourses about your own culture' (1994, pp. 119–120).

Writing in 2003, McArthur reiterates these views on *Local Hero* in his twin studies *Whisky Galore! & The Maggie* (2003a) and *Brigadoon, Braveheart and the Scots* (2003b). In these works, McArthur elaborates upon his views on what he sees as a group of films which show the tendency (which he terms the 'Scottish

Discursive Unconscious') to represent Scotland and Scottish people in the regressive terms of tartanry and kailyardism. The four eponymous films and others, including *Local Hero*, represent Scotland, particularly Highland Scotland, as being outside of 'the "real" world of politics and economics' (2003a, p. 77). Petrie takes a similar view on *Local Hero* to that expressed by McArthur. While recognizing more complexity in the film than is generally granted, Petrie argues that the film's 'externally constructed romantic vision of Scotland [. . .] serves to overpower the additional theme of existential loneliness and isolation associated with the character of MacIntyre' as well as overshadowing several significant departures from the narrative conventions of what have become known as kailyardic films (2000a, pp. 155–156).

Petrie adds ideological and historical dimensions to this reading of the film in *Contemporary Scottish Fictions*. Here he characterizes the film as a backwards step in an otherwise exciting, progressive epoch in the history of Scottish cultural production. Contextualizing the film within Forsyth's early output, which Petrie considers to be part of the 'Scottish cultural revival' of the early 1980s, he calls *Local Hero* 'a temporary retreat into a more stereotypical representation [of Scotland] for mass consumption' (2004, p. 61). The film is excluded from Petrie's section on Forsyth's early work, which is presented alongside the novels of James Kelman and Alasdair Gray as well as the television work of John Byrne, because Petrie is concerned with works which he feels show 'a creative engagement with contemporary experience' of Scotland in the 1980s (2004, p. 61). In other words, *Local Hero* is implicitly characterized as a film that exists outside the domain of 'important' history because it offers no reflection on the life of Scots during this period. It is thus not surprising that in concluding his study, Petrie counts the film amongst the 'market-driven distortions' which he excluded from his history of the period (2004, p. 209).

More recently, critics and historians have contested these claims, pointing out the extent to which Forsyth knowingly parodied and pastiched the conventions of kailyardism in the film (e.g. Meir 2004, 2008; Sillars 2009). Ian Goode has shown that the film offers a multifaceted treatment of Scottish landscapes that goes beyond the scope of tartanry and aspires to a progressive environmentalist discourse (2008). Martin-Jones has discussed *Local Hero* specifically and Forsyth's comedy generally as important components of

Scottish popular cinema in the 1980s (2009, pp. 24–30). Jonathan Murray (2011, pp. 71–100) synthesizes many of these insights into an auteurist account of the film that shows the ways in which Forsyth's unique brand of humour as well as his approach to mise-en-scène allows the film-maker to make powerful statements about national identity, globalization, environmentalism and life in an age of neo-liberal capitalism.

This chapter seeks to build on the fruits of this collective rethinking of *Local Hero* while also hoping to more thoroughly flesh out the ways in which the film is, contra McArthur and Petrie, in many ways a document of its time, reflecting on its political context and engaging with the lived experiences of Scottish people. As we see, this involves more than the film's pastiche of Scottish representational discourses, which is, nevertheless, crucial to appreciate as are the many jokes that Forsyth makes at the expense of national identity generally. The chapter also more thoroughly examines the relationship between Forsyth and the international market, an exploration that focuses on the genesis of the film from the partnership between Forsyth and David Puttnam (Figure 1) as well as issues

Figure 1 Bill Forsyth (left) and David Puttnam (right) on location for the filming of *Local Hero*

related to the marketing and distribution of the film. Importantly, all of these issues are shown to be interrelated and by the end of this chapter we see in the making of *Local Hero* a balancing act between the artist and the market that acts as a template for many of the case studies that follow in this book.

The film itself: comedy, nation and politics

In his study of Forsyth, Murray argues that in part because of the uniquely gentle tone of his comedy and his deferential and self-deprecating media persona, many have come to underestimate the seriousness of the director's work (2011, p. 3). In his view, this helps to explain the negative reception of *Local Hero* as it was easier to assume that an indigenous film-maker had succumbed to the pressures of the international market than to assume such a genial comedy – made by such a seemingly genial man – had any deeper critical agenda (p. 74). When it comes to many themes, including Scottish representation, this misapprehension has been thoroughly debunked. The kailyard ideal of Ferness is knowingly shown in *Local Hero* to be a myth manufactured by the villagers to sell the town to the rich tourist Mac (Peter Riegert), who has come on behalf of an American oil company to literally do just that: buy the town. The iconography of the tartan and kailyardic traditions of Scottish representation, from the magical Highland mists to the ceilidh and the outsider 'going native' and marrying a local girl, are systematically invoked by Forsyth only to be undermined or lampooned in the film. The film thus cannot be seen as a simple reiteration of what one critic called the '*Whisky Galore!* syndrome' (Brown, 1983, p. 158) but is instead more of a pastiche of that tradition, pastiche being a practice that acknowledges the historicity of its representational traditions whilst also enjoying the same pleasures of the original (Dyer, 2007).

Understanding Forsyth's pastiche of tartanry and kailyardism is extremely important to fully appreciating the film and its director, but the depth of Forsyth's satirical project goes beyond these discourses. As described above, McArthur has criticized the film's depiction of the village as existing outside 'the "real" world of politics and economics' (2003a, p. 77). Alistair Michie likewise places the film within the context of representations that present 'the isolated community, shut off from "reality", detached from

history' (1986, p. 258). By excluding the film from his study of
Scottish fictions which reflect upon the Scottish condition during
the Thatcher years, Petrie implicitly echoes these sentiments. Such
assessments, however, overlook the film's pointed satire of the economic and political realities confronting Scotland and Britain in
the1980s. *Local Hero* is actually very much a film of its time, and
the village of Ferness is anything but an isolated community set
apart from the world of politics, economics and history.

Reaganite/Thatcherite corporate capitalism is the narrative's
catalyst and Mac is in many ways the epitome of the 'yuppie', the
social class that became synonymous with the decade. British
economic and political complicity with America during this period
is likewise apparent in the film. Early in the film Happer's (Burt
Lancaster) secretary (Karen Douglas) is overheard connecting a call
from a female prime minister, a thinly veiled reference to Margaret
Thatcher. Forsyth takes this opportunity to poke fun at Thatcher's
'Iron Lady' persona when the secretary chats with the Prime Minister regarding a dessert recipe they shared ('Yes ma'am, I tried it
with the raspberries, it was delicious'). However brief this joke is,
it nonetheless lampoons the close relationship between the British
government of the time and American big business, the basic joke
here being that one of the world's supposedly most powerful political leaders must wait on hold to talk to the CEO of a major
American corporation. In that respect the film's Thatcher is no
more significant to American businessmen than the unnamed third
world leader ('his serene highness' as the secretary calls him), who
must also wait his turn to speak to the actual world power in the
film, that being American big business.

The presence of the British government in the film does not end
here. The occasional flyovers by fighter jets punctuating the film's
action remind the audience that the Highlands are not untouched
by the militarism that marked the Cold War era generally and
Thatcher's government in particular. Forsyth's script is frank about
the import of this motif. While Victor and Mac wander around
the town the morning after the ceilidh they idly watch the planes
overhead. Forsyth's directions in the script characterize the link
between those planes and the story's Cold War context: 'Beyond
[Victor and Mac] the rehearsals for the Third World War are
underway' (1981, p. 116). The fact that these jets sometimes test
their weapons so near to Ferness that the clouds from the explosions

are visible shows that the British government is also exploiting the remote Highland landscape for its own purposes, though without offering to compensate the locals. Keeping with the film's overall ironic tenor, Mac at one point comments on these training exercises by saying that they 'spoil a pretty nice country'.

The occasional appearance of the 'real' world's tools of mass destruction speak not only to Thatcherite militarism but also to the Cold War which provided the occasion for much of that militarism. Forsyth also draws on this aspect of the film's historical context. One of the film's most memorable characters is Victor (Christopher Rozycki), a sailor from the Soviet Union who comes to town to attend the local ceilidh and to check up on his investments, which are being managed by Gordon. Together with the town's African minister Reverend Macpherson (Gyearbuor Asante), Victor reminds us that Ferness is not an isolated town cut off from the outside world, but is instead 'globalized' in its own way (Murray, 2011, p. 85). Victor's presence in the film also allows for a number of jokes on Cold War-era international relations. When she hears Victor announcing his visit, the local shopkeeper (Ann Scott-Jones) tells Roddy (Tam Dean Burn) to tell Gordon that 'the Russians are coming'. Victor's sophisticated financial arrangements with Gordon undercut the idea that all Soviet citizens are ideologically homogenous socialists.[2] In fact, Victor seems to be the most unscrupulously capitalist person in Ferness, as he suggests at one point that Gordon sell the beach to Mac without telling Ben, and checks with Ben to make sure that he has a deed for it. This, of course, is just one instance of the film's many inversions of national stereotypes, but we should not overlook just how topical the film is being here in taking on the global geopolitical zeitgeist in memorable, effective and, well, funny ways.

Besides satirizing the tensions and militarism of the Cold War, as Murray and Goode have shown, the film also takes on environmental issues and the endemic poverty of Scotland's marginalized rural communities. Ben (Fulton McKay) is in many ways the moral centre of the film, standing up to the exploitation of the region. Embedded within the running joke of the villagers being so desperate to sell out to the Americans is a point about the economic condition of those living in the Highlands. Brown argues that the film does not 'dodge' the 'socio-economic' realities of remote village life (1984, p. 43), and it is important to appreciate this aspect of

the film as it is at odds with the picture presented by most subsequent Scottish criticism of the film. Though there is no extensive
treatment of the actual economic challenges facing the villagers,
there are several moments in the film to remind us that life in
small Highland villages is not as idyllic as one may think. In a very
pointed joke about the realities of global trade, Roddy, the local
lobster trapper, tells Mac he does not eat what he catches because
it is too expensive (Murray, 2011, p. 94). Later, Victor tries to allay
any doubts Mac has about buying up the town, on one occasion
saying, 'I like it here, but it is a tough life for the locals. You should
be proud of yourself, making them all millionaires.' And on another
occasion, he explains: 'It's their place, Mac. They have a right to
make what they can of it. You can't eat scenery.' This last comment
from Victor is an especially poignant reminder that, the beauty of
the area notwithstanding, life in a coastal village is very difficult
and that poverty is often a part of life for those in remote areas
of natural beauty.

Questions of national representation in *Local Hero* invariably
lead one to the group of films to which the film is always compared,
and has been described as imitating. Brown has aptly termed this
discursive context 'the *Whisky Galore!* syndrome' (1983, p. 158)
as critics have consistently named *Whisky Galore!*, *The Maggie*
and *Brigadoon*, as the specific films being imitated. But this aspect
of the film is also not as straightforward as has been described by
the film's critics. Just as the villagers of Ferness consciously manu-
facture a certain image of themselves and direct Mac and Danny
towards the more romantic areas of the town, so does Forsyth
consciously deploy many of the clichéd signifiers associated with
'the *Whisky Galore!* syndrome'. Throughout the film, Forsyth is
concerned with poking fun at the illusory nature of such representations of Scotland.

The use of the Highland mists is a good example of such a usage.
When Danny and Mac embark on the trip from Aberdeen to
Ferness their journey is delayed by a thick fog which causes them
to run over a rabbit and forces them to pull over and wait for the
fog to clear. They have to wait overnight, but once the fog does
clear they move along to Ferness and a world wholly set apart
from that of Houston or Aberdeen. The intertextual reference here
is, of course, to the mists of *Brigadoon* which precede the appearance of the magical town which happens only once every one

hundred years. Writing about the use of the mists in *Brigadoon* and throughout films set in the Highlands, Michie notes that they serve to dislocate the small Scottish community from the rest of the 'real' world and provide a convenient type of 'dream dissolve' between those two worlds (1986, p. 258). The mists in *Local Hero* do demarcate the boundaries between two different worlds, but their deployment is anything but mystical and wondrous, in fact the humour in the scene derives from the mundane nuances of a supposedly dream-like moment. It forces the two men into a somewhat awkward night sleeping in the car with the rabbit they have injured, eating chocolate and chewing gum while Danny begins to irritate Mac with his flair for languages. When the pair awake and the mists have cleared they are not overawed by their surroundings and there is a moment of surreal comedy as Mac does some early morning calisthenics which seem weirdly incongruous against the backdrop of the Highland landscape. The combination in this scene of the traditional usage of the mists to demarcate the boundary between two worlds with a joke about the lack of wonder in this particular moment is one of many instances in the film of the simultaneous usage of traditional iconography and ironic commentary on such iconography.

Another element of so-called kailyardic narratives that the film appropriates is the motif in which the outsider-figure 'goes native'. The film conveys this through a character arc over the course of which Mac gradually sheds the trappings of American corporate culture and begins to blend into the village's way of life. This is compared unfavourably by many to a similar character trajectory in *The Maggie*. In this film an American businessman Calvin Marshall (Paul Douglas) is the victim of multiple tricks and ruses at the hands of the crew of the eponymous Clyde puffer.[3] As the crew keep diverting Marshall all over the Highland coast to pick up passengers and go to a ceilidh, he slowly comes to understand the values of the simple folk he meets and finally shows his allegiance with the crew of the ship by agreeing to pay for the repairs required to keep the vessel sailing. A crucial scene in the film takes place at the ceilidh which the crew tricks Marshall into attending. Here Marshall meets a beautiful young woman who explains that given the choice between a rich suitor and a poor one, she would rather marry the latter as he would always be thinking of her and not his money. Noticing a close parallel to his own treatment of his wife, Marshall sees the error of his ways, setting the stage for his ultimate conversion. Though it still takes a knock on the head to get to that point, the ceilidh scene is nonetheless pivotal, as it foregrounds the nobility of Highlanders in contrast to the American businessman. The process of 'going native' in *The Maggie* is underscored by Marshall's change in costume. Just before he goes to the ceilidh he runs out of business suits and buys a thickly knitted turtleneck sweater in a local store and by the end of the ceilidh he is visually indistinguishable from the villagers.

This pattern of integration into the Highland community is repeated with some variations in *Brigadoon* and *Whisky Galore!* and is typically symbolically rendered through the marriage of the outsider figure to a local girl. In *Brigadoon*, Tommy (Gene Kelly) is persuaded to stay in Brigadoon and marry Fiona (Cyd Charisse) during the course of her sister's wedding celebrations. In *Whisky Galore!* the English soldier Sergeant Odd (Bruce Seton) is integrated into the community through his assistance in the plunder of the ship and his marriage to local girl Peggy Macroon (Joan Greenwood). Even Marshall's change in *The Maggie* has been described as a 'marriage' by Michie who describes the renaming of 'The Maggie' as 'The Calvin B. Marshall' as a symbolic wedding (1986, p. 261). In each scenario, nation is equated with gender, with passive Scottish female characters becoming the object of desire that in part motivates the outsiders to 'go native'.

A similar transition takes place in *Local Hero*. As Mac gradually comes to appreciate the beauty of the village and the tranquillity of its lifestyle, his costume is gradually transformed as he adopts the thick knitted turtleneck sweater – culminating at the ceilidh, when Stella gets him to take off his blazer, the last remnant of the suit he arrived in. At another point in the film, Mac leaves his wristwatch, with its timer set to conference time in Houston, in the surf, symbolically abdicating his life in the metropolis. Like Marshall, Mac has a drunken epiphany at the ceilidh and half seriously offers to trade lives with Gordon, taking Gordon's wife in exchange for Mac's salary and '$50,000 in mixed securities'. Crucially, the narrative of *Local Hero*, though it flirts with such a resolution, never arrives at the conclusion of its traditional counterparts. As Petrie points out, Mac 'unlike his predecessors in the genre, fails to cement his relationship to the magical environment by winning the girl, a theme crystallized in the relatively downbeat and somewhat unresolved ending with Mac back home in Texas pondering the superficiality of his materialistic existence' (2000a, p. 156). The village in *Local Hero* proves not to be a magical place of escape after all and Forsyth makes a point of reminding us that Mac can never actually 'go native'. When Happer orders him back to Houston, he takes a look at his employee and tells him to get a shave, undercutting and ridiculing the relaxed look Mac has cultivated in the laid-back confines of Ferness as Happer brings Mac's stay there to an abrupt end.

Commenting on the various contraventions of generic practices in *Local Hero*, Petrie argues that they fail to outweigh the tartan and kailyardic dimensions of the film. Acknowledging the novelty of having the villagers so eager to sell out to the oil company, he writes that 'despite this twist, ultimately the film conforms to the established tradition in terms of a reliance on the romantic and elemental appeal of the beauty and remoteness of the landscape' (2000a, p. 155). Later, in discussing the film's melancholic ending he writes that 'even this coda assumes the form of sentimental longing, stimulated by a romantic encounter with an idealised vision of Scotland' (2000a, p. 156).

As with other motifs of this group of films set in remote parts of Scotland, *Local Hero* makes landscape photography one of its main attractions, but just as it does with the portrayal of small-town folk and the process of 'going native', *Local Hero* uses romantic vistas in more innovative ways than is typically seen in 'the *Whisky Galore!* syndrome' films. The first image of the village that we see shows us that Forsyth is aware of the artificial nature of the film's village. In a sly Brechtian stroke, Forsyth jumps from Danny and Mac at the airport to what appears to be a landscape shot of the town. A sound on the audio track seems to be that of crickets chirping as the camera hovers over an impossibly green bay with waves lapping the shore. The shot holds for several seconds, a time span short enough to keep some viewers from realizing that this is a model of Ferness and not the actual town, before we hear a voice telling Mac and Danny to close the door to the laboratory, making the audience aware that this is in fact a model. As brief as the shot is, it nonetheless has the effect of reminding the viewer that what they are seeing is, after all, a constructed image. This is also possibly a subtle reference to the making of *Brigadoon*, wherein MGM head Louis Freed famously found the

Highlands to be not Scottish enough for his purposes and decided to film the picture on a Hollywood soundstage instead.[4] Forsyth turns this sense of the artificial construction of the Highland village into a running joke as the scientists at the lab tell Mac to 'hold Ferness for a minute' and then make a gift of the model to Mac, who takes it with him on his trip.[5]

There is, however, a great deal of more earnestly traditional deployment of landscape photography in the film, usually accompanied by swelling chords from Mark Knopfler's score. These shots typically originate from Mac or Danny's point of view and are coupled with comments from one of them relating to the beauty of the landscape and/or the beach. The film does not offer an alternative view of Scotland to balance out the rural vistas visible in the film. It does, however, feature a Scottish character who is just as enthralled as Mac by those vistas. Danny's presence in the film, among other things, reminds us that urban Scots are as mystified by the beauty of the Highlands as foreign nationals are.

It is important at this point to acknowledge that the film does not wholly discard the conventions of tartanry and kailyardism either. The landscapes are beautiful, the villagers are odd-balls and life in the village is presented as altogether more simple and appealing than life in Houston. Such a strategy can be usefully considered as a pastiching of the conventions of tartanry and kailyardism. Describing the aesthetic value of pastiche, Richard Dyer argues that it allows for the reproduction of pleasures from older representations while also acknowledging their historicity (2007, p. 138). For *Local Hero*, this means that the film is both a work of tartanry/kailyardism and an attempt to transcend these discourses. The former characteristic is that which has been seized upon by Scottish critics who have pointed to international address as its cause. The latter is less acknowledged, but was just as important to the film's international circulation.

Industrial contexts for *Local Hero*: a market-driven distortion?

Local Hero is thus a film that at the textual level is anything but a straightforward rehashing of the traditions of tartanry and kailyardism devoid of 'serious' content. What does this then say about the industrial and policy arguments that were once put forward about Scottish cinema, arguments that were predicated in part on the example of Forsyth and *Local Hero*. As noted at the outset of this book, much Scottish cinema historiography, particularly the works of the *Scotch Reels* writers and Petrie's work, has been oriented towards policy advocacy and this has had the unfortunate side effect of misconstruing the events of Scottish film history. Nowhere is this as manifest as in the case of this film and its relationship to external production resources and distribution markets.

To begin this industrial analysis of the film, it is first important to revisit the film's critical detractors, focusing on their concern with how the film's industrial position has been seen as determining its representational strategies. Though the critiques of the film by McArthur and Petrie cited above use terms like 'market forces' and 'international address' to describe this position, there is also a particular member of *Local Hero*'s creative team that is most closely identified with commercial forces, that being the film's producer, David Puttnam. In McArthur's critique in the 'Poor Celtic Cinema' article, the part that David Puttnam played in shaping *Local Hero* comes in for particular criticism when McArthur writes that the film was 'produced and packaged by David Puttnam' (1994, p. 119) for the international market as a way of explaining the ways in which Forsyth was led to utilize regressive discourses to represent Scotland.

Puttnam, and his relationship to the directors he works with, has also come in for criticism by Petrie. In his account of the British film industry during the 1980s, Puttnam is characterized by Petrie as a producer who is the dominant creative influence on the projects he oversees, in effect becoming a 'producer-auteur' (1991, pp. 177–178). This results, in Petrie's account, implicitly in the 'wrong' kind of producer and his influence on film texts is presented as something that is inappropriate. Discussing the work of producer Stephen Woolley, Petrie writes: 'In each case, the films produced reflect very much the vision of the director involved rather than the producer, as is arguably the case with David Puttnam' (1991, p. 181). Such sentiments find their way into Petrie's later writing on Scottish cinema. When Petrie writes of *Local Hero* that within the context of Forsyth's oeuvre as a whole it represented 'a temporary retreat into a more stereotypical representation [of Scotland] for mass consumption' (2004, p. 61), he also describes *Local Hero* pointedly as a 'more overtly commercial' film 'produced by David Puttnam and featuring Hollywood star Burt Lancaster in a supporting role' (2004, p. 41). The implication here, rendered in terms that recall McArthur's description of the film in *Scotch Reels* quoted above, is that the personnel mentioned, Puttnam and Lancaster, are evidence of the film being 'more overtly commercial', and, when taken together with his historical contextualization of the film, less nationally relevant.

There is no doubting that Puttnam is a producer who sought to wield a great deal of creative influence on the projects he worked on and *Local Hero* was no exception. As is now widely known, it was Puttnam who had the initial idea to make the film and all but commissioned Forsyth to write and direct it. Moreover, the producer had Forsyth watch *Whisky Galore!* so that the director knew exactly what kind of film Puttnam was looking to make (Murray, 2011, p. 76). Such a background to the making of the film can be seen as problematic for national cinema critics. After all, we potentially have here an instance of an Englishman taking creative control of a Scottish-themed film and possibly taking that control away from a Scotsman. More troubling could be an implicit problem from the point of view of film theory. Being inspired by the 'auteur theory', most film criticism assumes that the director should have creative control of a film and that there is something inappropriate about a producer usurping that role. In this school of thought the auteur director stands on the side of 'art' while the producer is cast in an adversarial role associated with 'commerce'. This way of thinking is now being challenged within film studies with greater attention and new respect being accorded to the producer.[6] More often than not, scholarship of this kind seeks to account for the creative contributions made by producers, contributions which sometimes consist largely of mitigating the constraints of the marketplace for the other creative personnel working on films. It is within this emerging vein of film historiography that we can locate this section of the chapter. Assessing the balance of power between Puttnam/ market forces on one hand and Forsyth's creative vision for the film is a historiographical task that can yield important insights into several related debates in film theory generally, and national cinema studies specifically. As Murray has shown, many in the critical community at the time of the film's production had wondered about how exactly the film would balance the creative visions of Puttnam and Forsyth (2011, p. 73) and here I attempt to assess just this.

In reconstructing *Local Hero*'s production context, I draw on a number of documents from the David Puttnam collection at the British Film Institute relating to the making of the film, including memos between Puttnam, Forsyth and others involved in the making of the film, as well as reports from test screenings and previous drafts of the film's screenplay. While these documents do not give us a complete picture of which creative decisions were made and why, when taken together they do provide enough evidence to suggest a number of things that, at times, both support and contradict the hypothesis that 'market forces' and the film's producer have had a more substantial impact on the film than Forsyth's personal vision. On balance, however, the contradictions outweigh the supporting pieces of evidence and indicate that Forsyth's creativity underpinned the majority of the final version of the film and that, somewhat ironically, that vision was thought by Puttnam to be highly important to the film's commercial profile.

The first documents I make use of are a number of screening reports from test audiences in Toronto and London. Test screenings and market research had by the early 1980s become an integral part of pre- and post-production practices among Hollywood studios and distributors (Wyatt, 1994, p. 19) and Puttnam's use of them to influence the final editing of the film indicates his emulation of the practices of the commercial industry's biggest players. This is not particularly surprising given that Warner Bros, who had a distribution interest early in the film's making, was involved in the production at this stage and actually conducted the North American test screenings. Such screening reports are, in my view, not evidence of audience reception per se as much as they are evidence of the production pressures that Warner Bros and others brought to bear on Forsyth. In order to determine if changes were made based on these reports, I also make use of a series of reports and memos that passed between Puttnam, Forsyth, Warners executive Richard Del Belso and independent market researcher Val Lyon.

What did the audiences think about *Local Hero* and how did their opinions end up influencing the film? The most prominent recurring problem that audiences both in North America and the UK had with the first cut of the film was with its pacing. The sample audiences were nearly unanimous in saying the film either seemed too long or dragged in parts. The North American test group specifically cited the ceilidh sequence, the negotiations with

Ben and the repetition of certain motifs to be particular moments when the film became monotonously long (Del Belso, 1982, p. 6). Puttnam was apparently concerned with this aspect of the film. Twenty-one of his twenty-seven suggestions made for changing the film in a memo to Forsyth are concerned with shortening the film, often expressed as 'trimming' or 'tightening' specific scenes. Using another version of this memo labelled 'post-production' and featuring handwritten notes as a guide, many of these editorial suggestions seem to have been followed. Some of these changes appear to have been fairly innocuous with no apparent damage being done to the film's major themes. An example of these would be Puttnam's suggestion that Mac's arrival at the airport in Aberdeen be sped up. There is not much, if anything lost in trimming this part of the film.[7]

There is also evidence, in some instances, that Forsyth resisted Puttnam's suggestions for shortening the film and by so doing, preserved portions that had thematic import. One of the suggestions marked with a handwritten 'No' in the margin suggests cutting a line from Victor where he says that Mac 'speak[s] a lot of sense for an oil man'.[8] Keeping this line in the film was apparently important to Forsyth and it is arguable that it is a part of the ecological/satirical project of the larger film. There are, however, very few 'No's in the memo and at least one moment when a major satirical element of the film was undermined in the name of 'trimming' the film. This pertains to the motif of military aircraft flying over Ferness – discussed previously as representing an instance of Forsyth critiquing Thatcherite militarism – and is worth looking at in some detail.

In his memo to Forsyth spelling out suggested changes to the first version of the film, Puttnam comments on this aspect saying that there are 'too many aircraft' in the film, and asking Forsyth 'can we lose one?' When considered alongside an explicit citation of the motif by Del Belso, this does indicate a fair amount of pressure on the part of the financiers to rein in Forsyth's usage of the bombers, and when one looks at the sheer volume of references to the flyovers in the second draft of the screenplay it is apparent that there was a great deal of 'trimming' of this element of the film throughout the production process. The bombing runs are vividly described in this version of the script and continue until much later into the narrative than is the case in the finished film. The bombings

then continue almost right up to the end of the film, with one of
the townsfolk jokingly asking how much it would cost to buy one
of the planes (Forsyth, 1981, p. 130). Given the thematic import
described above, the decision to cut out some of the bombings does
soften the political critique offered by the film and in that way
supports the contention that market forces contributed to the depiction of Scotland as being removed from the world of contemporary
politics. But it is also important to remember that they do not
completely nullify this aspect of the film and that some political
critique does remain in the finished film in spite of these objections,
even if it is arguably rendered less comprehensible by cutting down
on its usage.

Despite this pointed bit of commercial influence, the majority of
the proposed changes were not implemented. Also ranking highly
among the complaints of test screeners was the size of the cast of
characters and the number of subplots. Because of the large number
of characters and their various stories, test screeners found the film
somewhat confusing. The report from Warners makes mention
of several characters and plots which audiences had trouble with.
One that is significant for the critical reception of *Local Hero* is
their objection to the two main female characters, Marina (Jenny
Seagrove) and Stella (Jennifer Black). Del Belso's comments regarding the audience's take on the two female characters are especially
interesting in relation to the problem many critics have had with
the ideological handling of gender in the film:

> Young women had a tendency to express critical opinions about
> the portrayal of the female characters in the movie. They felt that
> both Marina and Stella were victims of a male chauvinistic attitude,
> treated as decorative objects rather than full-blooded characters.
> (1982, p. 6)

These comments seem to have occasioned very few changes in the
film. Despite such sharp criticism of this aspect of the film, which
is echoed in the UK screening report, Marina and Stella are not
given any further development in the course of the reworking of
the film. The screeners' reaction to the characters did not change
at any point in the production process, in fact audience antipathy
to Marina and Stella is surprisingly consistent in the UK screening
reports before and after the recutting of the film. The same percentage of each audience – 11 per cent – found the characters needing

more development. Moreover, the second set of screeners ranked Marina and Stella, along with the African pastor, as the characters which they enjoyed the least (Lyon, 1982b, p. 7).

Based on this evidence, the apparently objectionable depiction of Marina and Stella cannot be said to be an aspect of the film which Puttnam and Forsyth were unaware of, and, more interestingly, appears to be in direct conflict with the demands of the marketplace. The criticism of these characters and their lack of development is consistent and resounding, but they nevertheless appear in the final version of the film largely unaltered, serving as an instance of Forsyth's integrity to his own personal vision, even if it is seen by test audiences and later film critics as something unpalatable. This is particularly interesting for critical writing on the film as the overly symbolic usage of the female characters as analogues to the Scottish elements (Marina being associated with the sea and Stella with the Highland firmament) has been counted as an aspect of the film which links it to *Brigadoon* and *The Maggie* where female characters are used in a similar, albeit much more covert fashion. This similarity has been variously cited as evidence of Forsyth unconsciously succumbing to ingrained representations of Scotland (McArthur, 2003a, p. 8), or his consciously trying to mimic the sexist use of gender of his predecessors to similar commercial effect (Petrie, 2000a, p. 156). The evidence presented here suggests instead that Forsyth, in this aspect of the film at least, was not naive or overtly pandering to commercial concerns, but was instead knowingly acting in opposition to them. Furthermore, Murray has argued that using characters and subplots which defy classical narrative conventions of development and resolution is one of Forsyth's auteur signatures (2011, p. 6) and this makes the case for Forsyth sticking to his authorial vision – in spite of pressure from the Americans – all the more apparent.

Another issue in the development of the film which will interest those interested in national representation is related to the usage of landscape. The second draft of the screenplay features a great deal of often very lyrical description of the Highland elements and landscape, pausing at one point to describe the unique Highland evening light which has become known as the 'gloaming' (Forsyth, 1981, p. 79). It is also quite explicit in conflating these 'tartan exteriors', to once again borrow a phrase from McArthur, with a certain sense of Scottishness, remarking at one point that the

Highland landscape is the most 'typical Scottish image' (1981, p. 32).
The deployment of landscape in the finished film has been a target
of criticism for some of the film's detractors, who see it as another
part of the film which was derivative of its tartan/kailyardic predecessors, and as a continuation of an inauthentic view of Scotland
which is oriented towards tourism rather than 'genuine' national
representation. In their treatise on Scottish heritage and tourism,
for example, David McCrone, Angela Morris and Richard Kiely
refer specifically to *Local Hero* as an example of films which use
the iconography of the Scottish landscape in a manner similar to
Scottish tourism advertisements (1995, p. 65).

Criticism about the use of landscape as an attraction for for-
eigners is validated somewhat by the contents of the production
files. The North American screening report lists 'entrancing settings'
among the film's main 'sources of satisfaction' (Del Belso, 1982,
p. 2). It is important to note, though, that this reaction was not
confined to North Americans, as the report from the British test
screening indicates that 48 per cent of the audience specifically
mentioned that they enjoyed the film's landscapes and scenery (Lyon,
1982a, p. 2). Puttnam himself comments on the use of landscape
in his first set of suggestions to Forsyth, but he urges Forsyth to
cut some of the scenery. Referring specifically to the exteriors during the ceilidh sequence, he suggests the removal of some scenic
shots, saying about the deployment of landscape in general in the
film, 'I don't think we need to milk it.'[9] The suggested judiciousness
with landscape shows just how much Puttnam thinks of it as one
of the film's attractions, one that was too valuable to overuse. It
also points to the ways in which Puttnam wanted to keep the film
from being too mainstream and commercial. 'Milking' the scenery,
making the film more like a tourist advert would have been detri-
mental to the film's credibility as a work of art, something that
Puttnam was very concerned about.

The final aspect of the film that I would like to comment on
here in relation to commercial pressures is one that remained largely
unchanged throughout its making: that is the ending. In his
memoir *The Undeclared War* David Puttnam refers to his own
experiences in the making of *Local Hero* to illustrate the balance
he sought throughout his career between commercial and artistic
demands. In so doing he mentions a particular incident that is
worth quoting at some length:

Warner Bros. offered us additional funding to reshoot the ending [of *Local Hero*], so that the American, Mac, remained in Scotland, removing the lingering ambiguity. Were we to do so, they felt, we would have a film more 'sympathetic' to the expectations of the audience. This they believed could add 10 or even $20 million to its eventual box-office performance . . . I have absolutely no doubt that they were right; had we reshot the ending, *Local Hero* may well have grossed an additional $20 million in the international marketplace. In accepting their offer both myself and the director, Bill Forsyth, felt that we would have been betraying the spirit of the film. After all, the movie itself dramatizes an unresolved conflict between a pastoral view of the world and a more hard-edged commercial ideology. I still think that, given its impact on those who came to love the film and the integrity of its long-term reputation, we were right to decline. (1997, p. 335)

This anecdote has been reiterated by Forsyth himself in interviews promoting the film's twenty-fifth anniversary re-release. Here, Forsyth also notes that a new shot of some sort had to be added to the ending, leading to the now famous shot of the red phone box with Mac's call going unanswered (Murray, 2011, p. 98). Though there is no mention of this offer in Puttnam's files, there is a great deal of evidence that shows how uncommercial the ending was perceived to be. The ending occupies a prominent place in the 'Specific Dislikes' section of the North American report. Del Belso goes into some detail explaining why audiences did not like the ending, listing at one point four different issues viewers wanted the film to resolve, these being, in preferential order, the fates of the town, Mac, Ben and the villagers (1982, p. 7). Speaking about Mac in particular, the audiences felt that he should have run away to Ferness in the end, and complained about the downbeat tone of the film's denouement in relation to the rest of the film (Del Belso, 1982, p. 8). The report from the UK screenings likewise shows audience discontent with the ending which was found to be too 'open' and 'unresolved' (Lyon, 1982a, p. 4).

In spite of these audience objections/commercial pressures, it is clear in the production files that Puttnam was a strong supporter of leaving the ending unchanged throughout the production, even before the offer would have taken place. In his first memo to Forsyth he directly praises the film's ending for leaving the audience feeling unfulfilled, saying: 'This is something all too seldom done in our self-indulgent industry.'[10] The film's ending, which breaks so sharply from its *Whisky Galore!*-type predecessors, is thus one that remained largely intact despite the pressures of the marketplace. When this is considered alongside what several critics have argued is one of Forsyth's thematic signatures – an obsession with loneliness and personal alienation – we can see in the making of *Local Hero* the familiar story of the film-maker adhering to their vision in spite of the demands of the film's financial backers.

Marketing and reception: From kailyard to cross-over

Characterizations of the development of *Local Hero* as either a project which was unduly influenced by commercial concerns or, conversely, as an instance of artistic independence in the midst of a profit-driven industry would thus both be inaccurate. There is, however, another way in which commercial concerns did strongly affect the film, though not in terms of how it ended up being assembled, but over how it was received by audiences upon its release. By this I am referring to how the film was sold to audiences around the world. While the writers I have cited comment mainly upon the film's production context, there is another facet of commercial cinema that, at least in part, informs the negative reception of *Local Hero* among Scottish film critics. This facet is closely intertwined with the film's status as 'internationally oriented', that being the way it has been marketed and promoted. McArthur, for one, explicitly takes issue with this aspect of the film, as he criticized the way it was 'produced and packaged' for the international market (1994, p. 119). Being exportable, or trying to be exportable, inherently puts emphasis on a film's status as global commodity, and the ways in which that commodity is made alluring to consumers can often lend insights into the intercultural issues raised by nationally specific cinema in a global context. It is thus important to look more closely at how *Local Hero*'s advertising constructs the film, especially in cultural terms.

A concern with how films set in Scotland have been marketed can be seen in Scottish film criticism in McArthur's works *Brigadoon, Braveheart and the Scots* and *Whisky Galore! & The Maggie*. To buttress his ideological critique of these films, McArthur examines their marketing in order to offer it as evidence of the films' ideological projects. Writing in his study of *Whisky Galore!* and *The Maggie*, he lays out the reasoning behind this methodology: '[marketing documents] constitute useful evidence as to how the company involved viewed the film at the time' (2003a, p. 80). Although he is writing specifically here about pressbooks from studios, McArthur's rationale is applied to his study of other promotion materials including posters, film-related clothing and memorabilia, and even events and activities organized to promote the film. While many of McArthur's conclusions, drawn from his analyses of these documents, are persuasive, they do not constitute evidence that a film itself is necessarily always of the same ideological persuasion as its marketing suggests. Instead it is more fitting to say that marketing documents constitute useful evidence of how the company involved *saw easiest to sell the film to audiences*. The profit motive governing film promotion means that a company will market the film in the terms it finds most appealing to audiences at large and not necessarily the terms in which it understands the film being promoted.

The distinction between these views is particularly crucial when studying films that are subject to accusations of cultural misrepresentation. If one were to scrutinize the marketing and promotion of *Local Hero*, at least in its early stages, it would be possible to come to similar conclusions as those McArthur draws from his examination of the marketing and promotion of *Brigadoon*. Those involved in marketing *Local Hero* drew on many stereotypes about the Highlands and its inhabitants and encouraged the sort of readings of the film which much recent criticism has been concerned with debunking. This can be seen through an examination of some of the more conventional marketing devices as well as more unconventional ones.

The strategies of simplifying a film's complexities and latching on to its most internationally recognized discursive qualities can be seen in *Local Hero*'s trailer. The condensed version of the film's narrative can likewise be very telling. *Local Hero*'s trailer, as featured on its Warner Brothers 1999 DVD release, is a remarkable example of just how a trailer can flatten out the subtle irony of a film and manipulate the film's contents to make it seem like a completely different work. As flute and drum music plays slowly on the soundtrack, we see Mac in Happer's planetarium as the roof opens, we hear that voice-of-God narrator that seems to only exist in trailers say, in a monologue interspersed with clips from the film (narration in bold, images and scenes shown in brackets):

> **There is a place where the Northern Lights transform the sky** . . . [Happer tells Mac to watch the sky and to phone him about what he sees] . . . **Modern mermaids spring from the sea** . . . [Cut to Marina meeting with Danny on the beach] . . . [Cut to Ben saying to Mac and Gordon that he finds amazing things every two or three weeks] . . . [Cut to Mac and Danny's car in the mist] . . . **The land breathes with an ancient mystery** . . . [Cut to Mac in the car saying 'Where are we?'] . . . [Cut to Mac watching the meteor shower] . . . **And all who witness its wonders come to believe in its magic** . . . [Cut to Happer receiving Mac's call about the Northern Lights] . . . [Cut to Mac in the phone booth watching the lights trying to explain them to Happer] . . . [Cut to the villagers on the beach seeing the light of Happer's helicopter in the sky; it is never made clear in this clip that this is Happer's chopper and instead gives the impression of a divine light in the firmament] . . . **This is the new film from the producer of** *Chariots of Fire.* *Local Hero* . . . [A montage of images summarizing the oil company's plan to buy the town and Mac as its agent; Gordon is shown dancing on the chair saying, 'We're gonna be rich'] . . . **Peter Reigert and Burt Lancaster** . . . [Montage now shows Mac's desire to stay in the town, offering to swap lives with Gordon; cut to shot of Danny, from behind, running into the water to Marina. The editing makes it appear to be Mac running into the water, going native][11] . . . *Local Hero* . . . [Cut to Ben laughing in front of the fire] . . . **The story of an ordinary man who cared enough to do something extraordinary** . . . [Cut to a continuation of Danny swimming to Marina, implication remains that this is Mac we're seeing] . . . *Local Hero.*

As Lisa Kernan argues of trailers generally, the trailer for *Local Hero* 'accentuates the film's surface of cinematic spectacle, displaying the film's shiniest wares, or most attractive images, positioning it as a commodity for sale' (2004, p. 10). Some of these are the creative personnel, the stars and the producer specifically. Others, though, are the sometimes laughable clichés which are generally associated with tartanry and kailyardism: the Northern Lights, 'modern mermaids', a land that 'breathes with an ancient mystery', and so on. The images selected by the trailer-makers likewise emphasise these aspects of the film: meteor showers and the Northern Lights are on display; the Highland mists feature prominently; Mac appears to go native even more than he did in the film as the editing has him running into the water to embrace a woman, and so on. Other documents relating to the film's promotion use similar strategies. The film's main advertising poster, which graces the case for its DVD release, is the most common image associated with the film's promotion. The image here is a painted picture of Mac and Happer in full business suits, except for shoes and socks as they are wading in the water of a Highland bay, complete with seagulls circling overhead and far-off mountains visible in the distance. Romantic landscape is thus juxtaposed with 'going native', shedding one's business suit and getting into the water, just as was the case with the trailer's deceptive montage, which makes it seem to be Mac who is swimming out to Marina. The poster's illustrator, Allan Manham, in a memo to Puttnam, described the guiding thought behind the paintings as showing 'the contrast between the smart and sophisticated world of international business and the refreshing values of the little community'.[12] Other existing poster images – including Mac in the phone booth with the villagers surrounding it peering in and another which features a stretch limousine parked on the beach outside of Ben's shack – offer variations upon this kailyardic theme.

In addition to these standard marketing devices, the film also had a tie-in marketing promotion with the Scottish Tourist Board and John Menzies Outfitters, a retailer that specialized in outdoor clothing and supplies. Shoppers at John Menzies could win tickets to see Local Hero and some would be eligible for a free holiday in the Highlands.[13] David Puttnam arranged special screenings all over Scotland for schoolchildren on the pretext of showing them what the Highlands were like.[14] Special screenings were arranged for radio disc jockeys seeking to market the film's soundtrack, which featured Mark Knopfler's arrangements of traditional ceilidh music as well as his swelling romantic compositions, which accompanied many of the film's landscape shots. Newspaper articles, such as one in an Aberdeen newspaper,[15] offered accounts of the film's production focusing on the rascally behaviour of the inhabitants of Pennan, the village where the film was shot, as they played 'kailyardic' tricks on the producers in hope of getting more money out of them.

The ideological slant of this marketing is by now very clear. It offers precisely the sort of exoticized Highland environment that many critics accused the film of offering. But this is, of course, not an accurate summary of *Local Hero*'s representational tendencies. Marketing is always a reductive practice. Film commercials and trailers are, after all, two minutes long at the most and commonly condense narratives into the most accessible storyline imaginable, all in the name of attracting viewers to the theatres to see the rest. Furthermore, as Kernan has argued about trailers and Wyatt has argued about marketing generally, when the film in question is more complex and unconventional than standard generic film-making, advertising the film requires simplifying the film, fitting it into recognizable patterns and doing so in such a way that is often a distortion of the film itself (Kernan, 2004, p. 51; Wyatt, 1994, p. 10). The reductiveness of the film's marketing campaign can also be attributed to the 'high concept' approach to film-marketing which Wyatt argues was at its peak in the early 1980s (1994, p. 15). Such an approach places emphasis on presenting films in simple terms, with the ideal, according to Wyatt, being a film plot that can be summarized in one sentence and is relatively consistently used from the 'pitching' of a project to a studio through to its marketing to audiences (1994, p. 9).

But the film was not just marketed for the masses. Though the marketing materials described above constitute the main branch of the film's marketing campaign, the promotion of the film did change over time as it remained on release and later posters and trailers incorporated critical praise from reviewers in quality newspapers. Leading critics, such as Andrew Sarris in *The Village Voice* and Pauline Kael in *The New Yorker*, advised readers that the film was 'not just' another formulaic small town comedy (Kael, 1983, pp. 116–118; Sarris, 1983, p. 55). Sarris praised the film's 'exquisitely modernist melodies and bittersweet half-notes' and expresses a reluctance to provide a plot summary of the film lest the reader come to 'anticipate a series of cute highland flings and picturesque poses of facile anti-materialism' (p. 55). Kael likewise takes on genre directly and writes that Forsyth's 'style is far more personal and aberrant than that of the popular British comedies of the 1950s' (p. 116). Such a differentiation brings us back to the Puttnam's reasons for not changing the film's ending. The film's break from generic precedent, Puttnam argued, was a distinctive touch that lent it an integrity that would have been lacking had he and Forsyth opted for a happy ending. The artistic integrity and innovation inherent in the film's ending, in which critics have also found Forsyth's auteurist sensibilities, were necessary according to Puttnam as a method of product differentiation, making it a more intellectually upscale product than it would otherwise have been.

Such an impetus to market the film in artistic terms is consistent with what Hill argues was an increasing trend in the 1980s, which saw British films circulate internationally as art cinema even if their content was not always in keeping with the aesthetic practices of traditional art cinema (1999, p. 66). It is also in keeping with how the film was distributed and promoted over the longer timeline of its global release. The film, which opened in selected cities on 17 February 1983 and gradually distributed more and more widely in a so-called 'platform' pattern in North America and the UK, was still playing as late as 11 July 1983 in Scotland (*The Herald*, 1983) and, according to memos in Puttnam's production files, was intended to be re-released in early 1984 to cash in on any Oscar nominations it may have garnered.[16] Such a distribution strategy (gradual release of the film, reliance on 'word of mouth' publicity, extended run in cinemas) indicates that the film circulated in a manner akin to prestigious art films rather than 'high concept' commercial films, which generally look to generate most of their revenue at the box office in the opening few weeks of a wide simultaneous release.[17] Crucially, this distribution strategy did dovetail with the film's aesthetic approach, which as we saw blended some aspects of the popular traditions of kailyardism and tartanry with the narrative and thematic tendencies of art cinema. With this realization in mind, we can now draw some conclusions from this exploration of *Local Hero*.

Conclusion: *Local Hero*, 'the cross-over' film and Scottish film historiography

Local Hero is a film that rewards further textual and contextual consideration than it had for a long time been given in Scottish cinema studies. Looking more closely at both the text and industrial contexts of *Local Hero* shows the film to be neither a tragic example of a promising Scottish film-maker perpetuating cultural stereotypes to meet the demands of the international market, nor an industrially determined simple-minded remake of films like *The Maggie* or *Brigadoon*. Though it was made with English money and was marketed to international audiences, *Local Hero*, nonetheless, interacts with Scottish national culture in ways that challenge stereotypes and reflect on the lived reality of contemporary Scots, all while addressing 'universal' themes such as personal and social alienation.

At the same time, *Local Hero* was also not completely immune to market pressures. It was neither able to exist as an auteur-oriented art film nor was it a completely crass attempt to cash in on stereotypical images of Scotland. Instead the picture that has emerged in this analysis is of a film that has occupied a position somewhere in between art cinema and commercial cinema, at times drawing on aspects of both to reach audiences. In this way the film epitomizes the 'cross-over' form, a type of film-making that will be seen again and again throughout this book and within Scottish cinema as a whole. Writers such as Christine Geraghty, in her study of the 'cross-over' hit *My Beautiful Laundrette* (Stephen Frears, 1985) (2005), and Andrew Higson in his study of British costume drama (2003) have used this term to describe films which commercially depend on a blend of both critical prestige and popular appeal. This model has been the ideal for many Scottish film-makers.

Crucially for our concerns in this book, we also see the practices and strategies employed by Enigma and Goldcrest, two private companies, continued in projects supported by public institutions. In Chapter 2 we see a different manifestation of the same phenomenon in relation to a film made with the backing of a public service broadcaster. *Mrs Brown* will be shown to be a project with similar critical and ideological baggage to *Local Hero*, coming this time in relation to its status as a so-called 'heritage' film.

2

Mrs Brown: Scottish cinema in an age of devolved public service broadcasting

After *Local Hero* and *Trainspotting*, *Mrs Brown* ranks as the most prominent indigenously produced contemporary Scottish film in terms of both popularity and critical prestige. Despite this position, the film is only briefly discussed, if at all, within writing on Scottish cinema, until now garnering only brief mentions in survey histories and a short analysis in a dossier publication (Neely, 2005). More extensive treatments of the film can be found within British cinema studies, but such writing overlooks the film's Scottish content, focusing instead on the representation of the monarchy. This chapter attempts to fill these gaps. It is not simply a matter of international prominence that makes *Mrs Brown* such an important film. The film also presents an opportunity for discussing a number of concerns at the heart of contemporary Scottish cinema as a whole. These include the depiction of Scottish national identity among the groundswell of devolutionary sentiment; the representation of Scottish history on screen; and the roles that genre and taste formations have played in Scottish cinema.

Besides these cultural issues, there are a number of industrial issues that *Mrs Brown* can help to illuminate, issues that are also central to Scottish cinema during this period. These include the unique problems associated with balancing the apparently discordant impulses relating to export and domestic relevance, as well as public service and mass appeal; and the devolution of production resources such as public service broadcasters in the 1990s. In order to discuss these issues, we must begin with the institutions themselves, those being the BBC and its devolved incarnation BBC Scotland. Before looking at the importance of devolving the BBC we should begin by briefly examining the role that television networks, especially public service broadcasters, have played within the British and Scottish film industries. In so doing, we see a number of institutional shifts towards 'cross-over' models that closely mirror larger trends in public and private sector funding for filmmaking. As is the case with all of the films under consideration in this volume, we see throughout this study of *Mrs Brown* that these industrial issues are inseparable from the cultural and aesthetic issues that are also occasioned by a critical analysis of the film.

Film and television in Britain and Scotland

Writing in the mid-1990s, Andrea Calderwood, then head of BBC Scotland and executive producer of *Mrs Brown*, claimed that the best way to describe the industry in Scotland at that time was as one of 'a film and television industry' rather than a 'film industry' proper (n.d., p. 190). The credit for the existence of any media industry at all in Scotland is attributed by Calderwood to investment by broadcasters, namely Channel 4 and BBC Scotland. Such a description has been echoed by Ivan Turok who notes: 'Television provides more continuity than feature films in Scotland and has had a bigger impact on local jobs and infrastructure. It has done more to develop creative and technical talent and to help establish production companies with the capacity for growth' (2003, p. 558). Looking further back in history, Duncan Petrie devotes an entire chapter of *Screening Scotland* to detailing the importance of television drama in the 1970s and 1980s for maintaining a Scottish presence in British television and training a generation of film technicians and professionals (2000a, pp. 123–147). Scotland is not unique in this regard. As work by John Hill and Martin McLoone (n.d.), and John Caughie (1986, 2000) has shown, the industrial situation in Britain in recent history has been characterized by increasing convergence between the film and television industries, and not just in terms of training and employing creative personnel.

Besides its capacity to act as a training ground for its personnel, Calderwood also points out the more direct dependence of the Scottish film industry on television money as a source of production finance, as nearly every Scottish film has benefited from broadcaster investment, an observation demonstrated by the fact that four of the six films produced in 1995 were funded at least in part by broadcasters (n.d., p. 193).[18] This pattern has been consistent throughout the history of indigenous film production in Scotland, before and after Calderwood's account was written. Channel 4 has supported the production of canonical 'new Scottish' works such as *Trainspotting*, *Orphans* (Peter Mullan, 1999), and *The Last King of Scotland*, while BBC Scotland has played major parts in funding works such as *Small Faces* (Gillies MacKinnon, 1995), *Ratcatcher*, *Morvern Callar* and *Red Road*. Even preceding the establishment of Channel 4, which has historically been the broadcaster most involved in the British film industry, television played an important part in getting Scottish films made, as Petrie points out regarding STV's support for Bill Forsyth's *Gregory's Girl* (2004, p. 41). Hill, whose work has sought to dispute the initial apocalyptic anxieties which greeted the increased imbrication of the film and television industries, has expressed hope for the progressive potential of public service broadcasters getting involved in national cinema production: 'there is the possibility that television films can draw sustenance from television's public service tradition and speak to their own cultures in a way that Hollywood films increasingly do not' (n.d., p. 166). Hill's hopeful comments are very important for my analysis of *Mrs Brown*, and for much of this chapter I ask if this can be said to apply to this particular film. But before considering whether or not this has been the case for Scottish cinema, we should look a bit more closely at BBC Scotland's 'limited but very significant involvement' in the Scottish film industry (Petrie 2000a, p. 140) as well as the importance that the devolution of Britain's dominant media institution has had in historiographies of Scottish cinema.

The BBC started local television broadcasting in Scotland in the early 1950s, and established a studio in the country around the same time that the ITV companies, with their emphasis on regional production, took to the airwaves. Turok describes original production by BBC Scotland as gradually emerging from this point on and doing so largely in response to fears of losing Scottish audiences to STV (2003, p. 558). Both Turok and Petrie cite the devolutionary movement of the 1970s as the source of a push for an increase in indigenous production, a push which eventually led to the establishment of a new drama production unit in Glasgow in 1979 (Petrie, 2004, p. 4; Turok, 2003, p. 559). Petrie describes the creation of the unit as one of the 'key institutional developments' of the period, one which laid the groundwork for the beginnings of a 'new high profile era of Scottish television drama' beginning in 1984 under the leadership of Bill Bryden and continuing after the appointment of Andrea Calderwood as head of the department in 1993 (Petrie, 2000a, pp. 140–142; 2004, p. 4). This was an epoch which saw the production of TV series such as *Tutti Frutti* (1987), *Your Cheatin' Heart* (1990) and the film *Ruffian Hearts* (David Kane, 1995), works that have become constitutive of a sort of 'new Scottish television' canon.

There are, however, problems with such a view of BBC Scotland's dramatic production. The corpus of television drama produced by BBC Scotland and included in Petrie's overview of the Scottish cultural renaissance is not a complete listing of the department's output during this period, nor does it include some of its most prominent works. Neither the dramatic serial *Hamish Macbeth* nor the Oscar-nominated *Mrs Brown* are mentioned within the context of the 'Scottish cultural renaissance', and *Monarch of the Glen* is only mentioned as an example of the 'market-driven distortions' that Petrie omits from his study (2004, p. 209). While I will leave the analyses of works such as *Hamish* and *Monarch* to other writers, overlooking the case of *Mrs Brown* as a product of BBC Scotland's drama department will be shown to have had the effect of writing a deceptively complex and significant film out of the new Scottish period, thus only telling a part of the story of institutional policy and Scottish national cinema, especially in the 1990s, a period which saw the concept of public service broadcasting undergo such fundamental change. As this ethos is, theoretically at least, at the heart of the BBC's production policies, it is worth looking more closely at the historical specificity of its inflection in the 1990s at the time when *Mrs Brown* was commissioned and produced.

There are few terms within television and media studies that are as contentious as public service broadcasting. A great deal of literature on this subject has emanated from policy-makers, journalists, academics and cultural critics attempting to define the essence of the concept with some degree of precision. Though some reflection on the history of the term in relation to British broadcasting is necessary in order to appreciate the degree of change the term has seen, I am not concerned here with providing a comprehensive overview of the evolving meanings attributed to the concept – an undertaking that would require a book (at least) to itself. Instead, I attempt to sketch out the debates around the term's meanings as they were manifest in the 1990s. As we will see, these debates echo those in the realms of film policy and film historiography in terms of balancing what can be roughly termed 'cultural' and 'commercial' concerns.

Public service broadcasting in the earliest Reithian formulation has long been seen as one oriented towards Arnoldian social amelioration through the famous trinity of information, education and entertainment. Crucial for such a purpose for broadcasting in Reith's view was protection from market pressures, pressures which would have theoretically led to lower standards and meant appealing to the basest of human sensibilities, the dreaded 'lowest common denominator'. As Paddy Scannell writes:

> Broadcasting [in the Reithian mould] had a responsibility to bring into the greatest possible number of homes in the fullest degree all that was best in every department of human knowledge, endeavour, and achievement. The preservation of a high moral tone – the avoidance of the vulgar and the hurtful – was of paramount importance. Broadcasting should give a lead to public taste rather than pander to it. (2000, p. 47)

While Reithian-inspired broadcasting was never completely dour and simplistically didactic in nature, the monopoly that the BBC enjoyed until 1955 meant that audience tastes were less important to the broadcaster than they were after the advent of commercial broadcasting in that year. Faced with competition for the first time, the BBC had to appeal more directly to audience desires in order to maintain a presence in public life (Franklin, 2001, p. 8). Such competition has only increased throughout the half century since the introduction of commercial broadcasting as the number of broadcast networks has increased to five and the number of digital and satellite networks has increased exponentially.

Within such a larger trajectory, it is possible to see the 1980s and 1990s as a particularly crucial period when the definition of public service broadcasting itself began to be imbued with what were originally considered to be contradictory demands of market pressures and cultural high-mindedness. With the convening of the Peacock Committee in 1986 under the auspices of the free market oriented Thatcher government, commercial pressures became a more prominent concern for the corporation. Though the Committee did not recommend the introduction of advertising as a means of financing the BBC and actually reaffirmed some of the network's Reithian principles, this was largely viewed as a surprise, as it was widely believed that advertising would be introduced to finance the BBC (Franklin, 2001, p. 25). Though the Committee left the licence fee system intact and reaffirmed public service as a goal for broadcasters, it did however prioritize commercial considerations and consumer choice above public service (Scannell, 2000, p. 55). Attempting to balance these goals became the official line at the BBC. As Bob Franklin notes, in the 1992 Green Paper *The Future of the BBC*, the corporation outlined two options for its future, one which would see it 'identify and colonise the "high ground" of broadcasting' with news, art and science programming or conversely, one which would see it move towards maximizing audience appeal, options that the corporation would eventually claim to be pursuing concomitantly (2001, p. 100). Public service broadcasting was explicitly described in the Green Paper as having eight objectives: focus on the audience; quality; diversity and choice; accessibility; editorial independence; efficiency and value for money; accountability; and national identity (reproduced in Franklin, 2001, pp. 29–30), thereby effectively subsuming commercial and cultural impulses into a single category.

In addition to these explicit criteria for public service broadcasting to meet, there is also the implicit idea that such broadcasting should act as a mechanism of market correction, providing content that would not be available if market forces were to completely control the creative agenda of broadcasters. Such a position can be seen in the Peacock Committee's report when they write that one important reason for the continuation of public service broadcasting was that 'many people would like high quality material to be available even though they would not willingly watch or listen to it themselves in large enough numbers for it to be paid for directly' (reproduced in Franklin, 2001, p. 26). A later report on the BBC, the Davies Report in 1999, stated this reasoning more directly: 'some form of market failure must lie at the heart of any concept of public service broadcasting' (reproduced in Franklin, 2001, p. 33), but the thinking has always in some senses been a part of the ethos behind the institution.

Accompanying this principle of market failure and correction through public service is the duty of public service broadcasters to cater to minority interests, sections of the population which on their own would not constitute large enough audiences to make such programming economically viable. Minority in this case could apply to ethnic minority groups such as British-Asians or those of Afro-Caribbean descent, but it could also be said to apply to the national regions of Scotland, Northern Ireland and Wales, which would be alienated by a broadcasting regime which only served the English majority of the British market. A provision for such specialized market correction can be seen in the Green Paper of 1992, which stated that 'as a public service broadcasting organization, the BBC might be expected to continue to broadcast services for people in Scotland, Wales and Northern Ireland, reflecting their interests, activities and cultural heritage' (reproduced in Franklin, 2001, p. 101).

Export pressures and BBC drama: who is British television for?

Such a set of criteria was in place at the time of *Mrs Brown*'s commissioning and production, but there is another dimension of the film's production context that must be accounted for, that being its status as a co-production with American public television.[19] Though the 1992 Green Paper argued for the importance of the BBC programming as an alternative to the products of 'organizations with multi-national interests for transmission in more than one country' (reproduced in Franklin, 2001, p. 101), this was not an unusual production arrangement for the corporation to participate in. Co-production of dramas with American public television had by this point become a common practice for the BBC as deals were made regularly with the producers of the programme *Masterpiece Theatre* and flagship PBS stations such as WGBH and WNET. This became such a common practice that, by the 1990s, one could say that much BBC drama production was economically dependent on such American investment (Steemers, 2004, p. 112). Such deals allow American partners to secure British content whilst increasing the budgets available to producers at the BBC. For some these arrangements were, and continue to be, somewhat problematic given the national remit of the BBC.

In detailing the position of British television production in the global marketplace, Jeannette Steemers notes that since the 1980s literary and historical dramas have been one of the most consistent British television exports, but argues that they have largely failed to achieve ratings successes at home (2004, p. 33).[20] Such productions continued, Steemers writes, because literary and historical dramas 'sold in the USA and fulfilled a public service obligation in respect of "cultural heritage"' (2004, p. 33). In the case of drama production generally, export pressures, for Steemers, are inherently at odds with domestic needs. She writes that there is 'a marked discrepancy between what works internationally and what works in the domestic marketplace' (2004, p. 33).

For John Caughie, the relationship between the BBC and American television partners is one that has a direct influence on the content of the network's dramatic production. He argues that such co-production agreements invariably determined the types of representations that would be created – see his description of the pressures inherent in the deals: 'The price [the BBC] paid was that the American end of "the deal" had to be assured that what was produced would be what American producers believed American audiences wanted to see from Britain' (2000, p. 208). Such an economic relationship has, for Caughie, had the effect of dictating the vision of the British past available in television. There is thus a suspicion in Caughie's writing that British television costume drama no longer 'belongs' to Britain and that these images are largely for foreign consumption; as he writes in an earlier essay, 'It is fairly clear that the rush to foreign markets leaves a large gap in the BBC's inherited policy of public service and the national cultural mission' (1986, p. 198).

Such views of the influence of export pressures, particularly those coming from American markets, bear eerie similarities to concerns found throughout critical writing on British and Scottish cinema. This leaves *Mrs Brown*, a film that started out as a television drama co-produced with American public television, doubly exposed to complaints about audience and cultural address. Many of these issues come into focus as we move into a discussion of the film itself, a discussion which begins with a consideration of costume drama, a genre long held to be made in Britain but not necessarily for British audiences.

Picturing Scottish 'heritage': genre aesthetics in *Mrs Brown*

Genre, with its status as an industrial as well as a critical category, is an ideal way to bridge the institutional and aesthetic analyses of

Mrs Brown. There are few generic modes in British film and television studies as widely commented upon and debated as that which we can broadly term historical costume drama. Such is the degree of scholarship on costume drama in Britain that a number of critical distinctions have been made between its different manifestations. Two such sub-categories that have developed a degree of critical currency and which are useful for a discussion of *Mrs Brown* are the 'historical film' and the 'heritage film'.

The appellation 'historical film' is useful in this regard because of the film's concern with actual persons and events, a concern which is not true of all costume dramas. That the film's depiction of actual historical persons, and more specifically British royals, was one of its perceived attractions is evidenced by the fact that Miramax initially distributed the film with the title *Her Majesty Mrs Brown* in order to emphasize the fact that Queen Victoria was actually the title character (Sloman, 1998, p. 15). One of the ways in which historical fiction is commonly seen as operating on a thematic level is through the interpretation of those lives and events, which in historical fiction analyses is generally seen as being a commentary on the time in which the film itself was made (Chapman, 2005, p. 3). Thus the reverential treatment of Victoria seen in *Victoria the Great* (Herbert Wilcox, 1936) can be viewed as an affirmation of the monarchy at a time when the abdication crisis had undermined public confidence in the institution (Chapman, 2005, p. 8). James Chapman (2005), Kara McKechnie (2001, 2002) and to a lesser extent Julianne Pidduck (2004, p. 169) have each written about *Mrs Brown* within such a framework, focusing on how the film depicts the life of Victoria and comparing it to other depictions of English monarchs such as Wilcox's Victoria films, as well as *The Madness of King George* (Nicholas Hytner, 1994) and *The Private Life of Henry VIII* (Alexander Korda, 1933). Such readings are useful as far as they go, but are exclusively concerned with Victoria and Englishness. There is no in-depth analysis by either author of what the film says about Scottishness or about the relationship between Scotland and Great Britain. A significant part of my analysis is thus concerned with trying to determine what the film has to say through its depiction of one crisis in the history of Britain, while also having been produced during what could be perceived as another, namely the second devolution referendum in 1997. Before coming to such an analysis, we need to look at the other major aesthetic/industrial/critical context within which *Mrs Brown* can usefully be placed. The 'heritage film' is one of the most controversial categories in British cinema studies. Such is the level of debate around the paradigm that several writers, including Claire Monk (2002), Andrew Higson (2003) and Belén Vidal (2012) have devoted large portions of their works to recounting the history of the term itself and its usage. Though many of the points raised in these debates are germane to understanding the nuances of the films somewhat monolithically known as 'heritage' works, I use the term here in a relatively straightforward way that draws on Higson's influential descriptions of both the aesthetic and thematic tendencies of this mode of film-making. This is not to imply that all costume dramas made in Britain adhere to the conventions that Higson describes in his work. There is, however, an extent to which most British costume drama since the success of *Chariots of Fire* (Hugh Hudson, 1981) and the films of James Ivory and Ismail Merchant – the films which have become the focal point of much of the heritage paradigm – have been in some ways a continuation of, or a reaction to, the kind of film-making found in those films. *Mrs Brown* is no exception to this rule and the paradigm of heritage can thus be usefully brought to bear on the film, in both aesthetic and industrial terms.

In analysing *Mrs Brown* in terms of its representation of history, we should begin with the view of the film articulated by Petrie (2005a), Neely (2005) and McArthur (2001) that its main stylistic strategy is based around the opposition between the robust energy of Brown (and, by implication, Scottishness) and 'an England marked by genteel restraint and repression that is characteristic of conventional heritage representations' (Neely, 2005, p. 244). In order to develop these insights to a greater degree and to offer a reading of what exactly the film is trying to say through this opposition, we can look at some of the stylistic conventions associated with heritage cinema. We can begin with visual style and mise-en-scène, aspects of the film which, when taken together, can be usefully compared to what Richard Dyer has called the 'museum aesthetic' of heritage films (1995, p. 204). Heritage film-making in the core works of the 1980s and 1990s is distinguished from much previous costume drama by its painstaking attention to period detail and historical accuracy in creating simulacra of the past through set design and costume. These meticulous recreations are then showcased through a particular camera style, one described succinctly by Higson, who says that in heritage films 'camerawork generally is fluid, artful and pictorialist, editing slow and undramatic. The use of long takes and deep focus, and long and medium shots rather than close-ups, produces a restrained aesthetic of display' (1996, pp. 233–234).

Such an aesthetic is present in *Mrs Brown* and it is associated almost exclusively with the film's English characters. Victoria and her attendants, especially early in the film, are seen mainly in interior shots inside the decorous rooms of 'heritage' locations such as Balmoral or Osborne House. When they do venture out of doors they are seen in medium and long shots as they walk in the ornate gardens of either estate. Brown, in contrast, is associated with the outdoors and with a mise-en-scène dominated by landscape photography. In his first appearance in the film, for example, he is framed against the rocky shores of the Isle of Wight complete with choppy seas lashing the coast. When he appears in 'heritage' spaces, Brown acts as a disruptive force. This can be seen in a sequence early in the film, when Brown, having offended the Queen with his frank comments about her emotional state, decides to force her to make use of his services by waiting with her pony in the courtyard, an act which is viewed by the court as open insubordination. The sequence begins with the camera moving through the sculpted hedges and comes to follow several nurses and children, as the group wanders through the garden until they meet Brown who is waiting with the pony. The interruption of courtly manners by Brown is represented by means of a marked break from the camera style which has been in use for much of the sequence and the film as a whole, as the camera stops on Brown and moves in from a medium shot to a close-up of his and the pony's faces, depriving the viewer of the finery of the garden which customarily marks the heritage mise-en-scène.

Brown's effrontery is enough to disrupt other heritage settings, as seen when at this point in the sequence the Queen notices Brown standing in the garden. Framed against the backdrop of a hallway full of paintings and sculptures, the Queen is frozen in her tracks when she sees Brown and gazes out the window, taken aback at his behaviour. The use of space here is very pointed in terms of generic conventions. The scene follows a pattern Pidduck describes as common in costume drama, a pattern she calls the 'woman at the window', 'a generic spatio-temporal economy of physical and sexual constraint' (2004, p. 26). Brown will later provide a source of sublimated sexual release for the Queen, but at this point it is important to see that mise-en-scène and camera style are the devices that mark him as the object of desire, the thing lacking in the Queen's life.

Another way in which Brown disrupts what would have been conventional heritage camera style is seen by the fact that all of the (very rare) occurrences of hand-held camera in the film – which are jolting within the context of the smooth, steady camera style of the film as a whole – coincide with Brown, whether he is running through the wilderness with a pistol or fighting with the ruffians in the stables at Balmoral. Such a camera style corresponds to Brown's vigour and physicality, which are juxtaposed with the stiffness and rigidity of his English counterparts. This can be seen in the film's matching scenes in which we see first the Queen, and then later Brown, go swimming. In the first of these we see the Queen and the princesses, clad in very covering Victorian swimming costumes and filmed using static camera shots, go into the still, tranquil water (Figure 2). When we see Brown and Archie (Gerald Butler) go swimming, on the other hand, the cinematography switches to hand-held as the camera follows them as they leap naked into the choppy waters. The contrast between the two leads is clear: nudity and vigour on Brown's part versus restrictive dress and rigidity on the part of the Queen. It is significant, however, to note the differing camera style associated with each character. Recognizing this aspect of the film's style helps us to appreciate the ways in which the film uses visual style to subtly communicate changes in the characters and their relationship to one another from this point on.

As previously described in the discussion of the film's 'woman at the window' moment, longing and a corresponding suppression of (e)motion are associated with the film's presentation of the Queen. The extent to which Brown's dynamism is presented as desirable, and indeed necessary, in the film is encapsulated in its opening shots. Following the opening title cards which situate us historically and give us the biographical context necessary for understanding the film's plot, we see a bust falling in slow motion from the edge of a castle. Such an opening immediately creates a sense of crisis for the monarchy as the 'heritage' sculpture cascades and

Figure 2 'Heritage' Action: Queen Victoria (Judy Dench) goes for a swim in *Mrs Brown*

crashes to the ground, shattering. This sense of crisis is amplified by the feeling that the bust must be that of Albert, as we have just been told of his recent death. (We later find out that is the sculpture of Brown that the Queen commissioned, and which Bertie [David Westhead] has destroyed in celebration of his death.) Then comes a jump-cut to Brown, identifiably Scottish as he is clad in his kilt, running through the night, pistol in hand. Cutting from slow motion to the hand-held, frenetic and disorienting camera work which characterizes the shots of Brown charging through the forest creates a jarring effect, especially as a scene of such action would not be among viewers' expectations when watching a historical costume drama in 1997. Brown shouts 'God save the Queen' and fires into the darkness, and we flash back to 1861 and the beginning of his and Victoria's story. With the sequence's foreboding tone and the image of this Scotsman rushing out in to the darkness to confront whatever force is supposed to be threatening the royal household, this sequence establishes the energy and vigour of Billy Connolly's Brown as seemingly the only force protecting the monarchy.

As the film progresses, Brown's movement and energy come to be portrayed as the antidote to the Queen's frozen, static crisis. A tentative first encounter takes place when Brown slowly leads the Queen away from the palace and into the woods. Both visual style – in this case, increased but steady movement as the camera swoops from above the house to follow the pair – and mise-en-scène, with Brown and Victoria moving through the sculpted garden off into a less carefully tended copse in the woods, underscore the gradual movement of the Queen's affections towards Brown. The high point of their friendship later in the film comes as they ride through the Highland hills at Balmoral (Figure 3). The camera style here shows a nearly perfect, in the film's terms, synthesis between Brown's dynamism and the heritage concerns for displaying attractions as the camera sweeps through the Highland landscape following the pair at a greater speed than seen earlier and yet still with enough

Figure 3 England and Scotland in harmony: Queen Victoria and John Brown riding in the Highlands in *Mrs Brown*

perspective to appreciate the grandeur of the landscape scenery. Later in the film, when we return to the scene showing Brown charging out into the darkness around Buckingham Palace, the same hand-held camera sequence from the film's opening, we see the balance in style has been lost as a series of disorienting, visually jarring shots create a sense of confusion and uncertainty. This mirrors Brown's mental state as his protective feelings towards the Queen have given way to a mania of sorts. As for the Queen, she was last seen before this sequence, sitting at the head of an ornate dining table unable to acknowledge Brown personally for saving her life. She has returned to the stasis from which Brown had tried to rescue her.

As indicated by some of the disparaging nicknames for films of the heritage cycle listed by Higson (2003, p. 9) – 'frock flicks', 'bodice rippers' and 'white flannel films' – as well as the more neutral critical term 'costume drama', the films are most commonly associated with clothing, specifically the lavish and detailed costumes on display in the films. *Mrs Brown* is no exception to this generalization, but the use of costume in the film, and indeed in many other heritage works, does not consist solely of presenting elaborate costumes for viewers to admire. As several scholars, including Pam Cook (1996), Stella Bruzzi (1997) and Sarah Street (2001) have argued, costumes are best understood not just as the 'eye candy' in any given film, but instead as part of the aesthetic system of a film text, contributing to the process of making meaning just as much as editing, dialogue or any other element of film style. Cook, in her case study of Britain's Gainsborough melodramas, has linked uses of costume in period dramas to the ways in which films project images of national identity. Such an approach dovetails nicely with my current line of argument because, as she points out, tartanry is a discourse that in visual terms is closely intertwined with dress and costume (1996, p. 29). McArthur picks up on the relationship between the film and the discourse of tartanry when he describes it as 'one of those so-called "kilt films"' (see Figure 4) and places it alongside works such as *Rob Roy* (Michael Caton-Jones, 1995) and *Braveheart* (2001, pp. 184–185).

The mere presence of the kilt in the film and its association with its hero is significant. Along with the Highland landscape shots which dominate the film's mise-en-scène during the Balmoral sequences, the kilt has the film entering the iconographic space of

Figure 4 A 'kilt film': Queen Victoria and John Brown (Billy Connolly), in tartan regalia, in *Mrs Brown*

tartanry. For many Scottish cultural critics this discourse has been described as an inauthentic and regressive pattern of representation of the national culture. Tom Nairn, for instance, in his *The Break-Up of Britain* laments the 'unbearable, crass, mindless philistinism' of the tartan displays seen on international nights at London pubs (1981, p. 160). He has also commented on the persistence of the discourse and the relationship of that persistence to a very negative view of popular culture, saying that 'Tartanry will not wither away, if only because it possesses the force of its own vulgarity' (1981, p. 165). The use of the kilt and the Highlands in *Mrs Brown*, however, invest the discourse with significant dignity and respectability. Unlike films like *Local Hero* or *Shallow Grave*,[21] the tartan icons of Scottishness – the Highlands and kilts – are handled in *Mrs Brown* without a hint of irony or subversion, instead they play a major part in the proud projection of national identity and difference.

More than simply proudly utilizing the kilt, Madden makes use of the costume to make larger statements about Brown's position in the Queen's world. Over the course of the film we only see Brown not wearing a kilt on four occasions: once he is seen nude while swimming (itself an important costume choice), and on three occasions he is seen in trousers. Of these, one is particularly the-matically pointed in its usage of costume. This comes late in the film after Disraeli (Anthony Sher) has prevailed upon Brown to take action and convince the Queen to return to public duties and, by so doing, stem the growing tide of republicanism which threatens the Tory government as well as, Brown is led to believe, the Queen's reign. Arguing with Victoria over whether or not he has betrayed her by suggesting she answer Parliament's calls to return to public duty, Brown appears indoors in trousers instead of his customary kilt. Making a pained plea that the audience knows he does not want to make, Brown's costume here suggests a new-found alliance with the English members of the court who, throughout the film, have been trying to coax the Queen into such a return. Brown's discomfort at having to assume such a position is underscored by his seemingly awkward movements in the trousers, an awkwardness which is amplified by the jarring effect that his alien appearance has to an audience which is, at this point, unaccustomed to seeing Brown dressed in such a fashion. The growing distance between the characters is clear at the end of the argument when Victoria chastises Brown for referring to her as 'woman', something which he has done throughout the film, saying, 'Do not presume to speak to your Queen in such a manner.' This answer is one of rigidly formal language and is spoken by Judi Dench in a tone of voice that is regal and condescending, far from the intimate tones that characterized the pair's conversations up to this point.

'Dame Judi' and the 'Big Yin': stardom, performance and national allegory

This climactic scene, in which Dench and Connolly communicate so much through their nuanced performances, allows us an oppor-tune moment to observe the importance of acting and star persona in *Mrs Brown*. Discussing the issue of 'quality' in public service broadcasting, Charlotte Brunsdon has noted that televised costume drama is a programming format that has 'come to figure [. . .] as the acme of British quality' (1990, p. 85). Writing specifically about the Granada serials *The Jewel in the Crown* (1984) and *Brideshead Revisited* (1981), Brunsdon notes the importance of casting certain types of actors who lend such dramas an air of 'quality'. She terms this aspect of the dramas 'the best of British acting': 'the presence of name theatrical actresses and actors' which 'adds the international dimension of British theatre to the programmes' (1990, p. 85).

Mrs Brown adheres to this convention by virtue of Judi Dench's casting and performance as Victoria as well as the casting of other British theatrical actors in supporting roles, such as Anthony Sher (who plays a memorable Disraeli) and Geoffrey Palmer (who plays Ponsonby). But the use of stardom in *Mrs Brown* goes beyond just conforming to genre conventions and also opens up questions of national representation. Though this was Dench's first leading role in the cinema, it came after a long career on the English stage and in television, most notably in the sitcom *As Time Goes By* (1992). Dench had also played a number of supporting roles in canonical heritage films such as *A Room with a View* (James Ivory, 1987) and *A Handful of Dust* (Charles Sturridge, 1988). Such a career has led Higson to include her among his list of the repertory players of heritage cinema in Britain (2003, p. 30) (a group which also includes Geoffrey Palmer), and led to an appointment as Dame Commander of the British Empire in 1985. This title has since been taken up frequently by the journalistic media in reviewing her work, as she is now commonly known as 'Dame Judi'.

Whereas the English characters are played by theatrically trained actors, Brown is played by Billy Connolly, a casting decision which draws on his persona as a working-class Scottish comedian who is widely known to have worked in a shipyard before moving into the world of comedy. Though an actor like Dench might be considered to be the more 'bankable' star in a heritage film, it was actually a desire to feature Connolly that led to BBC Scotland's interest in making the film (Meir, 2012, p. 55). Connolly's persona as an outspoken, ultra-masculine Scot and his large stature have earned him the nickname 'the Big Yin'. His casting alongside Dench is very significant and can be seen as taking the film in the direction of national allegory. The pairing of Dench, arch-English stage actress, and Connolly, arch-Scottish masculine actor, lends the film an international, class-crossing character. Such can be seen in the press coverage of an altercation at the film's Edinburgh Film Festival premier involving Connolly and a reporter from a Scottish newspaper. Reports on the incident invariably mention that the incident occurred in front of 'Dame' Judi Dench, implying shockingly inappropriate behaviour on the part of Connolly in front of such a regal personality as Dench (e.g. Bradshaw, 1997, p. 13).

The pairing also brings an element of pan-Britishness to the film, as noted by one reviewer who describes the two actors as showing 'two sides of the same coin – the heads and tails of the kingdom' (Walker, 1997, p. 27). In the film, the contrast in the personae of the respective actors translates into contrasting performance styles. Again we can look to generic conventions to describe and explain this difference. Caughie gives a particularly insightful description of the appeal of acting in costume drama, and one that is apropos of Dench's Victoria, when he writes of the

> [P]leasure in watching performance rather than the more seductive pleasure of losing oneself in the fantasy of identification: a pleasure in the observation of the details of gesture and inflection, in watching skill with the relaxed judgement detachment and critical judgement which Brecht associates with the aficionado of boxing. (2000, p. 224)

The kind of showy acting that Caughie sees as characterizing performances such as Peggy Aschcroft's in *The Jewel in the Crown* also characterizes Dench's performance in *Mrs Brown*. One such instance that is brief enough to discuss here is the scene in which Victoria seeks out the advice of the Dean of Windsor (Oliver Ford Davies) about the guilt she feels over her relationship with Brown. For reasons of rank and title, the Queen cannot speak directly to the Dean regarding her mixed feelings of attraction to Brown and guilt towards Albert's memory. So Dench must communicate this subtext through opaque dialogue that allows Victoria to avoid speaking directly. The conflicting feelings apparent when Dench's voice catches in her throat while saying that she has 'come to rely more on the comfort of living friends' are moving to the audience in that they are able to both appreciate the extent of emotional repression the Queen is feeling, but are also able to delight in Dench's ability to convey so much with these slight gestures and modulations of voice, to dab her eyes with a handkerchief when we realize her character must want to break down sobbing. It is little wonder then that Dench received the BAFTA and Golden Globe awards for Best Actress and was nominated for an Oscar in the same category: not only is her performance highly skilled, but the film's appeal is largely based on it, something Miramax chief Harvey Weinstein was very aware of as he aggressively campaigned for the film and Dench individually to be nominated for Oscars (Higson, 2003, p. 7).[22]

Billy Connolly's performance as Brown, on the other hand, is seemingly not marked by the subtlety or nuance found in the performances of the English actors. Petrie says of the film's acting styles that Connolly's 'energetic performance' overshadows 'the *longeurs*' of 'typical heritage style' (2000a, p. 212). McKechnie also notes this divide in performance styles, saying: 'There is a very poignant contrast between the refined southern English courtiers and the ruddy Scotsman, who "speaks as he finds" and seems to be the embodiment of [quoting Robert Burns] "the honest man, tho' e'er sae poor, [who is] King o' Men, for a' that"' (2002, p. 229). There is much truth in these characterizations, especially when it comes to contrasting Englishness and Scottishness. Brown says exactly what is on his mind and, although it initially shocks the Queen, it ultimately charms her and leads to the casual intimacy between the two. The extent to which this is presented by the film as a Scottish character trait is seen early in the film when Brown's brother Archie warns him about his lack of manners in directly addressing the Queen. Brown defends his speaking out of turn at the first meeting with the Queen in the film, saying: 'I speak as I find, Archie'; Archie responds, 'Not down South you don't, John.' Brown's bluntness and often boisterous tone of voice also highlight a class divide which accompanies the cultural divide between the Scottish and English in the film.

But this is only one aspect of Connolly's performance as Brown. Just as there is a play in the film with dress so that Brown appears uncomfortable in the clothes of the English so does he at times poignantly struggle to express himself in the formal dialogue that characterizes courtly speech. One instance of this comes when he attempts to resign his post following the scandal caused by his alleged involvement in a drunken fight ('I had foreseen that you would not . . . but Your Majesty should understand that I will not be changed in this', he labours to say). Another comes when he must assume a 'stiff upper lip' when hearing his work in stopping an assassination attempt denigrated by Bertie (David Westhead). At these moments we see that, despite the blunt directness that has characterized his performance to this point and which has been the subject of most of the commentary on that performance, Connolly is still capable of considerable subtlety and reserve. The difference between the performances is thus not that Connolly's lacks the kind of technical skill that Dench demonstrates in abundance but that because of his persona, it is not recognized by the critical community in quite the same way.

Scottish film, Scottish history

Having established how the film mobilizes both textual and intertextual generic conventions of costume drama to project cultural difference within Britain and, at points, to suggest a balance between those cultures, we can now turn to issues of history and its representation in the film. As the film takes Scotland's role in the British national past as one of its explicit subjects, more so than any film of the so-called new Scottish cinema period, I would be remiss if I did not examine exactly how that national past is imagined and what relevance that has for the time in which it was produced, a period described by all as one of momentous political change for Britain and Scotland.

One of the most pervasive criticisms of the heritage cycle of the Thatcher years was that it failed to engage critically with history or to offer any substantial commentary on the present day. Hill sums up the positions of those criticizing the political disengagement of heritage cinema with the present when he writes about the initial debates regarding heritage culture in the late 1980s: 'Heritage culture is often regarded as a form of retreat from the present, providing satisfactions which the present does not provide or compensation for what it lacks' (1999, p. 74). Later commentators on the genre, though, have argued that heritage does comment on the present, if only to attack the way in which it does so. Monk notes that because it maps national identity on to the trials and tribulations of upper-class characters, heritage cinema, like heritage culture at large, was accused of 'promot[ing] a false notion of historical reality' (2002, p. 179). This is among the complaints that McArthur has about *Mrs Brown*: that despite its projection of a complimentary sort of Scottish heritage, its claims about the relationship between Brown and Victoria 'actually confirm [the Scots'] subjection' (2001, p. 185).

An examination of the interpretation of history in *Mrs Brown* does well to begin with some account of the 'history' it takes as its subject. The film centres on a long-standing rumour that Queen

Victoria, who lent her name to an age renowned for its sexual repression, had a love affair with her Scottish ghillie during a lengthy period of mourning for her late husband Prince Albert. Though Victoria is of course a well-known figure in British history, her relationship with Brown has remained relatively opaque to historians and obscure to the lay person. Commenting on the selection of this particular relationship for the subject of the film, and its treatment by the film-makers, McKechnie notes that 'the way [the film's] love story is foregrounded over the "demands" of history and biography takes advantage of gaps in historical recording. *Mrs Brown* does not take its historical responsibility lightly; but rather than merely reproducing, it interprets' (2002, p. 228). Indeed, much of the journalistic coverage of the film (and, one suspects, the industrial positioning of the film by publicists), both in the UK and abroad, included some explication of the gap in the historical accounts of Brown and Victoria's relationship which the film uses as its point of departure (e.g. Janusonis, 1997, p. E-6; Wakefield, 1997, p. 26). Because not many viewers would have been aware of the John Brown controversy, much less of its particular details, the film-makers would not have faced the sort of pedantic nit-picking in the name of 'accuracy' that usually accompanies the reception of historical biopics. At the same time, however, the film can claim to make a statement on an actual historical controversy, suggesting that Victoria and Brown shared a very passionate, but in the end, chaste friendship. Crucially, given the BBC's public service ethos, it can also claim to be an 'educational' film, informing the public about obscure events in the life of an otherwise well-known monarch.

Embedded in this interpretation of the life of a British monarch is a foregrounding of the role that a Scottish servant played at a moment of great historical importance, heroically forgoing his own wishes, sacrificing his closest friendship and by doing so, saving the monarchy. Even if Brown is only provoked into doing so by the unscrupulous Disraeli, and even if Disraeli acts only out of self-interest, the film nonetheless presents the preservation of the monarchy as a good thing. This is underscored by the sweeping parliamentary address by Disraeli which follows the Queen's decree that Brown will be given an award for devoted service. As Victoria solemnly reflects on Brown's service and Brown himself is seen stoically accepting his fate to be relegated to the shadows, the film moves to Disraeli's swelling oration praising the decision to keep the monarchy intact, ending on the words 'power and glory' while the Parliament erupts in applause.

Brown's noble act of self-denial and loyalty takes on a particular importance when one considers the film's own historical context, as the political concerns of Great Britain in 1997 are writ large in the text of *Mrs Brown*. Chapman and McKechnie point to the travails of the House of Windsor as being the film's main objects of contemporary commentary (Chapman, 2005, pp. 315–316; McKechnie 2002, p. 219), but the film can also be productively seen in light of anxieties over the 'break up of Britain'. Knowing a devolutionary movement was in the air, Victoria's angry reaction when she learns of the ecclesiastical 'devolution' of Ireland from the Church of England ('The Irish must be told very firmly to stay exactly where they are. It's the thin end of the wedge Mr Disraeli. The next thing you will be telling me is that I no longer rule this nation') takes on a special resonance, especially as the 'nation' being referred could be interpreted as Scotland, given that she is still at Balmoral when she says this.

Simply choosing to make a film about Queen Victoria at this time could be seen as a significant statement in light of the context of devolution in Scotland and a similar groundswell of nationalist sentiment in Wales. It was Victoria, after all, who presided over the unprecedented expansion of the Empire abroad and who attempted to use her influence to create a truly 'united kingdom'. These efforts included the purchase of estates in Scotland and the Isle of Wight, the designation of the future king as the Prince of Wales, the granting of her children symbolic dukedoms throughout Great Britain (e.g. the Dukes of Cornwall and Edinburgh), and starting a popular craze for all things tartan and Highland. For all of this, Victoria was a sovereign who, more so than most others, is associated with trying to spread the monarchy throughout the kingdom (Richards, 1997, p. 8). An invocation of her legacy at such a point in history thus recalls a united Great Britain at a moment which some would have considered to be the precipice of its irrevocable break-up. This invocation is especially resonant when the film's narrative presents a pan-British historical allegory which positions Scotsman Brown as the force that gets Victoria back to her public duties and in effect saves the monarchy from the threat of republicanism.[23]

Though the film presents Brown and the Queen as forgoing their private desires for the public good, there is still some ambivalence about Brown's treatment at the hands of the British establishment. The view that the film projects of Brown as noble in his self-sacrifice can also be seen as supporting a postcolonial reading of his role in Victoria's life and reign. In order to develop this reading we can begin by returning to McArthur's comments on the film, which compare Brown to the 'house nigger' of slavery stories and in which McArthur argues that the film is an 'ideological con trick', saying that Brown's apparent high standing in Victoria's court serves to mask a 'discourse that confirms [the Scots'] subjection' (2001, pp. 185–186). There is much in the film to support McArthur's view of the film. Brown's physical vigour, represented by the numerous shots of his naked or bruised body, can be seen as the, by now, recognizable erotic subject of the colonizer's (the Queen's) gaze. In this respect, Neely is correct to make a parallel between the film and those of the so-called Raj revival of the 1980s, in which imperial history was represented sexually through various permutations of colonizer and colonized (2005, p. 244). Even the word 'noble', which I have used in describing Brown, is in postcolonial circles all too easily linked with 'savage'. Such a view of the film would interpret Brown's sacrifice as one procured through the Machiavellian trickery of Disraeli and, subsequently, historically suppressed through the intervention of the equally Machiavellian members of court.

Any critical reading of the film along these lines is problematized, however, by the melodramatic pull of Brown's deathbed scene. When Victoria comes to see Brown on his deathbed she offers what the film presents as a heartfelt apology for her neglect of Brown in the intervening years since the stay at Balmoral and says that she is desperate at the thought of losing him. The tenderness with which this scene is filmed and acted, with rising music, soft candle-light and Dench's teary eyes, presents the apology as genuine. Though it cannot be said to cancel out all of the colonially charged images we have seen to this point, the deathbed apology does illustrate the fact that the film wants to show Brown's devotion to the Queen as something that was recognized and appreciated – not simply disregarded by a capricious, egocentric ruler – and finally as justified and rewarded, despite the final act of betrayal by Ponsonby that keeps the truth about Brown and the Queen from ever being known. Brown really was Victoria's best friend, as he somewhat pitifully argued to Archie, and his sacrifice was appreciated. Whether or not it is received as such will vary, according to the viewer, but at least the film is trying to make us believe as much.

The nationalist allegory that underpins the film is presented then as one of nobility, not subjection, one made from a point of view we can roughly call Unionist. That the film is attempting to engage with such issues is of great significance to Scottish film history. Within the body of work now known as the 'new Scottish cinema', this is the only film to deal with devolution. Though Martin-Jones (2005a, 2005b, 2009) has argued that films such as *Orphans*, *Regeneration* (Gillies Mackinnon, 1997), *The Last Great Wilderness* (David Mackenzie, 2001) and *Dog Soldiers* (Neil Marshall, 2002) reflect English and Scottish national anxieties regarding devolution, *Mrs Brown* is the only film that actually attempts to represent them, even if that representation is projected onto the past. Since Petrie's original narrative of 'new Scottish cinema' culminates with the cinematic achievements of *Ratcatcher* and *Orphans* coinciding with the establishment of the devolved Scottish Parliament (2000a, p. 191), suggesting a link between the two, *Mrs Brown* deserves more in-depth attention than it has heretofore received. The relative lack of attention that the film has received may be explained by its anti-devolutionary stance. After all, in the context of a movement that has been described as one towards national political and representational sovereignty, a film that can be seen as celebrating Unionism and, with its unashamed tartanry, revels in what most Scottish cinema critics would call 'incorrect' Scottishness, is somewhat troublesome from a historian's point of view. This is especially the case when that film found such a large audience at home and abroad. It is with such an understanding in mind that we can now return to its production context.

Mrs Brown as public service

In what ways are the changing goals of public service broadcasting realized by *Mrs Brown*? What does the film's circulation at home and abroad tell us about the role that public service broadcasters such as BBC Scotland have played in Scottish cinema? *Mrs Brown* is not only the story of one of Britain's most celebrated monarchs, but also that of an important Scottish figure whose exact story remains somewhat shrouded in mystery. Despite the generally obscure details of his life, Brown is a figure with some cultural cachet in Scotland, but he is also one that, in a way which mirrors his removal from history in the film, remains marginalized within British film representations of history. The two major biopics of Victoria before *Mrs Brown*, Herbert Wilcox's *Victoria the Great* and *Sixty Glorious Years*, both relegate Brown (played by Gordon McLeod in both films) to a small role in which he appears to be no more significant than any of the Queen's (Anna Neagle in both films) other servants. Victoria's biographers likewise have mainly downplayed any rumours of an affair between the two and kept commentary on one of the central figures in Victoria's court to a minimum. Dulcie Ashdown devotes three pages out of 200 of her biography of the monarch to giving an account of Brown (1975, pp. 129–132); Lytton Strachey provides his version of the life of Brown in three pages of his 300-hundred page biography of Victoria (1921, pp. 271–274). Other attempts to bring the story to the screen, including one that would have had Sean Connery playing Brown opposite Julie Christie as Victoria, were reportedly scuppered by the royal family as, out of fear of bringing scandal upon Victoria, they threatened to bar the film-makers from using royal palaces as locations for shooting (Flynn, 1997, p. 24). The significance of getting this story of a famous Scotsman on to the screen is thus one that should not be underestimated.[24]

Another important historical context for *Mrs Brown* has less to do with political history and more to do with the tonal history of Scottish representation. Going by Connolly's description of Brown's reputation within Scotland, we should take note of the 'lowest common denominator' description that he gives that reputation: 'In Scotland he's loved. He's looked on as "One of our guys nailed the Queen, yes!"', one newspaper story quotes him as saying (Bickelhaupt and Dezell, 1997, p. E2). This aspect of the film's historical interpretation, which runs counter to that particular version of Brown's reputation, brings to the fore not only issues of 'quality' in the sense of tastefulness, but also, within the Scottish context, the issue of market failure and correction. With its status as a costume drama in the 'heritage' mould, with the attendant connotations of taste and decorum and its use of traditional representational discourses, the film's place in the history of Scottish film representations is also important to consider. As noted above, by the late 1990s *Mrs Brown*'s insistence on a tartan vision of Scotland could be seen as a bit anachronistic. Non-ironic use of kilts and Highland vistas would have appeared to be somewhat passé in 1997, following the success of culturally iconoclastic films such as *Shallow Grave* and *Trainspotting*. These films forever changed the way Scotland is imagined on the screen, particularly among international audiences. Suddenly kilts were not the only images associated with Scotland, much to the dismay of some. If Scottish cultural critics once worried that the nation would be too much known as the land of *Brigadoon*, following the international success of *Trainspotting*, the fear was, especially among Scottish tourism interests, that the world would perceive the nation as being plagued with crime and drug addiction; that instead of the Highlands, one would imagine Scotland in terms of the urban squalor depicted in films like *Ratcatcher* and *Small Faces*, or in the best-selling novels of Irvine Welsh and Ian Rankin (Nash, 1998, p. 286).

This goes for the style and tone of the film as well as its content. As opposed to the amorality of (anti)hero Mark Renton (Ewan McGregor) in *Trainspotting*, Brown is a hero because he does his duty, and this is a conscious interpretation of a controversial historical figure by the film-makers. To return to Brown's reputation as Connolly describes it, it hardly needs pointing out that *Mrs Brown* does not interpret the figure in this way. Again, Connolly explains the film's conception of Brown: 'I don't think he [slept with Victoria] . . . He was a servant for twenty-five years, and his father was one before him. He knew the rules; he knew not to cross that line' (Alberge, 1997). Though we cannot take Connolly's account as necessarily reflecting the views of the Scottish nation as a whole, his usage of this anecdote in promoting the film (it crops up in other interviews with him and Dench),[25] tells us that the perception was meant to be communicated to the film's audience.

Framed in such a way, Brown is not the class and culture bounding Lothario that Connolly describes as being the historical Brown's popular persona in Scotland, nor is he the rude, mean-spirited alcoholic which some of Victoria's biographers have described him as. For the sake of comparison, one could easily imagine how the story of Brown and Victoria could have been handled by writers like Irvine Welsh and *Trainspotting* screenwriter John Hodge. Viewed in such a context, the conscious effort to evoke stylistic 'quality' and the fusion of tartan dress and Scottish working-class masculinity with a narrative arc which associates duty, self-sacrifice and knowing one's place, has the film assuming the historical role of attempting to reinscribe a certain 'tasteful' vision of Scotland and Scots into the popular imagination. There is no toilet-diving in *Mrs Brown* and the heroic act of its protagonist is putting duty ahead of personal gain, a far cry from the climactic act of betrayal in *Trainspotting*. We thus see competing views of Scotland and Scottishness, disparate visions described astutely by Murray Smith as those of 'heritage' on the one hand and 'garbage' on the other (2002, p. 25). Given the emphasis on the latter in Scottish cultural production during this period, the evocation of 'heritage' through such a high-profile film is, in its own restrained way – quite a bold statement indeed.

Neely discusses this aspect of Scotland's film and television output through a discussion of heritage cinema's role as 'cultural ambassador' and writes that works such as *Mrs Brown*, *Rob Roy* and *Monarch of the Glen* acted in such a capacity (2005, p. 245). While I agree with Neely's general framework, I would argue that in fact only *Mrs Brown* among these works acts as a heritage 'cultural ambassador'. Though *Rob Roy* and especially *Braveheart* have had an enormous impact on Scottish tourism, their generic status as action films with a wholly different set of generic conventions distinguishes them from the sort of tasteful products that are associated with quality costume drama. As for *Monarch*, the fact that it remains a television series also inhibits its comparison to *Mrs Brown*. Though they share a common production context, even having been made by the same company, as Neely points out (2005, p. 243), their distribution contexts are crucial: whether justified or not, the aura of quality that theatrical distribution has outstrips that of television. In the media climate of the 1990s, and even still today, 'Oscar buzz' is a prestigious brand to which television simply does not have access. A work's ability to act as cultural ambassador is infinitely magnified within such a context. Thus *Mrs Brown* is, in terms of production and distribution, the only true 'heritage' cultural ambassador for Scotland during this period.

This position as cultural ambassador raises a number of other issues related to export, issues which often arise not only in relation to British costume drama film-making but also British television in the age of increasing co-production with American television partners. As Monk has shown, much of the critical animosity at 'heritage' films was based explicitly upon the films' success in export – particularly American – markets, to the extent that costume dramas which were not successful abroad were spared the pejorative label of 'heritage film' (2002, p. 180). Such a critical reaction echoes that found within the critical literature on the BBC and the export of British television discussed above, particularly in the case of Caughie's writing on costume drama. While there is no disputing the popularity of British costume drama among American audiences, writers on this topic seem to overlook the fact that such representations are considerably popular within Britain as well, and the works thus do not look the way that they do just because of these co-production agreements.

What about those agreements – do they indeed represent a threat to the creative control of British and Scottish television and film? Executive producer Andrea Calderwood has said that neither WGBH nor equity investor Irish Screen had any direct creative input on the film (Meir, 2012, p. 57). At the same time, however, she does acknowledge certain expectations on the part of WGBH that the film feature 'classy stars' and the other trappings of British 'quality' costume dramas. This point raises larger questions of generic expectations on the part of American production partners. In her study of British television exports, Steemers agrees that such creative pressures exist, but her example of American intervention in the production of British costume dramas is hardly alarming from a cultural point of view, this being the intervention of WGBH's executive producer Rebecca Eaton asking the British producers of *Persuasion* (Roger Michell, 1995) – another film which the BBC opted to distribute theatrically – to have the film's romantic leads kiss at the film's climax. This suggestion, according to Steemers, was greeted apprehensively by the British producers who felt it would have been anachronistic as people at the time that the film was set would not have kissed publicly. For her part, Steemers acknowledges that this change probably made the film better (2004, p. 115).

Export pressures have thus not been shown to have negatively affected the capacity of costume dramas to cater to British tastes and sensibilities. In all likelihood many British viewers, like Steemers, agreed with what Eaton suggested. When it comes to the export of British film, Street has shown that there is no easy distinction between indigenous and exportable pleasures in films (2002, p. 221), and a similar thing can be said about the content of British costume drama made for television. So if it was that WGBH (and later Miramax) wanted a 'classy piece' – to use Calderwood's phrase – that would garner critical acclaim and possibly awards, would this really be any different from the expectations that British and Scottish backers and audiences would have?

Such objections to the increasing involvement of American producers are not necessarily creatively minded fears as much as they are objections on principle to who exactly British television (and, by extension, film) are made for. The assumption in much national cinema study is that national cinema is meant to serve the domestic culture first and foremost (Street, 2002, p. 3), and such can also be said to be the case with national television production. In the realm of television drama, Steemers writes of such a tension existing, pointing particularly to costume drama that is more popular abroad than at home (2004, p. 33), but based on the evidence available this was not the case with *Mrs Brown*. Though the film attracted more admissions in the USA than in Britain (1.8 million in the USA compared to 900,000 in Britain [Lumiere Database, 2013]), the proportional audiences in each nation shows that a higher percentage of Britons saw the film at the cinema than did Americans (14.93 per 1000 of Britons compared to 6.61 per 1000 in the USA [Lumiere Database, 2013]). In fact, the film was, relatively speaking, a bigger hit in the UK than any other national market in North America and Europe. This is before taking into account the film's audiences on television, where the film, like all BBC Films productions, has been regularly broadcast in the UK.

Conclusion: BBC Scotland and the funding of Scottish national cinema

Mrs Brown is a film that, in a manner intricately related to heritage aesthetics, seeks to establish a polarity between Scottishness and Englishness. This articulation of national and cultural difference gives way to a loose allegory depicting Scottishness as the saviour of the British Crown during a time of royal crisis. Given the film's references to devolutionary pressures during Victoria's reign and its own production in the shadow of the second devolution referendum in Scotland, the film offers an ambivalent view on the historical relationship between Scotland and Britain, one that represents the devolutionary tensions of the period more than any other film in the 'new Scottish' canon. *Mrs Brown* is also a film that ran counter to the representations of Scotland that dominated screens around the time of its release, reasserting a certain tasteful vision of the nation that distinguished it from the bleak squalor of *Trainspotting* and similar representations.

How does this all relate to the commissioning activities of BBC Scotland, itself a devolved institutional body? In *Mrs Brown* we have a film that explores Scottish cultural history, offers a fresh viewpoint on Scotland in light of contemporary representations, and was successful in reaching local and international audiences – all while managing to reflect and comment upon a time of momentous political change in Great Britain. It is also a film which, with its royal story and casting of Dench alongside Connolly, can be said to have pan-British, cross-class appeal while still possessing the traditional textual markers of 'quality', making it popular with critics and winning it prestigious nominations and awards.

As a brief comment on the continuing convergence of television and film in Britain, it is worth pointing out how the film shows another instance of such convergence. As discussed above, John Hill particularly has asserted that the film industry in Britain could benefit from the injection of the public service tradition into film-funding decisions. Though one suspects Hill was thinking of more overtly stylistically innovative and politically left-wing films such as *My Beautiful Laundrette*,[26] his prediction could be seen as appropriate to the economics of film and television in Britain generally. In some ways it makes perfect sense that Channel 4 and BBC Films are the biggest players in the British film industry, which has seen numerous 'cross-over' successes throughout the 1980s and 1990s: there is a sense in which public service during this period has itself become a term with the idea of 'crossing over' at its heart. The films which seek to be mainstream enough to reach audiences on a large scale while also dealing with historical and cultural issues fit perfectly into programming schedules, just as they do into cinemas at home and abroad, and just as they do into government reports giving examples of public service broadcasting. Costume drama, which Steemers cites as a type of production that is perceived to fit easily into public service requirements while still holding some audience appeal (2004, p. 33) and which Higson describes in similar terms of achieving critical prestige and audience appeal (2003, pp. 123–127), is a particularly prominent example of this convergence. *Mrs Brown* is thus a work that is in cultural and industrial terms typical of Scottish film and television in this period.

3

Lynne Ramsay, cross-over cinema and *Morvern Callar*

'Young, gifted and Scottish': the auteur as national cinema milestone

Implicit in the titling of 'new' cinema is a privileging of director-driven film-making such as that found in the French *Nouvelle Vague*, or the 'new German cinema', each of which have become historically synonymous with names such as Godard, Truffaut, Varda, Herzog, Fassbinder and the like. It is thus not surprising that Petrie's account in *Screening Scotland* culminates with author-ial cinema, portraying the emergence of distinctive writer/directors as the apex of the 'new Scottish cinema' period. Hence the book begins and ends with the release of Ramsay's *Ratcatcher* and Mullan's *Orphans* (2000a, pp. 1, 226). The two are described as having 'iconoclastic visions' and 'distinctive style and thematic concerns' (2000a, p. 181). Besides the artistry and innovation that their films may display, for Petrie's account it is just as important that they simply have emerged and are distinctive artists. Such artists have long been held to be lacking in Scottish cinema, as can be seen in the call for distinctive film-makers which concludes McArthur's essay in *Scotch Reels* (1982b, pp. 67–68), and in his later essay on 'Poor Scottish Cinema' (1994, p. 112). These calls seemed to have been answered by the emergence of Ramsay, Mullan and, to a lesser extent, David Mackenzie. It was not just Scottish cinema historians who took notice. *The Independent*'s Deborah Orr – whose persona as a columnist includes a strong sense of Scottish identity – spoke for many Scottish cultural observers when she published a column on Lynne Ramsay entitled simply 'Young, Gifted and Scottish' (1999, p. 2).

A great deal of significance is attributed by Petrie, as well as by later writers, to the emergence of Ramsay and Mullan besides simply providing the nation with auteur directors. Their emergence is described as showing the formation of a discernible tradition of Scottish art cinema (Blandford, 2007, p. 77; Petrie, 2000a, p. 161; Petrie, 2004, p. 167) and as being emblematic of Scotland political devolution from the United Kingdom (Petrie, 2000a, p. 191). Blandford's account in particular posits *Ratcatcher* as the culmination of a tradition of art cinema beginning with Bill Douglas (2007, p. 77) and describes the importance of *Morvern Callar* as residing in its 'extension of the idea of Scotland as the chief outpost of serious, demanding independent cinema which in turn can be connected to the broader desire to foster cultural independence post-devolution' (2007, p. 79).

Embedded within these narratives of Ramsay's career are views on the effectiveness of policy interventions in positively shaping Scottish national cinema production. As discussed at the outset of this book, Scottish cinema historiography has throughout its own history placed great emphasis on the policy interventions of the late 1990s which created the subsidy mechanisms that ostensibly allowed for the flowering of the 'new Scottish cinema'. Within this narrative, Lynne Ramsay's career is particularly significant. *Ratcatcher* is listed among the films that Petrie cites as examples of funding structures increasing access for women to film-making in Scotland, and in cultural terms, 'engage[ing] in important ways with female experience' in an otherwise masculine-orientated tradition (2000b, pp. 167–168). In this vein it is highlighted as only the second feature written and directed by a woman in Scotland (the first being Margaret Tait's *Blue Black Permanent* [1992]) (Petrie, 2004, p. 66). Petrie's accounts of institutional interventions in the careers of Lynne Ramsay and other newly emerging directors also praises the role that short film schemes, such as BBC Scotland's *Tartan Shorts*, have played in developing the film-making skills and industrial profiles of such directors, especially Mullan and Ramsay (2000b, pp. 160–162).

Petrie is not the only historian to describe Ramsay's films as realizing the promise of film policy in Britain and Scotland. Mike Wayne has described *Ratcatcher*, along with *Beautiful People* (Jasmin Dizdar, 1999), as the 'only successful films' funded by the National Lottery in Britain (2002, p. 41). John Caughie, though, has gone furthest in citing the development of an art cinema auteur such as Lynne Ramsay as an important achievement for Scottish cinema and connecting that achievement to policy interventions. For Caughie, the film must be understood in relation to devolution generally and the search for a Scottish national identity specifically. Caughie compares the film to the 'great achievements of European art cinemas' (2007, p. 111) and writes of the 'strategic, tactical and imaginative value that the film brings to the possibilities of being creative in Scotland' (p. 113). In contextualizing the emergence of the film, Caughie points to 'the familiar institutional lineage – or patronage – of a national cinema whose claims on public funding rely less on a return on investment than on a desire for a national cinema of quality' (p. 112), the 'lineage' here referring to BBC Scotland, Scottish Screen and the Glasgow Film Fund (GFF). Caughie then offers a circumspect, but still optimistic view of the public funding of Scottish cinema, saying of the effects of an industrial mandate such as that held by the GFF:

> Thinking only of facilities, services and capacity for growth rather than the big, defining issues of culture and identity which preoccupy the desire for a national cinema, agencies may end up – even if only occasionally – supporting the creativity and individual talent through which difference leaks and on which an experimental art cinema depends. (p. 106)

While Caughie here offers a nuanced view of one institution with an industrial mandate, he leaves the rest untouched, implicitly suggesting that these are 'patrons' supporting artists like Ramsay.

In some ways these versions of Lynne Ramsay's film-making career cannot be disputed. All of her films have depended on public support, typically a combination of Lottery subsidy and funding from BBC Scotland, and it is thus difficult to imagine that she would have been able to make films without these institutions. But this does not tell the whole story. In this chapter, I argue that Ramsay's relationship to policy is significantly more complex than simply providing the financial basis for a new artist to succeed, and in doing so I also seek to explore what Ramsay's career after *Morvern Callar* tells us about the optimistic narratives presented by Scottish cinema historians. I begin by looking at the funding of *Morvern Callar*, an examination that necessarily focuses on the involvement of public subsidy bodies, particularly Scottish Screen, in the making of the film. As was the case with *Mrs Brown*, I argue that the involvement of the BBC in making the film, and generally supporting Lynne Ramsay's career, merits close attention. But, unlike the existing accounts in the field, the chapter also looks closely at the involvement of Alliance Atlantis, the now defunct Canadian sales and distribution company that acted as a co-producer of the film. As we will see, the involvement of this company once again brings with it thorny questions regarding the influence of the inter-national market on indigenous Scottish film-making, an issue that has received surprisingly little attention in discussions of the film.

Far from being a case of policy, or indeed the private sector, seeking to support the vision of a local artist, the evidence here suggests that *Morvern Callar* was seen not as a Scottish version of *The Passenger* (Michelangelo Antonioni, 1975) or Camus's *The Outsider* (Williams, 2002, p. 23), but instead as the latest 'cross-over' youth-themed drugs and raves film, expectations that the film ultimately disappointed. This view of the making of *Morvern Callar* leads us to the shadow of *Trainspotting* the film, which obviously did a great deal to kick-start Scottish film-making, but which at least in the cases of *Morvern* and *Young Adam* also set a precedent that was arguably as limiting as it was enabling for young Scottish film-makers.

Central to the examination of *Morvern Callar* and Lynne Ramsay generally are questions of genre. Just as kailyardic comedy and heritage cinema were important generic contexts to discuss in Chapters 1 and 2 respectively, so too art cinema acts as an important category for us here to unite issues of culture, aesthetics and indus-trial positioning. As we will see, tensions between the institutional dimensions of art cinema, its aesthetic tendencies and the increas-ing demand for hybrid forms of film-making that have placed more emphasis on popular pleasures have all shaped the making and reception of this film.

Making *Morvern Callar* I: BBC Scotland

Morvern Callar began its life as a film project before it had even been published as a novel. As is common practice with highly anticipated novels, Alan Warner's book was optioned for film adap-tation in 1996 by BBC Scotland before it had been published (Forde, 2002, p. 21). The BBC also commissioned the novel's author to adapt the screenplay. The buzz surrounding the novel at the time was closely related to the success of *Trainspotting* both as novel and film. Alan Warner was regarded as part of the 'chemical generation' of writers who came in the wake of Irvine Welsh's great commercial success (Dale, 2002, p. 77) and the hope was that the book and film would emulate the success of its predecessor. Ramsay was brought on to the project in 1998 before she had finished work on *Ratcatcher*. The buzz surrounding her work on that film and her award-winning short films *Small Deaths* (1996) and *Gasman* (1998) led the company to commission her to take over the project. (It also helped that the BBC had funded *Gasman* and provided some of the funding for *Ratcatcher*.) This decision was also affected by ongoing creative differences with Alan Warner, whose drafts of the screenplay were found to be uncinematic by the executives within the company (McCance, 1996).[27]

Among the executives at the BBC Films at this time were Charles Pattinson and George Faber. When these two left the BBC to form Company Pictures, they negotiated to take *Morvern* – along with other projects – with them, with the BBC retaining credit as co-producer for its work in developing the project (Slovo, 2012). Company Pictures kept the creative team of Lynne Ramsay and co-writer Liana Dognini in place and brought in Robyn Slovo to take on some of the producing duties for the film. They also began to seek additional funding for the project, looking both locally and internationally.

Making *Morvern Callar* II: public subsidy and a 'female *Trainspotting*'

As part of this search, Company Pictures applied for and received a production subsidy of £500,000 from Scottish Screen for the making of *Morvern Callar* in 2000, hot on the heels of the critical acclaim for *Ratcatcher*. Before examining the application in detail, it is important to note that the funding application accessed for this book is not complete. Though the main body of the application is currently accessible, other key materials, such as the statement of the Lottery Panel explaining their reasons for supporting the application, could not be obtained. Without this statement it is not possible to be certain what exactly the Panel found attractive in the application. Nevertheless, it is possible from looking closely at the language of the application to at least determine what it was that the applicants thought the Panel would want to read in such an application. That is to say that, by noting the points of emphasis in what was after all a successful application, it is possible to at least observe the discursive patterns within which Company Pictures sought to frame the film. Such patterns can then be inferred to reflect the criteria that Scottish Screen was looking for. With this in mind, we can begin with one question and answer in particular, a question that reads: 'Please give a brief summary (no more than 30 words) of the film you plan to make with lottery funds.' The applicants' response:

> Based on Alan Warners [*sic*] novel ('Morvern Callar'), Lynne Ramsay's rites of passage film about love, lust, growing up and escape, describes the extraordinary journey of a teenage girl from the West Coast of Scotland to the clubs and villages of Spain. (Scottish Screen, 2000)[28]

This opening description of the film immediately invokes the film's two major indigenous talents and describes the film implicitly as one which will capitalize on the vogue for youth rave culture that had been ushered in by *Trainspotting*. This dual strategy of seeking support for indigenous talent and promising a commercially viable film continues throughout the application. Appeals to Ramsay's cachet as a director can be seen in the applicants' response to question 37, 'How have you found out whether there is a demand for your film?':

> Given the excitement, critical acclaim, and festival prizes generated by Lynne Ramsay's first full length film *Ratcatcher*, we feel confident that there is already a demand for *Morvern Callar*. Lynne Ramsay is an unusually talented and exciting director who will ensure that this film will be strikingly original, memorable and accessible. (Scottish Screen, 2000)

The desire to present Ramsay as the project's major attraction can be seen by the sheer number of adjectives for both film-maker and film used in a passage consisting of only two sentences. In terms of the film-maker, we have 'critical acclaim' and 'festival prizes' as well as terms such as 'excitement', 'unusually talented' and 'exciting', with built-in audiences being all but promised in connection with all of these attributes. Likewise, we have a similar effusiveness to describe the film itself, with 'strikingly original, memorable and accessible'. Especially significant in this passage is the use of the word 'accessible', a word that would only be used if there was some reason to doubt that it would be so. This reflects a desire on the part of the applicants to frame the film as one that will not be stuck in the 'cultural ghetto' that art films sometimes fall into, and that the film will instead 'cross over' to mainstream audiences.

Illustrative of the tensions inherent in the discourse of the funding application is the strategy on the part of Company Pictures that sees them invoke protectionist rhetoric in relation to Ramsay's development as an artist. Rhetoric relating to Ramsay's 'genius', and the need for Scottish Screen to help develop it, is seen in the passages discussed above referring to her success on the festival circuit and her 'unusual' talent, but also in more subtle passages such as one that comes in response to question 47, 'How will lottery funding add value to your project?':

> This highly visual, teenage inspired film, set in both Scotland and Spain, seems the perfect next step for director Lynne Ramsay. We believe we have achieved a realistic budget and schedule to enable Lynne to make a visually stunning and emotionally powerful film. The lottery funding will be essential for us to achieve this project. (Scottish Screen, 2000)

Noteworthy here is the phrase 'the perfect next step' for Ramsay, which seems to be directly referencing Scottish Screen's mandate to develop promising Scottish talent. The second important thing here is the reiteration of the word 'visual', which like 'strikingly original', is a way to emphasize Ramsay's cinematic artistry. Again, we should note how this promise of a 'visually stunning' film is immediately followed by a promise to also be 'emotionally powerful'. This shows that the applicants are once again carefully trying to present the film as one with both artistic and audience appeal.

Carrying on from the last sentence of this passage, 'The lottery funding will be essential for us to achieve this project', we can see the applicants implicitly making the case that visionary artists such as Lynne Ramsay, as they have described her, can only fulfil their potential with the help of bodies such as Scottish Screen, thereby appealing to the body to act as an instrument of market protection. This is made more explicit in the response to the next question (Q48), 'Why can you not make your film with money from other sources?':

> We feel that Arts Council funding is vital for this film: It is important that the production process of *Morvern Callar* is not compromised by the demands of purely commercial backing. The lead roles are both for young Scottish actresses, and we believe that the film will suffer if Lynne is forced to go for marquee 'star' casting. (Scottish Screen, 2000)

The plea here is one that recalls one of the most basic arguments for the cultural necessity of subsidizing film production: that artists need to be sheltered from the demands inherent in the marketplace in order to be able to fully express themselves. Instead of using non-commercial aspects of the film – such as its indeterminate ending or lack of access to character psychology – as examples of potential commercially oriented changes, the applicants provide an example that is simply illustrated but also works as a significant act of flag-waving. By suggesting that commercial backing would threaten the 'Scottishness' of the film or hurt the Scottish film industry by compelling the film-makers to hire non-Scottish actors, the applicants manage to align artistic integrity with national concerns, thereby simultaneously appealing to a number of Scottish Screen's mandates.

This rhetoric thus frames the film as one with a number of attractive qualities for Scottish Screen: supporting an emerging indigenous writer/director, helping to bring the work of a Scottish novelist to the screen and making a film with great commercial appeal, particularly among younger demographics and particularly women. Such promises collectively frame the project as a sort of 'female *Trainspotting*', a term used later to describe the film by critics such as Sarah Neely (2008, p. 160). Indeed, the film-makers present the film as being even more alluring than *Trainspotting* for Scottish Screen; after all, now there was a Scottish auteur director involved and not another English director.

Alliance Atlantis, co-production and commercial pressures

Also prominent among the backers for *Morvern Callar* was Alliance Atlantis. The now defunct Canadian-based distributor and sales agent invested in the making of the film in return for sales rights in territories such as the UK, Canada, France and Spain and other countries (Slovo, 2012). The firm was at the time seeking to make a push from being known as a producer of art-house films and some television programming (including the wildly successful *CSI* franchise) to a 'mini-major' with interests in sales, distribution and production, a company in this respect along the lines of independent film powerhouse Lionsgate Films.

Distribution is of course a crucial component of the international film industry and is typically where most of the money and power are to be found. Despite the reputation that distributors have generally within film history as completely market oriented and only tangentially interested in the artistic side of cinema, Alliance Atlantis were not any more interfering in the project than any of the other backers. According to producer Robyn Slovo, the company itself had little input on the making of the film itself, instead leaving Ramsay for the most part to make the film she wanted to make (2012). For Slovo this was in part because of the corporate culture at Alliance Atlantis, which despite its base in Canada was very stereotypically European when it came to art-house cinema, but also because of the complexity of the co-production agreement that was put together by Company Pictures. The deal – which featured one public broadcaster, three governmental subsidy bodies (including the GFF, Scottish Screen and the Arts Council of England) and several equity investors as well as Alliance – spread the equity in the film so thin that no one single partner had a controlling stake in the project (Slovo, 2012). We thus see in the involvement of companies such as Alliance Atlantis an instance in which the 'international market' – long the villain in Scottish cinema historiography – helped to protect an indigenous artist from creative interference.

This is not to say, however, that Ramsay faced no commercial pressures. One area that was affected by commercial concerns, at least initially, was the casting of Samantha Morton, who had by this time been nominated for an Oscar for her role in *Sweet and Lowdown* (Woody Allen, 1999) and was at the time also playing a major part in Steven Spielberg's 2002 film *Minority Report*. Casting an established actor like Morton was a distinct change from Ramsay's working methods. Up to this point in her career as she had exclusively cast non-professional actors in her short films as well as *Ratcatcher* and, with the exception of Morton, continued to do so in *Morvern*. Ramsay had at the outset wanted to continue with these practices but opted instead to cast Morton in part because she represented some 'commercial comfort' for the film's backers (Slovo, 2012).

Figure 5 Marquee casting? Samantha Morton as the eponymous heroine in *Morvern Callar*

Such an enforced change is surprising and ironic given that Company Pictures had appealed to Scottish Screen for funding to protect Ramsay from exactly this kind of scenario and the fact that it happened should give us pause when we think about the efficacy of policy to blunt the impact of the market. But there is also a question here of whether or not the film would necessarily have benefited from market protection when it came to casting. Despite what appears to be a case in which the pressures of the market altered a Scottish film, interfered with the intentions of a Scottish film-maker and deprived a Scottish actor of a job, nothing has really been said against Morton's casting (Figure 5). Instead, her performance has received almost universal praise for its subtlety, its depth and perhaps most surprisingly, its Englishness. Similar textual and contextual dynamics to *Morvern* can be seen in the case of *Local Hero*. As seen in Chapter 1, *Local Hero* shows the Highland community of Ferness to be home to a surprising number of transnational wanderers. Like *Morvern*, it is also a film with its own transnational production context, one that called for foreign actors and characters. But whereas Burt Lancaster's casting in *Local Hero* drew the immediate ire of the *Scotch Reels* critics, Morton's casting, and the subsequent alteration of a Scottish story, has been warmly received. For Teresa Grace Murray this opens up an implicit postcolonial dimension of the film, allowing it to touch – albeit obliquely – on the relationship between the English and the Scottish (2006, p. 265). For Caughie, what he jokingly calls the 'scandalous transgression' of Morvern being English in the film 'cannot be innocent' and instead allows the film to wilfully break from the tradition of the Highland landscape acting as a restorative force for English characters (2007, p. 107). Moreover, Caughie argues this generally allows Ramsay to show Oban as a sort of post-national space where some characters just happen to be from other places.

Caughie suggests that it must have been an intentional decision for Morton not to learn a Scottish accent, which she could have easily done (p. 106). But the case may not have been as straight-forward as Caughie suggests. Morton has said in interviews that there was not enough time for her to learn the accent, implying that it was not intended that she speak with her Nottingham accent (*Morvern*, 2003). Neely also notes that there were rumours during the making of the film and immediately after its release that Morton was in fact unable to master the accent (2003, p. 251). Such doubts combined with the pressures of the film's backers for a marketable star combine to suggest that perhaps the decision to cast Morton and to have her speak with an English accent was not just a stroke of genius on the part of Ramsay, but that instead the film benefited, ironically, from the inability of Scottish Screen to protect an artist from the market.

Marketing *Morvern Callar*: authorship, soundtrack and adaptation

Unsurprisingly, the parallels to *Trainspotting* carried over into the ways in which *Morvern Callar* was marketed, but unlike the earlier film *Morvern* was also clearly branded as an auteur work in ways that *Trainspotting* was not. The campaigns for the film in the UK and North America (the film's two biggest markets) centred around two key 'tie-ins' for the film: its soundtrack and Alan Warner's novel. The importance of the former can be seen in the film's North American distributor, Palm Pictures, as well as the record label that handled the soundtrack, Warp Records. Palm Pictures was launched in 1998 by Chris Blackwell, who also founded Island Records, and considered itself to be 'a leader in the converging music and film markets' (Palm website). As such, its catalogue includes normative music albums as well as hybrid film/musical products such as compilations of music videos, filmed concerts and 'soundtrack' films. While this latter term is sometimes used derisively to mean films whose existence seems to be only a way to sell original soundtrack records, Palm's catalogue includes critically prestigious art films such as *Sex and Lucía* (Julio Medem, 2001) and *Noi the Albino* (Dagur Kári, 2003) as well as other soundtrack-driven films. Palm's favoured business model is thus one that seeks out opportunities for commercial synergies between music and film, a strategy that *Trainspotting*'s distributors followed to great commercial effect. But Palm also has a distinctly auteurist bent, taking on projects such as the works of directors like Julio Medem, Michael Haneke and Pablo Trapero. It also produces a home video series called 'Director's Label' which repackages short films and music videos by auteur film-makers such as Spike Jonze and Michel Gondry, among others.

Warp Records, who produced and distributed *Morvern Callar*'s soundtrack, offers another case study in the convergence of the film and music industries. At the time of film's making, the company was exclusively a music producer and one with a particular niche in the cerebral end of the British electronic music scene. Among their stable of talent at the time were Aphex Twin and Boards of Canada, two bands which would feature prominently on *Morvern*'s soundtrack. While the film was in production, the label would form a subsidiary to make films and more directly cash in on the synergies between independent music and independent cinema. Warp Films is now a major force in the British independent sector and has helped to produce cross-over hits like *This is England* (Shane Meadows, 2006) and *Submarine* (Richard Ayoade, 2010), films which were, like *Morvern*, reliant in part on auteur directors and original soundtrack sales for their commercial appeal.

Music was thus a major part of the film's commercial life – and also a major part of its aesthetic design – but another crucial tie-in was Warner's novel. As we saw in the discussion of the film's production story, the funding application was predicated in part on the popularity of the novel and the BBC had originally optioned the novel before it was even published, such was the buzz surrounding the book and the author. It is thus not surprising that the book should also feature prominently in the marketing of the film. Though due to disagreements between the publishers and the film-makers, there was no co-branded edition of the novel (as was the case with the campaign for *Trainspotting* and indeed many independent films based on popular novels), the publicity campaign for the film nevertheless made much of the process of adaptation and Warner's approval of the film.

Though Warner was largely pleased with how the film turned out (Dale, 2002, p. 79; Neely, 2003, pp. 240–241), the relationship between and himself and the film-makers was not always amicable. This can be seen in an interview with *The Times* in which Warner claimed to have gone for two years during the making of the film without speaking to Ramsay, and that he 'went f****** nuts' when Ramsay suggested changing the title of the film, which would have effectively erased the most obvious signs of Warner's authorship (Rees, 2002; asterisks in original). He then goes on a diatribe in which he calls adaptation 'every writer's worst nightmare' and says that film-makers only use published fiction as source material 'because they can't write good scripts' on their own (Rees, 2002). The writer of the piece, Jesper Rees, also paraphrases Warner as comparing Ramsay to the novel's Morvern as they both stole the works of other writers and passed them off as their own (Rees, 2002). Though Warner has expressed regret over this interview and has since given his unconditional support to the film, his comments here point to the other major force in the marketing discourses surrounding the film, that of Ramsay herself.

Ramsay has always featured prominently in the marketing campaigns for her films. Indeed, one indication of the extent to which she has been discursively constructed as an auteur is not just that she grants interviews as a part of the promotion of her films, but in the sheer number of interviews that exist. Dozens of filmed and written interviews over the years have informed readers about everything from her class background (e.g. Brooks, 1999), to her experiences at the NFTS film school (MacDonald, 2002, p. 115), to her favourite movies and film-makers (Donaldson, 2002; Ramsay, 2000) and the ways in which her gender has affected her career (Leigh, 2002). In keeping with the discursive tendencies of auteurism, Ramsay's publicity interviews have typically stressed the personal dimensions of her films. This is fairly straightforward in the case of *Ratcatcher* as the film was modelled on her experiences growing up in Glasgow in the 1970s. As a work of another author, *Morvern Callar* presented more of a challenge to the 'personalizing' project. The 'personal' issues here revolved around gender as writers, critics and Ramsay herself pointed to the ways in which her point of view as a woman made her able to tell Morvern's story in ways that Warner himself could not (e.g. D. Leigh, 2002).

Lynne Ramsay's *Morvern Callar*: narrative, score and art cinema

The discourses surrounding the production and packaging of *Morvern Callar* thus framed the project as one that combined the edgy, accessible generic aspects of *Trainspotting* with the auteurist sensibilities of Lynne Ramsay. So how did the film actually turn out? Was it indeed able to balance these demands and expectations? This section of the chapter takes on these questions by looking at both the textual operations of the film itself as well as the ways in which the film was received by critics and audiences.

We begin with the ways in which Ramsay and her co-writer Liana Dognini adapted the film's narrative from Warner's novel, starting with what is arguably the most significant difference between the film and the book, that being the change in narrative perspective. The book is written from the point of view of Morvern and its narration consists of a virtual monologue that dictates all of the action of the plot as well as Morvern's thoughts and observations of the world around her. Despite the alignment of the audience with her, the book does not provide much direct psychological access to Morvern. She simply records the events and experiences of the book's events without much in the way of commentary or explanation. The onus is then on the reader to decipher the significance of what is being described. Sophie Dale describes this aspect of the novel rather succinctly when she writes that, 'As a narrator, Morvern conceals her thoughts and works through indirection such that the reader is intrigued by what she *doesn't* say, and it is this withheld emotional power, as much as the events of the plot, which compels you to read on' (2002, p. 35).

This 'indirection' is a quality that the film shares on one level. It also never explains anything: Morvern's feelings and motivations are only obliquely hinted at, in a very similar fashion but to a more extreme degree than those of James (William Eadie) in *Ratcatcher*.

At least in that film, we do receive some glimpses into his psychology, however fleeting they are: a tear shed here, an attempt to help Margaret-Anne (Leanne Mullan) there, and so on. In *Morvern*, there are no such moments and enigma is placed ahead of access to characters, a narrative decision most typically illustrated by the haunting motifs of extreme close-ups of insects. This strategy does not just show a contrast with *Ratcatcher*, it also is sharply opposed to the approach taken in *Trainspotting* which sees the extensive use of first-person voice-over narration in the form of Mark Renton's (Ewan McGregor) explanations of elements of the plot and characterizations of his friends and himself for the audience. There are no moments when Morvern explains her decisions on a par with Renton's famous 'Choose Life' monologue, nor is there an explanation of Morvern's future in the way that we find one for Renton and this brings us to a key aspect of the film's narrative, that being the ending.

Warner's version of the story has a pregnant Morvern returning to Scotland after four years of raving in Spain to visit the grave of her foster mother and to find work now that her money has run out, leaving the narrative at a point from which *These Demented Lands*, Warner's sequel to the book, continues. The film, on the other hand, is much more ambiguous about Morvern's fate. The closing images of the film, which show Morvern striding through a rave listening to The Mamas and Papas' song 'Dedicated to the One I Love' on her headphones, isolated from what is going on around her, are open to a number of interpretations. One could assume that she has returned to the rave scene in Spain, as someone who knows the novel may think. Or the scene could be viewed as a flashback to earlier in the film just before her disgust with the youth club scene in Spain led her to flee the resort. Indeed, any number of readings are possible, as this is an open ending that, Caughie points out, is typical of the European art cinema tradition, one in which the alienation of the protagonist from the world around them is more significant than classical narrative closure (2007, p. 111).

For Caughie, this is one of the film's great strengths, but combined with the lack of access to character psychology it is also a decision that makes the film more challenging to mainstream audiences and therefore contributes to the film being less likely to 'cross over' in the way that *Trainspotting* was able to. The commitment to contemplative, apparently non-dramatic narration goes even deeper when it comes to issues of adaptation as Ramsay and Dognini omit many of the most suspenseful moments in the novel (e.g. a scene in which roofers nearly discover the corpse in the attic [1996, pp. 77–80]) and defuse the dramatic confrontation between Lanna and Morvern over the former's revelation of an affair between herself and Morvern's boyfriend. Unlike the visits from the neighbours, this latter plot point is at least in the film, but is handled so abruptly and in such unclear terms that it is easy to miss (a guilt-plagued Lanna shouts at one point 'it was just a fuck, and a crap one at that' in response to an innocent question from Morvern) and therefore lacks the impact and melodrama that more conventional scripts would have made from such a betrayal.

The narrative strategies of enigma and alienation can also be seen in the ways in which the film uses music. As noted previously, the film is in many ways a 'soundtrack film' and though this term has long been used as a pejorative industrial term, *Morvern*, like many 'soundtrack films' does attempt to use its popular music soundtrack to artistic ends. To get a sense of just how this is done we can once again compare the film to *Trainspotting*. In relatively superficial ways there are a number of parallels between the song selections on the films' soundtracks. Each draws on an interrelated blend of frenetic club music – a parallel that is rooted in the rave culture milieu that each attempts to evoke – the use of more hallucinatory electronic music and popular music with a built-in cult following.

Despite these parallels at the level of musical selection, there are a number of fundamental differences between the films when it comes to the specific aesthetic deployment of those songs. Boyle's usage of techno music, for example, is fairly straightforward as it is used to both develop settings (i.e. it is played when the characters are in clubs) or it is tightly synchronized to frenetic movement and montage patterns, such as is the case in the famous hallucinatory sequence in which Renton attempts to quit heroin while being haunted by an array of incidents from his past as an addict. This scene not only coordinates montage with the tempo of the music but also utilizes the music to narrate Renton's intense feelings of physical pain. A similar use of music is found near the end of the film when Renton steals the money from Begbie (Robert Carlyle). Here the steadily building drumbeat and baseline from 'Born Slippy' narrates Renton's tension – effectively standing in for his heartbeat – while he carefully slips the bag from the murderous Begbie's sleeping arms. Boyle also uses cult musicians such as Iggy Pop and The Stooges in ways that likewise closely match the on screen action, such as the opening sequence of the film when we see Renton and Spud (Ewan Bremner) being chased by the police, an action sequence which is 'mickey moused' to The Stooges' drum and bass heavy 'Lust for Life', and which goes on to intercut rapidly between footage of Renton and his friends playing football and Renton himself taking heroin.

A final memorable musical sequence in *Trainspotting* worth discussing here is the scoring of Renton's overdose with the Lou Reed song 'Perfect Day', a song choice that draws on Reed's persona as a songwriter inspired heavily by his use of opiates (Smith, 2002, pp. 67–68) while utilizing the tonal continuity between the song's slow, placid arrangement and the slow editing and static camera shots in the sequence. This all, of course, helps to form an ironic counterpoint between the song's lyrics ('It's such a perfect day / I'm glad I shared it with you') with the grim suspense regarding whether or not Renton will indeed survive the overdose.

Ramsay's use of music in *Morvern Callar* differs dramatically from Boyle's. For a film ostensibly concerned with rave culture there is precious little techno music to be found in the film itself. The only piece of music that fits this bill is heard when Morvern is at a club in Spain with Lanna and then we hear only a short bit of the song while the image track is slowed down, creating a feeling of alienation between sound and image. The other time one would logically expect to hear techno music comes at the film's ending, but here the music of the rave is drowned out for Morvern – and the audience – by the sounds of the aforementioned Mamas and the Papas song 'Dedicated to the One I Love', signifying Morvern's final alienation from the club scene.

Most of the other music utilized in the film can be roughly described as hallucinatory electronic music and usually works against the emotional tones that one would expect to find in the diegesis. An example of this would be the scene in which Morvern and Lanna attend an impromptu party at the home of some men they meet at the pub in Oban shortly after Morvern discovers her boyfriend's dead body. Instead of the high tempo, perhaps even frenetic music that would realistically be playing at such an event, the soundtrack here features the Holger Czukay song 'Fragrance', a song that is slow in tempo and dreamlike in orchestration. This is paired with a visual track which is slowed down to the point of almost being step printed while the découpage features a number of jump-cuts and disorienting changes in camera angle and focus. While this song choice could initially be ascribed to the development of the setting (i.e. the partygoers could all be listening to it), it is distorted throughout the sequence and then continues playing as the scene moves from inside the house to outside. The song choice here is thus not 'objective' to the diegesis but instead 'subjective' to Morvern. While the effect created here is on one hand fairly straightforward – to simulate the drug and alcohol induced states that Morvern and Lanna find themselves in – the tonal balance between sound and image is far less straightforward than was seen in Boyle's film and carries with it a further development of Morvern as being out of touch with her surroundings. This is not to say that there is no complexity to *Trainspotting*'s soundtrack, the point is that *Morvern Callar*'s is more clearly one that is used almost exclusively as a tool of character development, helping us to understand the alienated consciousness of the film's title character.

Adding a layer of complexity to the film's use of music is the addition of the Walkman that Morvern wears and the mix tape (made by her boyfriend as a final Christmas gift) to which she listens. Changing the volume levels on the music coming from the Walkman becomes a motif in the film that allows Ramsay to repeatedly create distance between Morvern and her surroundings and to play with expectations regarding diegetic and non-diegetic music. The subjective effects created with this device show a greater degree of complexity than was seen in *Trainspotting*, for example in the 'Some Velvet Morning' sequence in which Morvern walks through the grocery store where she works while listening to Lee Hazelwood and Nancy Sinatra's somnambulistic-toned duet. As Caughie shows, this sequence consists of a rich interplay between objectivity and subjectivity in terms of camera position and editing (2007, p. 109). This sequence both recalls and differs sharply from the Renton overdose sequence in *Trainspotting*. Both sequences utilize pieces of music with similar hallucinatory and surreal moods, but whereas Boyle's sequence utilizes those moods to correspond to an appropriately hallucinatory and surreal incident – a drug overdose that visually features special effects and trick photography in the form of the sunken carpet and point-of-view shots from beneath that carpet – Ramsay's sequence plays on the contrast between the mundane reality of Morvern's environment and the extraordinary, hallucinatory situation in which she finds herself.

These acts of distantiation on Ramsay's part not only place Morvern at a far remove from her surroundings, but they do the same to the film's audience. These decisions come in stark contrast to *Trainspotting* in which the film's characters and its audience are immersed in the world of drugs and music. This allows for vicarious pleasures in the case of *Trainspotting* (no matter what the film-makers may have said in the wake of the controversies surrounding the film's depiction of drug use), but *Morvern* makes a calculated effort to keep us away from those same pleasures and instead focuses on the interior conflict at the heart of the film's narrative. This difference is crucial for appreciating the larger distinction between *Trainspotting* as a film that blends elements of the popular and the art cinemas (Smith, 2002, p. 88) and *Morvern* which is more clearly entrenched in the art cinema tradition.

We Need to Talk About Kevin and Ramsay's re-emergence as cross-over film-maker

Given such textual difficulty and insistence on subjectivity, alienation and the aesthetic strategies of modernist art cinema, it is perhaps not surprising that *Morvern Callar* was both a hit with film critics and a failure with film audiences. Many of the leading figures in the Anglo-American critical community, including Roger Ebert, Phillip French and Mark Kermode, shared Caughie's enthusiasm for the film's uncompromising art cinema orientation. But no amount of 'marquee casting', auteur publicity, cult music-laden soundtracks or literary tie-ins could bring audiences to the film. Indeed, despite its prestigious place in accounts of Scottish cinema, it remains one of the lowest grossing films of the so-called 'new Scottish cinema' epoch. Despite critical praise from the likes of Petrie, Blandford and Caughie – the latter of whom sees the film and its director as 'expanding the range of creative practices within Scotland' (2007, p. 114) – Ramsay would be removed from her next project, *The Lovely Bones* (Peter Jackson, 2010), in part because commercial expectations for the project increased as sales of the source novel climbed, leading the producers to seek out a more commercial director (Ramsay and Leigh, 2005). She would then return to writing/directing with *We Need to Talk About Kevin* (2011) a film which shows a significant evolution in Ramsay's style of film-making and its relationship to the international market. In this final section, I attempt to explore what Ramsay's career since *Morvern Callar* tells us about the possibilities of art cinema film-making for Scottish film-makers in this contemporary period.

Ramsay's return to feature film-making came in 2011 after a nine-year hiatus. The project was once again an adaptation of a cult novel, this one being Lionel Shriver's *We Need to Talk About Kevin*. The film, which like her two previous features began as a commission from BBC Films, proved to be something of a cross-over success achieving critical praise, numerous awards and nominations (including nominations for a Golden Globe, BAFTAs and others) and relative commercial success, grossing over $6 million globally as of the end of 2011 (Boxofficemojo.com). So what has changed between *Morvern Callar* and *We Need to Talk About Kevin* and what does this tell us about Ramsay specifically and the Scottish auteur film-maker generally in this contemporary period?

There are numerous parallels between *Morvern* and *We Need to Talk* at the level of style and technique, but the films differ in their approaches to character, narrative and theme. In the latter film, Ramsay once again makes extensive use of jump-cuts combined with slow motion, slightly out of focus cinematography to create phantasmagoric, surreal effects throughout the film. This stylistic tendency can be seen in the opening of the film which shows Eva (Tilda Swinton) at the Tomatina Festival (in Buñol, Spain) bathed in tomato juice and happily taking part in the festivities. Such images are never directly explained to the viewer and they set a tone of mystery and disquiet that will become crucial to the film. This scene closely recalls sequences in *Morvern* such as the party early in the film and the rave scene which ends the film. But at other points in *We Need to Talk* these exact same techniques are used in more conventional ways. This phantasmagoric style of cinematography and editing recurs throughout the film, including at key moments in the narrative such as Eva and Franklin's (John C. Reilly) drunken courtship and Eva's arrival at the scene of her son's mass killing at his high school.

In terms of techniques, these scenes recall the party scenes from early in *Morvern* but instead of creating a tonal contrast that distances the audience from the world of the film, here Ramsay is deploying them in order to simulate Eva's internal state at times of heightened emotions. In other words, these are melodramatic moments and Ramsay is creating those moments to facilitate spectator identification with the narrative and characters rather than distancing them as she did in *Morvern*. This is most clearly seen in the repeated flashbacks to the day of Kevin's rampage in which each of the flashback adds new narrative information that allow the audience to piece together the events of that day and to notice more grim details (such as the locks used by Kevin to seal the doors to the gymnasium) that haunt Eva. Looking back across Ramsay's oeuvre, it is important to appreciate just how differently rendered Eva's guilt and conflict are from the ways in which those same emotional states are represented in *Morvern* or *Ratcatcher*. Enigma in *We Need to Talk* is only used to create mysteries that are later solved; Ramsay's films up to this point had given their audiences no such hermeneutic pleasure.

We Need to Talk also features very auspicious use of sound design and scoring. Like *Morvern* (and indeed *Ratcatcher*) it contains moments when characters simply do not speak on screen, in which the audience is left to guess at their internal states by observing the actors' facial expressions, which are often held in the close-up. Unlike the earlier films which featured long periods of silence between characters, these moments are less frequent and are almost always imbued with suspense as the tension between Eva and Kevin builds throughout the film. Music choices in both *Morvern* and *We Need to Talk* consist once again of cultish popular music. In the former, it helps to deepen the mystery of Morvern and the off-screen boyfriend or to demonstrate her alienation from her world, unlike *We Need to Talk* where most of the musical pieces are used in relatively predictable – perhaps some would say clichéd and facile – ways. Examples of these moments would include the choice of The Beach Boys song 'In My Room' to accompany Eva's search of Kevin's bedroom or 'Nobody's Child' as the song to end the film with. Such transparently narrative and thematic use of music is echoed by the use of other elements of style, particularly colour – red being a logical and predictable one given the violence that unfolds in the film.

The approaches to narrative, character and theme generally in *We Need to Talk* are much more easily accessible than *Morvern*.

On the face of it, this may seem a very curious position to take on the films considering that *Morvern* – the uncertain temporality of the final scene notwithstanding – features a linear narrative while *We Need to Talk* is structured as a serious of flashbacks between a number of different timeframes. Despite the complexity of the handling of time in *We Need to Talk*, it is a much more clearly causally driven, goal-oriented narrative. The audience wants to know why Eva is living as a pariah in this small town, where her family is and so on. As the flashbacks play out we then want to piece together the events and figure out what exactly happened. Unlike the case with *Morvern*, we do eventually find this out and we are given a clear ending hinting at redemption for, and reconciliation between, Eva and Kevin. The flashbacks in the film are motivated by Proustian moments in which Eva spots something that sparks memories of the events leading up the massacre. *Morvern*, in contrast, is loosely structured and episodic in the extreme, leaving its audience with the work of attributing meaning (be it at the level of character or theme) to the individual scenes. Finally, the ending of *We Need to Talk* makes an interesting contrast with that of *Morvern Callar*. Not only is the former closed and somewhat optimistic – Kevin now regrets his actions and seeks maternal comfort from Eva – but it is also faithful to Shriver's novel. This, of course, is a very different adaptation strategy than the one Ramsay utilized in *Morvern Callar* where, as was seen previously, the ending was left very open.

Thus we can see that despite sharing of some of the aesthetic tendencies of its predecessor, *We Need to Talk* nevertheless constitutes a shift in Ramsay's approach to narrative that moves away from the art cinema traditions of European modernism and towards what Caughie calls the 'European quality cinema' ethos, which he says is typical of contemporary British cinema (2007, p. 104), one which mixes the stylistic flair of art cinema with the narrative accessibility of popular cinema. This approach at the level of text is echoed by many elements of the industrial contexts surrounding the film. Though Ramsay is central to the marketing of the film – and indeed is the focus of the film's featurette – stars and genre also feature prominently. Instead of the exclusive use of non-professional actors, *We Need to Talk* features two leads – Tilda Swinton and John C. Reilly – who are stars, and even perhaps 'marquee casting' within the context of contemporary independent cinema. Reilly and Swinton then appear throughout the film's publicity campaign along with Ramsay and Lionel Shriver and all of them make sure to use terms such 'horror' and 'psychological thriller' to describe the film whenever they can. This usage of stardom and genre in *We Need to Talk* combined with the topicality of the film's subject matter and its stylistic accessibility combine to make the film one with a great deal of mainstream audience appeal, one much more clearly poised to be able to 'cross over' than its predecessor.

Conclusions: Ramsay, *Morvern* and Scottish film history

Appreciating the significance of this shift on the part of Ramsay as a film-maker provides an opportune moment to return to Ramsay's and *Morvern*'s places in Scottish film historiography. As shown at the outset of this chapter, Ramsay has been seen as one of the great highlights of the 'new Scottish cinema' period and credit for her emergence has been implicitly and explicitly been given to the policy mechanisms that supported her work. What this chapter has shown is that this narrative needs qualification and nuancing. While it is undoubtedly true that Ramsay has benefited from the assistance of funding bodies such as Scottish Screen, it has been two London-based institutions that have been the steadiest supporters of her work: the UK Film Council and BBC Films, the latter of which I would argue has been the most important institution for her development as a film-maker. This is not to look past the role played by non-British production companies in the making of her films as Canadian and American firms invested in *Morvern* and *We Need to Talk*, respectively, and going further back a French firm (Pathé) invested in *Ratcatcher*. The international market has thus been crucial to Ramsay's career.

The political economy of Scottish cinema and Ramsay's place in that context is thus more complex than existing accounts would have it. Such can be seen in the arc of Ramsay's career as film-maker. Despite many of the hopes expressed for Ramsay as a leading figure for Scottish art cinema, what we have seen in this chapter is that *Morvern* was never intended by anyone involved in the making or marketing of the film, except Ramsay herself, as an art film. Instead, it was more likely a variation of *Trainspotting* that was sought. That Ramsay was able to make the film in a way that most critics recognize as powerful and aesthetically interesting should not be seen as the outcome of progressive film policy but instead as a moment of happenstance. While Caughie was correct to point this out in relation to the GFF, we must also see that this principle applies to all of the institutions involved in the making of the film. Ramsay's career between *Morvern* and *We Need to Talk* shows just how fragile the mode of cinema she deployed in *Morvern* can be, and it was only once the latter film showed the hybrid aesthetic form that *Trainspotting* typifies that Ramsay's career was once again back on the up. Ramsay, though, was not alone as an indigenous Scottish film-maker hoping to break into the world of features against such a complex industrial backdrop. In Chapter 4 we see in David Mackenzie another director who was both empowered and limited by the shadow of *Trainspotting* and who sought to make his film in the midst of a challenging terrain, all while guided by a London-based figure who would make all the difference.

4

The many authors of *Young Adam*

The pursuit of the auteur within contemporary Scottish film culture did not begin or end with Lynne Ramsay. Peter Mullan and Andrea Arnold are film-makers who have both been touted in such ways by the critical community and have, at times, been supported by subsidy programmes in various ways. Both have also found international success, though more so with their films set outside Scotland (*The Magdalene Sisters* and *Fish Tank* [2009], respectively) rather than their breakthrough Scottish films. As noted at the outset of this book, while Mullan and Arnold are certainly important film-makers, their familiarity within critical discourses leaves little to be said here. Instead, my concern here is with a figure who has been less successful in critical terms than his peers even if his films, particularly *Young Adam* and *Hallam Foe*, have resonated more with audiences than *Red Road*, *Orphans* or *Neds*.

Like Ramsay, Mackenzie makes an ideal object for examining the ways in which Scottish film-making talent developed under the auspices of the policy regime that is universally held to have underpinned the flowering of the 'new Scottish cinema'. Also like Ramsay, Mackenzie's career has not been without difficulties. Though he has been more prolific, Mackenzie has never reached the auteur heights that he perhaps might have attained and has been instead relegated largely to Hollywood genre work with only a few 'auteur pieces' to his name. Finally, both film-makers sought to make their names in the aftermath of the phenomenon that was *Trainspotting* and their films were, in ways that were both incidental and intentional, irrevocably shaped by this context. *Young Adam*, which was intended to be Mackenzie's debut feature before production delays led him to make *The Last Great Wilderness* (2002) first, vividly illustrates many of these issues.

In choosing to take *Young Adam* as my object, I am disputing Martin-Jones's argument that *Young Adam* was not as successful as an art film as *Red Road* (2009, pp. 229–230). This claim does not hold water when one looks at the popularity of the two films among audiences and critics[29] or the general high profile *Young Adam* enjoyed at the time of its release. By the time it was released in the UK in September 2003, *Young Adam* was already, by the standards of Scottish cinema, a very high profile film indeed. In the time leading up to its release, the film had been the subject of two major controversies on either side of the Atlantic. In Britain, Ewan McGregor, the film's lead actor, had been outspoken, particularly during press appearances at the Cannes Film Festival, in criticizing the UK Film Council for its reluctance to step in with additional funds when one of the film's backers pulled out just before shooting began, leaving a financial shortfall that threatened to derail the entire production. On the other side of the ocean, controversy arose when the MPAA gave the film an NC-17 rating – severely limiting the amount of distribution the film would receive in the United States – because of the distributors' (Sony Pictures Classics) refusal to cut a scene featuring male full frontal nudity.

Besides subsidy and censorship controversies, a number of Scotland's most famous actors were cast in the film and were heavily promoting it. These included McGregor, the actor most associated with the renaissance of film production in Scotland, as well as Peter Mullan, of *My Name is Joe* fame and recently making a name of himself as a director, and international art-house star Tilda Swinton. The film was also presented as one that promised to recuperate the reputation of forgotten Scottish novelist Alexander Trocchi, all while launching the career of Mackenzie, who was being promoted as an emerging directing talent. The film enjoyed a mainly positive critical reception both at home and abroad and then swept the Scottish BAFTAs in 2004, confirming its status as one of the most talked about 'event' films that Scottish cinema had seen since *Trainspotting*.

In this chapter I closely examine the 'moment' of *Young Adam*, focusing on a number of issues which speak to the importance of the film for understanding contemporary Scottish cinema. These include national representation as well as the predicament of the Scottish film artist within the economy of an international marketplace, in which national film bodies periodically attempt to intervene.

'Scottishness' and 'Britishness' were crucial to the discourses surrounding *Young Adam* and were also important to the film itself. This eventually leads us to the creative personnel involved in the film, some of whom were implicated in conveying the 'nationality' of the film. The opening section of this chapter introduces us to *Young Adam*'s two recognized 'authors', novelist Alexander Trocchi and director David Mackenzie. The relationship between the literary and cinematic authors is shown to be markedly different from that seen in Chapter 3 between Ramsay and Warner and brings us to a larger meditation on the material conditions of authorship in the case of Mackenzie. This, in turn, brings us to Jeremy Thomas, the film's English producer, who, I suggest, is the third figure that can be considered one of the film's authors. As such, my analysis of *Young Adam* is oriented towards illuminating a number of industrial, cultural and aesthetic issues that have surrounded film production in Scotland and Britain, a point that brings us back to the issues raised in my opening study of *Local Hero*, a film which also raised questions within Scottish film culture about the ability of the indigenous artist to navigate international markets. Such a multifaceted exploration of *Young Adam* begins with national identity, not within the film itself, but in the film's production context where being 'British' and/or 'Scottish' was arguably of much greater consequence than within the film itself.

An 'important' Scottish film: funding contexts and controversies

Being a film with national importance, whether it be for Scotland or Britain, is something that dominates every aspect of the discursive contexts surrounding *Young Adam*, from its press kit – which, among other things, quotes Thomas himself saying: 'If you're filming a book by a Scot in Scotland there is no one more suitable than Ewan [McGregor]' to play the lead character (Recorded Picture Company, 2003, p. 2) – to its application for subsidy from Scottish Screen, in part by pointing out its 'extremely strong Scottish credentials' (Scottish Screen, 2001b, p. 7), to the publicity surrounding the film which made great use of such 'credentials'. As the ways in which the controversies over public support manifested themselves in the press implicitly frame the film as nationally relevant, they are important objects for analysis here.

Accusations directed at the UK Film Council began with the film's promotional press conference at Cannes in 2003. A report in the trade press tells of a heated argument between Alan Parker, then head of the Council, and Jeremy Thomas after McGregor and Swinton dedicated part of the post-screening press conference to attacking the Council's decision not to intercede when the project faced the aforementioned shortfall (Minns, 2003, p. 10). This was just the beginning, however, as McGregor in particular continued to use publicity interviews for the film to criticize the Council, accusing the body of prioritizing financial concerns over cultural ones and general philistinism when it came to 'important' works such as *Young Adam*. In some cases these attacks even became the main story related to the film, as seen in such headlines as: 'McGregor Rages at Film Fund's Agenda' (Gibbons, 2003, p. 7) and 'McGregor in Attack on "Betrayal" of British Films' (Alberge, 2003, p. 11). These attacks typically feature critiques of the kind of cinema that the Council supposedly favoured combined with claims that, because of such policies, the body was not acting in the *national* interest. *Young Adam* was an important film for Scotland and Britain, according to McGregor, precisely because it was not an easily marketable film. Such a position can be seen in a piece in the *Guardian*, where *Young Adam* is considered alongside that of the Hanif Kureishi-scripted film *The Mother* (Roger Michell, 2003) – which also featured 'difficult' sexual content and faced similar funding difficulties – as springboards for inquiry into the values of the British film-making establishment: 'Their triumph [that of *Young Adam* and *The Mother*] will reignite the debate on whether Alan Parker's Film Council is too ready to spend its pot of lottery money on middle-brow, commercial projects rather than daring scripts' (Gibbons, 2003, p. 7). McGregor goes on to say:

> Had I gone to them [the Council] with a romantic comedy there would have been no problem. [. . .] We used to have a reputation of being able to do anything in British film. And I was lucky to be involved in two films that opened the door to that, *Shallow Grave* and *Trainspotting*. But the door has slowly closed behind us. (2003, p. 7)

Here McGregor positions the film as the opposite of implicitly less substantial genre production and the equal of the films that launched his career, and which of course have been so important to Scottish cinema generally. His rhetoric, as well as Swinton's, continually reiterated the view that the film was 'national', with consistent reiteration of the mantra that *Young Adam* was an example of film-making that offered 'British films for British people' (Macnab, 2003b, p. 10), and Swinton remarked on several different occasions that the film was distinctly 'Scottish' as opposed to British or American (e.g. Macleod, 2004; Mathieson, 2005; Martin-Jones, 2009, p. 228).

Besides qualities pertaining to artistic complexity and national address and importance, there are also claims of authenticity made in these polemics, authenticity which is presented as being at risk under the money-conscious regime at the Council. A piece in *The Times* features an allegation made by McGregor that the Council suggested that the makers of *Young Adam* lower their production costs by filming outside Britain, a suggestion that the makers apparently disregarded on specifically national grounds. He goes on to criticize the same body for being more forthcoming with support for a film shot entirely in France (*Chemins de Traverse* [Manuel Poirier, 2004]) (Alberge, 2003, p. 11). Characterizing the film in such a way plays on two interrelated national sympathies. One is that British institutions should support British films and thereby support local industry. The second important play on national sympathies has to do with the relationship between locality and nationality, as these comments rely on assurance that the film was in fact shot in the area that is claims to represent; in effect promising indexical authenticity, an authenticity that would have been lacking had it been shot in Eastern Europe or some other location even whilst ostensibly being set in Scotland. Though there is some doubt over how well McGregor's comments in these interviews reflect the reality of the dilemmas faced by the film-makers,[30] what is interesting for our present purposes is how this rhetoric about the cultural responsibility of funding bodies acted as a source of promotional discourses for the film, discourses which framed the film in very specific terms relating to national importance, 'difficulty', complexity, originality and authenticity.

The attempts to frame *Young Adam* as a 'national' film can also be seen in the application for production subsidy from Scottish Screen. The 'Meeting the Criteria' section of the Scottish Screen funding application for *Young Adam* begins with the following question: 'How many people will benefit from the project and in what ways will they benefit?' (Scottish Screen, 2001b, p. 7). In their response, the applicants list various forms of economic and cultural impact, including local spend and employment as well as a number of claims for the national relevance of the film for Scotland – or, to use the applicants' own language: 'an important cultural impact for Scotland' (Scottish Screen, 2001b, p. 7). This in itself is not surprising considering that the applicants were seeking funding from a Scottish cultural organization, but it is nonetheless interesting to look at just how they articulate that relevance: 'The nature of the screenplay and [the film's] extremely strong Scottish credentials should raise the interest and curiosity of the audience and might have a possible effect on tourism' (Scottish Screen, 2001b, p. 7). And later, in response to an even more pointed question ("How is your project culturally relevant to Scotland?"): 'The film is based in Scotland, it will be shot in Scotland and the writer of the underlying novel, the screenwriter, the director and the lead actor are Scottish' (Scottish Screen, 2001b, p. 7). While it is not explicitly stated here, it is not too much of a stretch to say that the latter response can be said to explain the first, effectively laying out the film's 'Scottish credentials'.

National representation in *Young Adam*: Clydeside and kitchen sink noir

These are responses which contain a number of promises and it is worth looking at their contents in relation to the film itself in greater detail, beginning with the assertion as to national representation, which is interesting for a number of reasons. First, it implies that national representation will be one of the film's attractions and that the nation will be a significant enough aspect of the film's mise-en-scène to arouse 'interest and curiosity' regarding the nation in audiences. Second, the application rhetoric implies that the nationality of its personnel will be another set of attractions, strengthening its projection of 'Scottishness'. Given such promises, in this section, I look more closely at national representation in the film. Is *Young Adam* somehow 'about' Scotland? Is the nation itself presented in a particularly exotic or interesting manner? To begin answering these questions, we must remember that it is a film with a historical setting, in this case Scotland in the 1950s, and that this raises issues of historical representation that require sorting out before moving on to analyse the film's national representational tendencies proper.

In its attempts to recreate the period being represented, the film can be usefully compared to films such as *Far From Heaven* (Todd Haynes, 2003) or *The Postman Always Rings Twice* (Bob Rafelson, 1981), which base their depiction of the period being represented on films from that time, while also interpreting and commenting on that period by means of critical discrepancies from the conventions of the films being imitated.[31] This is, of course, not without precedent in British cinema. Writing about British films from the 1980s which seek to represent the 1950s, John Hill draws upon Fredric Jameson's notion of 'nostalgia for the present' as it relates to depictions of the decade. Hill argues that a number of British films from the 1980s follow a pattern of 'remembering' the decade in mediated terms, in essence presenting not an attempt at a realistic view of what the 1950s looked like but instead simulating what the decade has come to look like in films made in the 1950s and drawing on the genres that are most associated with that period (1999, p. 124). Writing specifically about *Dance with a Stranger* (Mike Newell, 1985), Hill argues that the film uses the aesthetic and narrative conventions of film noir and the women's film to represent the post-war period (1999, p. 128). The film's themes also revolve around taking a critical view towards the 1950s as a period of sexual repression and social hypocrisy as well as rigid class and gender divides (1999, p. 125). Very similar things can be said of the representational tendencies of *Young Adam* with a nationally specific wrinkle. The film draws on the stylistic and generic conventions of noir, but with its concern for the Glaswegian working-class male milieu of the 1950s, also draws on the 'angry young man' film of the British new wave, while also recalling the Scottish representational tradition of Clydesidism.

Noirish aspects of the film can be seen operating in *Young Adam* from just a cursory overview of its plot: Joe (Ewan McGregor), a handsome young drifter with a loose code of ethics comes between an unhappy housewife, Ella (Tilda Swinton), and her deeply flawed husband, Les (Peter Mullan). The drifter and the unhappy wife carry on a passionate and dangerous affair under the husband's nose and it is gradually revealed that the drifter is involved in the death of a woman who was his lover – with the wrong man executed for the crime. Along the way the wife's marriage is put at risk, only to be repaired in the end after the drifter is out of the picture. All this plot needs is a deliberate murder or two to be almost identical to that of *The Postman Always Rings Twice*, the quintessential noir

Figure 6 Kitchen sink realism on the Clyde: Ewan McGregor (left) and Peter Mullan (right) in *Young Adam*

story that has been adapted numerous times, including once in Italy (*Ossessione* [Luchino Visconti, 1943]), and twice in Hollywood in 1946 (Tay Gannett) and 1981 (Bob Rafelson). Both stories feature transgressive sexual encounters with the spectre of death and destruction paralleling the moral transgressions of their respective protagonists, with *Young Adam*'s montage structure counterpointing memories of Joe's affair with Cathie (Emily Mortimer) – the woman who ends up dead – with his affair with Ella.

Going beyond theme and narrative arc, elements of the film such as lighting and the use of colour in *Young Adam* also recall film noir. One could point to a number of instances of the expressive use of shadow and chiaroscuro in the film, such as one of the many shots of Joe smoking in his darkened bunk, or barely lit faces peering through the walls of the barge to watch the various couplings taking place in Ella's bunk, or the dark blue hues lighting encounter between Joe and Cathie under a pier-side lorry, precedes her drowning, as notable instances of this influence. To these we could add other well-known noir mainstays such as the existential worldview of its main character Joe, the general feeling of physical claustrophobia on the barge and in the crowded Glasgow pubs and tenements that Joe frequents, which echoes Joe's feelings of entrapment first by Cathie and later by Ella when both women suggest marriage to him. There are also significant differences between the film and classical noir. To begin with, we actually see the sex between characters, something that did not occur in the original films, a discrepancy commonly found in neo-noir films (Dyer, 2007, p. 124). Also, when comparing Swinton's Ella – who is seen scratching her armpits and talking with her mouth full at various points during her affair with Joe – to the glamorous femme fatale characters of the original noir films, we can see another sharp difference between the film and its predecessors. Likewise, can Joe's lack of charm and seductive power in the film be compared to other noir heroes. Unlike someone like Walter Neff (Fred McMurray) in *Double Indemnity* (Billy Wilder, 1944), who seduces (or at least thinks he seduces) Phyllis (Barbara Stanwyck) with his witty and sexually-charged flirtatious banter, Joe simply thrusts himself upon the women in the film. He says only a few words before taking Cathie behind a rock to have sex when they first meet ('Would you like to go for a walk with me', he says after a brief exchange of pleasantries). His 'courtship' of Ella consists of thrusting his leg and hand against her leg at dinner one day. He only needs to wait for Ella's sister Gwen (Therese Bradley) to finish her drink before the two have a decidedly non-erotic encounter out in an alley next to an pub, one which concludes with Gwen saying; 'Look at the mess you made of me.' The graphic detail of the sex throughout the film – including the shot of McGregor's penis that caused difficulties with American censors – as well as the banality of the characters are differences from classical noir which signpost the film's attempts to reinterpret the 1950s. It was not, according to the film, a period of high moral standards or particularly beautiful or noble people.

The figure of the 'angry young man', lifted from British literature and cinema of the late 1950s and early 1960s, can also be seen as an intertext for the film's Joe. Hill describes this figure as being born out of the disaffection of the male working class in post-war Britain as the economy moved from a manufacturing base to a service-oriented one. When this occurred, the male breadwinner was threatened with a loss of his traditional occupations in heavy industrial labour. Further frustrating traditional masculinity in this period was the increasing prominence of the woman in the workplace as she began to act as the primary provider for many working-class families. The anger that all these changes occasioned was outwardly directed at the hypocrisies of post-war British society, which promulgated a myth of a new prosperity and egalitarianism, but it was also equally directed at the newly economically empowered working-class woman (1986, pp. 20–27). This figure has one of its most famous cinematic incarnations in Richard Burton's Jimmy Porter in *Look Back in Anger* (Tony Richardson, 1958). For all the political content of the film, Hill points out that at root, *Look Back in Anger* spends most of its time showcasing the virulent misogyny of Jimmy (1986, p. 25).

Young Adam's Joe, whose story is set at approximately this time period, is suffering from a similar crisis of masculinity. After the departure of Les from the barge – significantly, Ella owns the vessel – Joe's relationship with Ella becomes increasingly characterized as one of economic dependence. When Les comes to talk to Ella, she snaps at Joe saying: 'You got work to do', lording her position as his boss over him. Any romance there may be imagined to exist between the two is undercut when the film at one point jumps from the two beginning to make love to Ella paying Joe his wages. Joe is likewise economically beholden to Cathie during their affair and is also very resentful of this situation. His anger and resentment manifest themselves in the 'custard scene', in which the materials of domestic labour (foodstuffs and cooking utensils) become the instruments of misogynist assault and degradation. The critical discrepancy, the act of interpretation on the part of the film, of the 'angry young man' figure shows him to be violent and morally debased and not at all as heroic and romanticized as he was in many of the films of the British new wave.

The final representational context that can be usefully applied to the film is one that is specifically Scottish. Writing of Scottish-set films from the 1940s and 1950s such as *The Brave Don't Cry* and *Floodtide* (Frederick Wilson, 1949), McArthur describes Clydesidism as a discourse that places emphasis on the spectacle of working-class masculinity, thematically emphasizing community and unity among the working classes and portraying the Clyde as the centre of working-class life (1982b, pp. 52–54). Taken together these are tendencies that the film both employs and subverts in equal measure. The film's narrative is punctuated by moments of banal observation of men at work. These include Les and Joe shovelling coal, loading and unloading the barge, manoeuvring the barge down the Clyde, and washing coal soot off one another's backs. Besides just showing the men engaging in traditionally masculine pursuits, these spectacles, especially the final one, are imbued with a sense of community between the two workers, one that the audience knows, from very early in the film, is a false one. To return to national representation, the milieux of Clydeside Scotland (including the dockyards and shipyards that were still active at the time, the pointedly squalid pubs and flats of the urban working classes of the period, the canals and quiet rural stretch of land between Edinburgh and Glasgow) are what we see of Scotland in the film. In keeping with the film's bleak and nihilistic tone, these spaces are invested with a feeling of gloom and decay.

Authorship, adaptation and art cinema

Nationality and national importance were important dimensions of the promotion of *Young Adam*. This was the case despite Martin-Jones's argument that the film was, at the textual level at least, nationally non-specific enough to be exportable to other countries (2009, pp. 229–230). In promoting the film, much was made of some of the same 'strong Scottish credentials' that were used in the funding application, especially stars and authors. As we saw above, McGregor's rhetorical authority in criticizing the Film Council was based in part on his participation in the making of *Shallow Grave* and *Trainspotting*, and he is cited by Thomas as being the quintessential Scottish actor. Equally prominent during the promotion of the film was the nationality of Tilda Swinton, who defended the film as a specifically Scottish one (as opposed to British), and who used interviews to argue for the Europeanness of Scottish cinema and art in comparison to what she describes as commercialized British cinema, implicitly drawing on her cachet as an art cinema actress for directors such as Derek Jarman and Sally Potter (e.g. Michael, 2003; Pearce, 2003). Likewise were there numerous newspaper pieces on Alexander Trocchi, the, by now, obscure Scottish author whom the film was ostensibly bringing back into the fold of Scottish arts and culture (e.g. Burnside, 2002; Christopher, 2003; Cumming, 2003).

Among all of these figures, it is that of director David Mackenzie who is the most important for our concerns here. At the time of the film's release he was the least known figure among those involved in the project. Unlike Ramsay, who has been omnipresent in the promotion of her films, Mackenzie became a somewhat marginal figure in the promotion of *Young Adam* and further, when he did speak, he was almost always deferential to Trocchi. Mackenzie's status in the film's promotion stands in stark contrast to his discursive presence in the application for funding from Scottish Screen. Throughout the application Mackenzie occupies a prominent place, compared with the film's stars or by Trocchi. When asked: 'Why do you consider this project to be of high artistic quality', the applicants list Mackenzie's 'great talent' and 'award winning short films' before the project's 'Internationally renowned actors' (Scottish Screen, 2001b, p. 9). The only part of the project mentioned before Mackenzie in this response is the film's source novel, which is described (somewhat dubiously) as 'acclaimed' (Scottish Screen, 2001b, p. 8). The subsequent question in the artistic quality subsection goes further in placing Mackenzie ahead of his collaborators. Question 36 on the application asks: 'Why do you consider the creative team is appropriate to this project?', and is answered by the applicants with reference to only one member of that team:

> David Mackenzie, the writer of the screenplay and the director, has worked on this project for many years. We are very impressed with his vision for the project. His award-winning short films give rise to great expectations for his feature-film debut. (Scottish Screen, 2001b, p. 9)[32]

The rhetoric in this passage is clearly predicated on auteurist grounds, referencing Mackenzie's personal vision, his implicit longstanding devotion to getting the film made, his previous work and the prestigious awards it has received.

These references to Mackenzie's authorial vision for the project each seem to be calling on the portion of Scottish Screen's mandate that requires the body to assist in the development of Scottish talent. This is even more apparent in the applicants' response to a later question: 'Why can you not make your film with money from other sources?': 'Even though we view this project as a highly commercial proposition, David Mackenzie is a first time director and distributors are cautious in such cases. It is therefore necessary to source additional funding' (Scottish Screen, 2001b, p. 10). Without presenting the film as a potentially uncommercial project, the applicants do all they can here to call on the market protection mandate of Scottish Screen to intervene and ensure an unestablished Scottish artist is able to bring his vision to the screen. That this was a successful strategy for the applicants to deploy can be seen from the decision made by the Lottery Panel. The minutes which record the Panel's decision in favour of *Young Adam*'s application as well as the reasons for doing so, in whole, read as follows:

> A strong package: writer/director is David MacKenzie [*sic*] (*The Last Great Wilderness*), actors Ewan McGregor and Tilda Swinton. Very visual script but the Panel raised concerns indicating further development work was required to enhance the thriller content. It was thought that flashbacks could be moved around and the murderer's identity should be only given away nearer the end. It was noted that the film would appeal to a European Audience [*sic*]. On a whole the Panel were very supportive of this project and approved funds. (Scottish Screen, 2001b)

We can see that David Mackenzie qua auteur is a significant component of the Panel's discourse here, with his name and previous work being mentioned before stars Ewan McGregor and Tilda Swinton. We can also see a symmetry of sorts between the applicants' language in praising Mackenzie's 'vision' for the project, and the Panel's praise for the film's 'very visual script'. Though 'vision' is used in different senses in each of the respective passages, in both cases it implies that the film will be auteur driven.

The question is now whether or not *Young Adam* was seen as a 'Mackenzie film'. We can begin to explore this with the references in the promotion and reception of the film that deal with the other authorial figure involved with the project: Alexander Trocchi. In a situation that contrasts sharply with the relationship between Lynne Ramsay and Alan Warner, Mackenzie is almost always deferential to Trocchi when he discusses the film. Asked in an interview whether or not he was acting as a director-for-hire on the film, Mackenzie gives a response that is typical of his statements during the promotion of the film: 'No, it was a passion of mine. I read Alexander Trocchi's book about nine years ago and it's taken me that long to get it off the ground' (Bear, 2004).

Such avowed devotion and even subservience runs throughout Mackenzie's other comments on the film. Introducing the DVD's commentary track, Mackenzie says that the idea for the film was born out of his fascination with Trocchi's book, and particularly with the character of Joe. This quickly becomes more than just an interesting bit of trivia and instead introduces a concern with the fidelity of Mackenzie's script, which subsequently becomes one of the commentary track's main themes. As one of the 'talking heads' on the commentary track, Swinton explicitly grounds the theme of the fidelity of the adaptation in an auteurist discourse, immediately praising Mackenzie's script for realizing Trocchi's 'cinematic' novel. The theme of fidelity returns again and again throughout the commentary track as the various personnel involved in the track (Mackenzie, Swinton, the production designer Laurence Dorman and the editor Colin Monie) point out how various curious aspects of the film are included because they are in the novel. The 'faithful' aspects include extremely minute details, such as the number of cigarette stubs (nine) seen momentarily on screen in an ashtray in Gwen's apartment. Fidelity to Trocchi's novel subsequently features prominently in the press kit for the film (the opening sentence of the pack describes the film as 'a beautiful and faithful adaptation' of Trocchi's book [Recorded Picture Company, 2003, p. 1]), is mentioned in nearly every review of the film and is added as a term of praise in Blandford's account of the film (2007, p. 83). The image that is sought to be presented is of one artist channelling another, bringing to the screen the work of someone who has had a personal impact on Mackenzie, as faithfully as possible. Important for its auteur director is the obscurity of that inspirational artist, as it is the reclaiming of Trocchi that is presented as Mackenzie's triumph in both the promotional discourses surrounding the film and in Blandford's discussion of the film (2007, p. 83). It is thus worth looking more closely at the Trocchi's status before and after the film's release in some more detail.

Mentions of Trocchi and his work in the press surrounding *Young Adam* are conflicting in their accounts of his legacy, with some referring to him as a 'countercultural hero' (Hodgkinson, 2002), and others describing him as 'virtually forgotten by the time of his death' (Cumming, 2003). One particularly unkind commentator called Trocchi 'little more than a footnote in the history of the Beat Generation', stating that despite the publicity generated by the re-publication of his works in the early 1990s and the production of the film 'his name still means little or nothing outside of the world of the counter-culture anorak' (Burnside, 2002). While Anna Burnside's comments overstate the case somewhat (there had been a retrospective of Trocchi's life and work, *A Life in Pieces* [Campbell and Niel, 1997], published in 1997 and reviewed in *The Sunday Times* [Horovitz, 1997] and other mainstream publications) 'obscure' was nonetheless the right word to describe Trocchi in 2003. His name is not to be found in mainstream anthologies and textbooks on the literature of the Beat movement, and what was written about him before the film was released tends to dwell on his wasted potential and life spent in obscurity, rather than the quality or importance of his body of work.

In such a context, Mackenzie's continual praise for Trocchi becomes an instance of the director acting as someone with specialized knowledge who brings a forgotten figure to the attention of a larger national and international culture. One of the central promotional strategies for the film revolved around sparking public interest and curiosity about the figure of Trocchi and his place in Scottish literature. Hence, the film's press packet includes a section entitled 'The Life and Work of Alexander Trocchi' (Recorded Picture Company, 2003, pp. 5–7), an explanatory section that would not be thought necessary for a well-known author. Likewise, it is significant that a large portion of the film's 'behind the scenes' featurette is devoted to explicating the Trocchi's life and work. It is in such materials, in which Mackenzie is one of the 'experts' on the novel and its writer, that we can see Mackenzie himself promoted by virtue of his knowledge of a writer who is unknown to most audiences.

Though, in many ways, the film is indeed 'faithful' to the book in terms of presenting the story found therein, there are nevertheless a number of differences between the two texts that are worth looking at more closely. Besides simply correcting the widespread belief that the film was a slavishly faithful recreation of the novel, my analysis here also show show, as with Ramsay and *Morvern Callar*, these changes help to re-brand the film as Mackenzie's by both aligning it more with art cinema conventions, as well as by adding scenes that serve to personalize the film for Mackenzie, thereby shifting creative agency away from the ostensible subject of the publicity to the auteur writer/director.

As with *Morvern*, one of the major changes that occurred during the adaptation process was the removal of the novel's first-person narration. The decision to drop this device changes not only the way in which the film's story is told, but also how we understand Joe. From the outset of the novel, Joe hints that he knows more about the body than he is telling the reader. After he mentions a necrophilic thought he had about the corpse, Joe teases the reader by saying, 'Later you will see what I mean' (Trocchi, 1983, p. 9). Though there are flashbacks in the novel, the first-person narration does not slip into stream-of-consciousness, meaning that the flashbacks are clearly marked as such. This is in sharp contrast to the film, in which it only becomes apparent that the flashbacks were indeed flashbacks late in the film. The novel's Joe will typically say something like: 'There was a time I suppose when we were happy' before launching into his memories of Cathie (Trocchi, 1983, p. 134). The first mention of Cathie in the novel not only makes clear that she is outside of the present tense of the narration, but also goes on to spell out most of the shared history between Joe and Cathie.[33] On the possibility of the body being Cathie's, the book is likewise more explicit than the film is. Early in the narrative, before his second encounter with Ella, Joe addresses the reader directly, saying:

> Go back to the beginning.
> It's an odd thing, or rather it *was* an odd thing. Thank God it's not likely to happen again.
> I wanted to talk about Ella, about how she suddenly came to me, like a brainwave, on the very day we dragged the dead woman from the river. For that reason, and not to complicate the issue, I said nothing about Cathie. At least I didn't show where she fitted into the picture. She was there all the time of course, but you didn't know it. She was the corpse. (Trocchi, 1983, p. 82)

Not only does Trocchi here make it clear that the scene that follows will be a flashback, but with the first line also makes the reader understand exactly what point in the story's diegetic time Joe is speaking about. There is no ambiguity about when the flashbacks refer to, as there is in the film. Cathie's relationship to the other plots in the book is likewise overtly spelled out by Trocchi. There is no ambiguity as to whether or not she is the corpse that was found at the beginning of the book or that finding the body was linked to Joe beginning his affair with Ella.

In contrast, the film's flashbacks are not clearly signalled at all and it is only gradually that the actual timeline of events in the film becomes apparent. David Bordwell describes a convention of classical art cinema which is apropos of the film's structure: 'One common strategy is to use flashbacks in ways that only gradually reveal a prior event, so as to tantalize the viewer with reminders of his or her limited knowledge' (1986, p. 210). As fitting as it is for the film's use of flashbacks, this is only a partial description of the film's narrative design. *Young Adam* combines the reliance on flashback for conveying narrative information and the slow revelation of narrative details with an additional obfuscating tendency not to clearly demarcate the flashbacks as such, leaving the audience unaware that many of the scenes they are seeing do not take place in the film's present tense. Martin-Jones compares this stylistic decision in the film to the narrative practices of art cinema auteurs such as Federico Fellini and Alain Resnais (2009, p. 227). Conventional as it may be to the art cinema, what does this do to the film? It does make the film more complex and puzzling than it would have been if it had featured a standard, linear narrative, but does it do anything more than making the film more of a puzzle that the audience derives pleasure from intellectually reassembling? As Bordwell implies in a passage cited earlier on flashbacks and slowly revealing a story, tantalizing the audience with the details of a story is very much a power game, one which demonstrates the film-maker's authority over the audience, here asserting Mackenzie as the agent controlling the audience's knowledge of the events of the film's story.

These changes in narration also affect how Joe is understood. Comparing the film's Joe to that of Trocchi's novel helps us to appreciate the extent to which the former is more outwardly likeable. By doing such things as dropping the highly unpleasant first-person narration of events that is found in the novel, Mackenzie creates a Joe Taylor that is, almost by default, more appealing than his literary counterpart. But there are also changes to the events of the story which, when considered alongside the change in narrative perspective, create a distinctly more palatable Joe. One such change comes when Mackenzie adds a scene in which Joe heroically leaps into the Clyde to rescue James, Les and Ella's son, when he is accidentally pulled overboard. Besides increasing the ambiguity of Joe's character, making him more sympathetic than his counterpart in the novel, this addition also personalizes the film vis-à-vis Mackenzie himself. As he notes in the film's DVD commentary and promotional interviews, Mackenzie based this scene on an accident he had experienced as a child.

Another example of the cleaning up of Trocchi's novel and especially Joe himself is the film's 'custard scene', which for all of its build-up in the press is considerably less disturbing than its counterpart in the novel. This can be seen from looking at the novel's version of the scene at some length:

> I grasped her by one arm, twisted her about so her great big and now custard smeared buttocks were facing me and with all the strength of my right arm I thrashed at them with the rough slat of wood. I thrashed her mercilessly for about a minute. She was making shrill whinnying noises as she threshed about on the dusty floor . . . She was seated on her haunches, crying, wheezing and shaking. I emptied the bottle [of ink] over her head . . . I don't know whether she was crying or laughing as I poured a two-pound bag of sugar over her head. Her whole near-naked body was twitching convulsively, a blue breast and yellow-and-red one, a green belly, and all the odour of her pain and sweat and gnashing. By that time I was hard. I stripped off my clothes, grasped the slat of the egg crate, and moved among her with prick and stick, like a tycoon. (Trocchi, 1983, p. 137)

As much as McGregor's casting is against type in the film, it is impossible to imagine his version of Joe speaking (or even thinking) like the narrator in this passage. Whereas the book presented Joe as an outright repulsive character, the film does not do so and instead chooses ambiguity, making Joe into an enigmatic anti-hero, rather than repugnant villain. The changes from book to film, including these changes to narrative, character and tone, as well as the open-endedness of the film's ending, all serve to make the film more conventional in terms of traditionally conceived art cinema.

In describing the changes made in adapting Trocchi's novel as ones oriented towards producing more of an art film than would have resulted from a stricter adaptation, I am characterizing the film as the sort of personal, complex art cinema viewed by Petrie, Murray, Blandford and others as typical of film production during the 'new Scottish cinema' period – but is this what was intended at the point of subsidy? To begin to answer this question, we can start by returning to the decision minutes for the film's subsidy decision, discussed above. If those minutes present the film as essentially an auteur film dominated by Mackenzie's 'visual' imagination and aimed at the European market (which here reads as a synonym for the art-house market), the simultaneous mention of the film as a 'thriller' may be somewhat unexpected, not only because this is an unlikely characterization of the film itself, but also because one would think genre not to be especially important in a film that is praised in terms of authorial vision. As Elsaesser points out, the romantically conceived art-house director is traditionally seen as standing opposed to genres and formulas, instead relying on their own visions to create their films (2005, p. 52). The view of the film articulated in the minutes is thus apparently contradictory, as praise for the personal vision and art cinema qualities of the project are juxtaposed with suggestions for changes to that vision and a hope for greater popular cinema appeal.

The film's final incarnation makes it difficult to discern any thriller content at all, as the revelation of Joe's complicity in Cathie's death does not solve a mystery in the film as much as it develops his character as a tortured, amoral wanderer. In spite of this the film was promoted, and to a lesser extent received, in terms like those that surface in the decision minutes. The press pack describes the film as a 'moody, sensual thriller' (Recorded Picture Company, 2003, p. 1) and reviewers, including the *Observer*'s Phillip French (2003, p. 9) among others, subsequently pick up on this terminology (e.g. Christopher, 2003; Sandhu, 2003b). In this sense, such promotion and reviews participate in depicting the film in terms that bridge the art cinema/popular cinema divide in which artistic elements such as the 'custard scene' can be seen as erotic moments familiar from thrillers such as *Jagged Edge* (Richard Marquand, 1985), Rafelson's version of *The Postman Always Rings Twice*, or *Basic Instinct* (Paul Verhoeven, 1992) – films that are themselves often infused with noirish stylistic tendencies.[34]

Young Adam does not operate on the same textual level as *Jagged Edge* or *Basic Instinct*, but instead bears a more substantial textual and extra-textual resemblance to films such as *Blow Up* (Michelangelo Antonioni, 1966) or the films of Nicholas Roeg, especially his *Bad Timing* (1980), all of which deal with sexuality, violence and moral transgression in ways that are both visceral and cerebral. These films were, roughly speaking, art-thriller hybrids and were modestly successful in terms of achieving a degree of 'crossover' success. Taking into account the fact that Jeremy Thomas produced not only *Young Adam* but also *Bad Timing*, we come to the final member of the creative team mentioned earlier in the application, and are given grounds to begin to suspect that he is perhaps the most influential of the group, even if he is the least discussed in the final minutes.

The producer as author?: Jeremy Thomas and *Young Adam*

Reading the subsidy application form itself, it is impossible to overlook the discursive weighting given to the film's producer. A full nine of the twenty-five pages that make up the *Young Adam* application package are devoted exclusively to Jeremy Thomas and his production company Recorded Picture. This compares to four mentions in total of David Mackenzie which, taken together, would not add up to a single page of text. The portions of the application dedicated to Thomas include a two-page biography of the producer and a complete listing of the films he had worked on up to this point, as well as more mundane information such as VAT numbers and so on, all of which are the domain of the producer. The suspicion created by such a discursive imbalance between producer and director is that, even if the director is mentioned in the decision minutes, it is the producer who is the most important figure for this successful application. This suspicion is especially piqued by one particular question that reads in part: 'Who within the organisation will take core responsibility for [managing the project]'; the applicants' response: 'Jeremy Thomas will be the producer of the film and will oversee every aspect of its evolution', after which follows the aforementioned biography of Thomas that lists his box-office successes as well as the awards he and his films have received (Scottish Screen, 2001b, p. 11). The types of films that comprise Thomas's CV, including *Bad Timing*, *The Last Emperor* (Bernardo Bertolucci, 1987), and *Sexy Beast* (Jonathan Glazer, 2000) are particular types of film which have been successful in terms of both reaching audiences as well as winning festival prizes and other sorts of prestigious awards. Such a career underscores Thomas's ability to tap a market niche for films with high artistic credentials but which are also accessible and capable of 'crossing over'.

In her study of the history of the reception of films, academic and otherwise, Janet Staiger discusses a number of influential paradigms in film studies, including auteur study, genre analysis and national cinema, and terms such paradigms 'reading strategies' which can produce discrete sets of meanings from similar texts (1992, p. 95). Having already discussed national and auteurist reading strategies as they have been encouraged and applied to the film, could we also productively examine the film using a reading strategy that is centred around Jeremy Thomas and his previous work? As Andrew Spicer has noted regarding the general problems faced in researching producers, assessment of the achievements of individual producers who have worked with numerous directors is especially difficult (2004, p. 46), but by looking at Thomas's oeuvre as a whole a number of patterns in terms of the contents and discursive contexts of his films arise. In pursuing such a critical approach to Thomas's work, I draw on the work of one writer who has attempted to apply such a unifying authorial persona to the producer's films, journalist Tim Adler in his *The Producers: Money, Movies and Who Really Calls the Shots* (2004). Here Adler profiles a number of influential producers who have worked with auteur directors, such as Alberto Grimaldi and Andrew Macdonald, and attempts to establish each of them, and not the directors, as the most important creative agents involved with their respective films.

To see that the deployment of a producer-oriented 'reading strategy' can reproduce the hagiographic excesses of its director-oriented counterpart, one need look no further than one of Adler's comments on *Young Adam*: 'Thomas's production is one of the most satisfying elements in this dream poem of a film' (2004, p. 187). What exactly constitutes 'Thomas's production' is never quite explained but there are a number of similarities between the film and a number of other projects that Thomas was involved in either as the producer or an executive producer, particularly at the level of promotion and reception, areas in which I have elsewhere argued Thomas is most apparently influential on his projects (Meir, 2009). Within the promotion and marketing of *Young Adam*, there are three Thomas themes relevant for this discussion, those being the prominence of transgressive sexuality, the importance of adaptation and finally aesthetics and marketing that make the film both artistically 'serious' and accessible to mainstream audiences.

Among works such as *Bad Timing*, *Crash* (David Cronenberg, 1996), *Gohatto* (Ngisa Oshima, 1999), *Stealing Beauty* (Bernardo Bertolucci, 1994), *Naked Lunch* (David Cronenberg, 1991), *The Dreamers* (Bernardo Bertolucci, 2004), *The Sheltering Sky* (Bernardo Bertolucci, 1990) and *A Dangerous Method* (David Cronenberg,

2011) are to be found numerous instances of sexuality which is considered transgressive of mainstream filmgoing tastes and sensibilities, including full frontal male nudity, incestuous sex, homoerotic sex, ambiguously rendered rape scenes and necrophilia. Whatever form it may take in individual films, sexual explicitness is something present across Thomas's oeuvre and is always presented as something more than mere titillation, instead being used to develop characters and reinforce the themes of the films. The rape/necrophilia scene in *Bad Timing* shows Alex's (Art Garfunkel) obsession with Milena (Theresa Russell) to have consumed him to the point of lunacy. The multiple affairs embarked upon by the characters in *The Sheltering Sky* and *Crash* are expressions of their unhappiness with everyday married life (something that can also be said of Ella in *Young Adam*). Growing up and being initiated into the world of adulthood underpins the sexual encounters in *Stealing Beauty* and *The Dreamers*, and so forth.

The sex scenes in *Young Adam*, which even when not as extreme as the 'custard scene', are cruel at times and on the whole unpleasant and decidedly non-titillating (one reviewer described them as 'ghastly' [Gilbey, 2003, p. 18]), are especially similar in this regard to those found in *Crash*, which Adler describes as 'as sexually exciting as a gear box oil change' (2004, p. 184). Sex in the film becomes a matter of power and control, with the custard scene being one in which Joe reasserts his mastery over Cathie, as in an earlier scene where he threatened to drown her by rocking the boat they are rowing together, a scene that ends with the two making love. Similarly, the progression of Joe and Ella's affair is marked by her increasing control over when and how often the two have sex, culminating in the jump-cut from the two having sex to Ella paying Joe his wages.

Another, related similarity *Young Adam* has to Thomas's larger body of work is the use that is made of controversy as a tool for promotion and free advertising. Battles over censorship were responsible for raising the profile of *Crash*[35] – a film whose tagline was 'The most controversial film you will ever see' – as well as other Thomas projects including *The Dreamers*, *Bad Timing* and *Young Adam*. That the film incurred such controversy cannot be said to have been altogether unexpected. Indeed, controversy is something that the film-makers actively sought to cultivate, though they were thinking of a different part of the film than the full frontal nudity that eventually incurred the NC-17 rating in America. In introducing the 'custard scene', the press kit for the film claims that: 'There's one particular sex scene in the film certain to cause a stir' (Recorded Picture Company, 2003, p. 3). Later it says of McGregor: 'The actor is in no doubt that the film's sex scenes will cause a stir' and quotes the actor comparing his role to that of Marlon Brando in *Last Tango in Paris* (1972) (directed by Thomas's frequent collaborator Bernardo Bertolucci) and saying that he watched that film to prepare for the role, implicitly referencing the infamous butter and sodomy scene that provoked so much controversy and publicity in the 1970s (Recorded Picture Company, 2003, p. 8).[36] The press pack is also quick to assert that sex in the film is not just titillation, but is something very 'serious', saying for instance of McGregor: 'But, he contends, the sex scenes are far from gratuitous' (Recorded Picture Company, 2003, p. 8); Mortimer later calls gratuitous sex scenes in other films 'really sick and cynical' and describes them as 'merely appealing to people's basest instincts' (Recorded Picture Company, 2003, p. 13).

The promotional signposting of this scene, with its erotic content, potential to incur controversy and possibly censorship, presents the scene as one that can potentially attract curious audiences and contribute to making the film a *success de scandale*. Numerous commentators go on to note the comparison with *Last Tango*, naming the custard scene as one of the film's most memorable sequences, echoing the scene's description in the press pack. Some reviews, such as Nigel Andrews's in *The Financial Times* for example, mention it in the story's headline (2003).[37] The spectre of censorship is also raised by Emily Mortimer in a profile in *The Sunday Times*. Here she wonders aloud if the scene would be cut by British censors (Pearce, 2002). Also present in these reviews is the acknowledgement of Thomas's influence in presiding over possible censorship problems. One review quotes Thomas as saying that the film would likely face the same hostility and censorship problems that *Crash* did, in all likelihood due to the 'custard scene' (MacNab, 2003a). *Crash* controversies were also compared in one piece to those facing *Young Adam* as well as the similar difficulties that Thomas was facing with *The Dreamers* (Bamigboye, 2003).

Part of the promotional discourse surrounding the controversial aspects of the film is a repeated insistence of the artistic importance of sex in the film. The press pack quotes Thomas at one point as saying that 'sex is a crucial element in the film' and that: 'If you're making adult films, it's bound to be a central theme . . . Sex acts as emotional punctuation to the story. Joe is trying to lose himself in sex' (Recorded Picture Company, 2003, p. 3). The film's DVD commentary track features Swinton discussing the ratings controversy in the USA and criticising the 'prurience' of American audiences. These are only two examples of many, as this theme remains prominent throughout the film's promotion and reception. Sexual content, and the attendant issues pertaining to artistic freedom/integrity as well as the high art qualities of the film, thus serve to brand *Young Adam* in similar terms.

A final Thomas 'signature' can be seen in how the film was promoted in terms of adaptation. In his profile of Thomas, Adler presents *Young Adam* as part of Thomas's 'cult novel trilogy' along with *Crash* and *Naked Lunch* (David Cronenberg, 1991) (2004, p. 173), a group of films which in various ways made much of their literary origins. While I would agree that such is true of these three films, it does not quite account for the scope or the significance of adaptation among the films that Thomas has worked on. In addition to these three films, *The Sheltering Sky* (novel by Paul Bowles), *Everybody Wins* (play by Arthur Miller), *The Dreamers* (novel by Gilbert Adair) and *Fast Food Nation* (non-fiction exposé by Eric Schlosser) were all based on high profile books/plays. Such use of literary source material is of course not a new or unique practice for a film-maker to adopt, as these materials bring with them pre-constituted stories and characters as well as, in the case of very popular books, pre-sold audiences. But Thomas adaptations make much more of their literary origins than most other films, even more so than those of the 'heritage' canon which have been long held to trade on promises of fidelity to source novels (Higson, 2003, pp. 16–20). Much effort was made in the promotional campaigns around *Crash* and *Naked Lunch* to attract the fans of the two rather cultish novels. The case of *Naked Lunch* is particularly pronounced in this regard. Its trailer consists mainly of an interview with William Burroughs and the DVD release features a documentary on the difficulties of bringing the hallucinatory world of the Burroughs novel to the screen, as well as an interview with Thomas himself discussing, among other things, the experience of reading the book and meeting with Burroughs. Such a dependence on a book's pre-sold following was also seen in the promotion of *Fast*

Food Nation and *The Sheltering Sky*, the latter also featuring Paul Bowles appearing in the film as an on-screen omniscient narrator who speaks the novel's closing lines at the end of Bertolucci's film.

The difference between the status of Trocchi and writers such as Burroughs, Bowles and J. G. Ballard is in some senses an exception that proves the rule regarding Thomas's influence over the discourses surrounding his films. Despite Adler's grouping the novel and the film with *Crash* and *Naked Lunch*, the following for *Young Adam*, which had been long out of print at the time the film was made, cannot be said to be on the same level of popularity as the novels that inspired Cronenberg's films. Hence the necessity of a marketing campaign in which the press pack includes a section detailing the life and work of Alexander Trocchi (Recorded Picture Company, 2003, pp. 5–7), and which included DVD featurettes with sections dedicated to explicating Trocchi himself, as well as an audio recording of McGregor reading from the novel. Whereas the featurette and trailer for *Naked Lunch* could assume knowledge of Burroughs and his work, as was seen earlier, considerable effort had to be made in *Young Adam*'s promotional campaign to ensure audiences knew who Trocchi was. In other words, in the case of *Young Adam*, Thomas and his production company undertook a marketing campaign that made adaptation a conspicuous aspect of the film.

Besides the section in the press pack dedicated explicitly to introducing the life and work of Trocchi, there is one particular mention of the novel and its author that is revealing of the strategic usage of adaptation in the promotion of the film. In the part dedicated to interviewing Emily Mortimer, the actress is quoted in the following way regarding Trocchi and his novel:

> 'It reminds you of Camus' *L'Etranger* – it has the same existential quality. It's like a hipster version of Camus, but there's something more angry about this. This film will make people think differently and more aware of other points of view.' The actress, who has a BA in Modern Languages from Oxford, was drawn to the richness of her character. (Recorded Picture Company, 2003, p. 13)

Even before the comment on Mortimer's education, which serves to confirm her intellectual authority to provide this commentary, this passage is one of the clearest instances of the promotion of the film in overtly intellectual terms. The references to Camus, complete with the title in its original language as opposed to calling it *The Outsider*, and the references to existentialism, Beat literature and arguably the 'angry young man' figure all contribute to frame the film in a similar fashion. Such a strategy is apparent throughout the larger promotional campaign, with literary figures such as Camus, Jack Kerouac, William Burroughs and Leonard Cohen mentioned in the press pack and throughout promotional interviews with Swinton, Mullan and others.[38] This is in addition to the press pack's cinematic references to *Last Tango in Paris*, film noir (Recorded Picture Company, 2003, p. 1) and the films of the British new wave (Recorded Picture Company, 2003, p. 8), all of which are echoed in reviews of the film and interviews with the cast and director, many of which turn to the theme of 'Europeanness' (here again a crude synonym for art cinema) to distinguish the film from mainstream Hollywood and British cinema.[39]

Such a promotional strategy in the case of *Young Adam* and across the career of Jeremy Thomas, especially with regard to projects he worked on which were adaptations, can be usefully compared to Dudley Andrew's account of contemporary auteurism. Andrew describes a certain strand of auteurist film-making aimed at more 'discerning' filmgoers, a strand he terms 'literary cinema', a 'cinema which is meant to be "read" rather than simply "consumed"' (Andrew, 2000, p. 24). This type of film-making is meant to be received as something both accessible and in, some senses, 'educational' and though he means the term to apply to auteur-driven film-making, it can be applied to almost all of Thomas's films, which have been for the most part collaborations with established 'star' directors such as Bertolucci, Cronenberg, Oshima and others, or conversely emerging auteurs such as Jonathan Glazer and David Mackenzie. All of his films are at least branded in terms of intellectual cultural capital, hence his propensity to package the works with pedagogically toned promotional materials such as those regarding Trocchi described above, but also to the DVD extras included with *Naked Lunch*, the featurette on the events of May 1968 included with *The Dreamers* and the film on the life and work of Takeshi Kitano included with *Brother* (Takeshi Kitano, 1999), to cite just a few examples. All of these materials (which were produced by Thomas and some of which include appearances by the producer as a 'talking head') have the effect of rendering the films in question as more than 'just' entertaining films.

By the same token, neither are Thomas's films packaged solely as esoteric art films. Popular genres have been important to *Brother* (martial arts film), *The Last Emperor* and *Gohatto* (historical epics), *Merry Christmas Mr Lawrence* (Ngisa Oshima, 1980) (war film), and *Young Adam, Crash*[40] and *Bad Timing* (erotic thrillers). Casting is another element that broadens the appeal of Thomas's work with pop stars being cast in some of his early films (David Bowie in *Merry Christmas, Mr Lawrence*, Art Garfunkel in *Bad Timing* and Liv Tyler in *Stealing Beauty*, who was at the time known only for being the daughter of pop star Steven Tyler). All of his other films include at least one recognized international star. *Young Adam* includes two (McGregor and Swinton) and this has led to Blandford naming casting as the one element of the film which was aimed at broadening the film's audience appeal (2007, p. 83).

The blending of generic elements (the historic epic) with the use of recognized international stars (Peter O'Toole) are two of the reasons why Peter Lev includes *The Last Emperor* as one of the key examples of what he terms the 'Euro-American film', a category of film that attempts to combine elements of Hollywood production values (big budgets, star casts, elements of recognized genres, production in English) with those of European art cinema (auteur directors, narrative ambiguity, character-driven stories), and which target both specialist and mainstream audiences (1993, p. 31). Taking away the large budget, much of what Lev describes is true of *Young Adam* and indeed Thomas's oeuvre as a whole, with the drop in budgets being explained by the successive commercial failures of *The Sheltering Sky*, *Naked Lunch* and *Everybody Wins*, which shook investor confidence in his big budget productions (Adler, 2004, p. 178). The film conforming to a paradigm which combines some aspects of art cinema with mainstream appeal aligns *Young Adam* with the 'cross-over' film.

Conclusion

Young Adam, which has been described by Blandford as yet another example of publicly supported art cinema (2007, p. 83), under closer analysis yields a number of important insights into policy, Scottish national cinema, art cinema and the position of artists in the international film market; in short, into all of this book's core concerns. As such, there are two important parallels to point out

between this film and other case studies in this book. The first
relates back to the role of English producers in developing Scottish
films and Scottish creative talent. One of the major controversies
within Scottish film historiography surrounding *Local Hero* was
the role that David Puttnam played in the making of the film. No
such controversies greeted *Young Adam*, even though another internationally oriented English producer was involved in producing
and packaging the film. This difference in reception can perhaps
be attributed to the working methods of the two producers, which
differ greatly. Puttnam is publicly known to be very involved in
the creative aspects of his films, whereas Thomas is more self-
effacing, publicly taking the role of the supporter of art cinema
auteurs. But as we saw above, his influence was nonetheless crucial
for getting the film made and getting it out to international markets.
In addition to the central role he played in getting the production
subsidies from Scottish Screen and in all likelihood the UK Film
Council, Thomas also brokered the film's co-production arrangement with StudioCanal. Similarly, he utilized all of his marketing
nous to build audiences for the film. Even if this did not make the
film a wildly successful, cross-over hit, it still ensured that it was
one of the most successful art-house films to emerge from Scotland
during this period, outstripping the audiences for *Morvern Callar*,
Ratcatcher, *Red Road*, *Orphans* and many others. It is not overstating the case to say that without this producing talent, an emerging Scottish directing talent may never have got the opportunity to
make their attempt at a breakthrough film.

The other important parallel to make with *Young Adam* is *Trainspotting*, a parallel that is most evident in the casting of McGregor.
As shown, this casting provided a number of opportunities for the
film to be promoted in relation to that most important of all Scottish films. McGregor and Thomas both repeatedly compare the film
to Boyle's, if for no other reason than to chastise the film-making
establishment in the UK for failing to support another possible
Trainspotting. The parallels between *Trainspotting* and *Young Adam*
go much deeper than casting. As Caughie points out, adaptation
is also central to both films (as well as *Morvern Callar*), more
specifically adaptation of Scottish novels with cult followings (2007,
p. 105). *Young Adam* the novel had nowhere near the following
of either *Trainspotting* or *Morvern Callar*, but it is a work associated with the Beat movement, a movement perennially popular with

disaffected youth looking for counterculture icons. In that sense, Joe is not so different, in some ways, from loners like Morvern or Mark Renton who are irreparably alienated from mainstream society – he just comes along at a different time in Scottish history.

More than character, adaptation or casting, it is the industrial model represented by *Trainspotting* that can be seen at work influencing *Young Adam*. Thomas did his level best to frame *Young Adam* as a potential cross-over hit, even managing to brand it in both generic and art-house terms, but it was simply not taken up in this way, with the film's bleak themes and sombre style never managing to excite audiences in the way that Boyle's *Trainspotting* had. Like Ramsay when *Morvern* failed to cross over, Mackenzie has suffered commercially as a director. Though he has been much more prolific than his female counterpart, Mackenzie's films have yet to achieve the buzz as an 'event film' in the way that *Young Adam* did. *Hallam Foe* came close to doing so but other films, including *Perfect Sense* which also starred McGregor, fell far short of *Young Adam*'s stature. Moreover, except for *Hallam Foe*, Mackenzie has no longer featured as writer/director and has instead been largely relegated to the role of 'director for hire'. Subsidized film-making has thus not single-handedly created an auteur in the case of David Mackenzie; the demands of the marketplace have instead wielded the biggest influence in shaping his career.

5

Importing national cinema: Ken Loach, *Ae Fond Kiss* and multicultural Scottish cinema

In Scotland, we're a colony in more ways than one . . . For me the two most important directors in Scotland in the past 15 years have both been English, Danny Boyle and Ken Loach. They were the ones who let us out of the cage. (Peter Mullan, quoted in Murray, 2005a, p. 4)

One of the most widely discussed cycles of films within the 'new Scottish cinema' period has comprised the five films made by English director Ken Loach in Scotland. These films – *Carla's Song* (1995), *My Name is Joe* (1998), *Sweet Sixteen* (2001), the recent *The Angel's Share* (2012) and *Ae Fond Kiss* (2004) – have been viewed as some of the most important of the period. These films, along with the director's Scottish-themed contribution to the portmanteau film *Tickets* (Ermanno Olmi, Abbas Kiarostami, Ken Loach, 2005), have featured prominently in accounts such as Petrie's two survey histories (2000a, pp. 200–203; 2004, pp. 170–173) and Martin-Jones's survey (2009, pp. 53–63; 175–187). John Hill has been the foremost Loach scholar in recent years and, as such, has also detailed the his contribution to Scottish cinema in his own study of the director (2011, pp. 182–193) as well as his contribution to the collection *Scottish Cinema Now* (2009). For reasons that I will discuss in detail, these works assign great importance to Loach's Scottish films. In fact it would not be overstating the case to argue that, with now five feature films made in Scotland over the last seventeen years, Ken Loach has been the most accomplished 'Scottish' film-maker of the period, a seemingly paradoxical situation that begs closer examination.

This chapter takes as its object Loach's fourth Scottish-set feature, *Ae Fond Kiss*. Prominent in my discussion of the film is the role of Scottish film policy in supporting an established English film-maker and the problems and debates inherent in this situation. The examination of the industrial contexts surrounding Loach's work also offer insights into the role that transnational co-production has played in contemporary Scottish cinema. Loach, with the help of his producer Rebecca O'Brien, has benefited enormously from the support of European distributors who have supported all of his recent work.

Beyond the industrial questions surrounding the film are other questions relating to film history. These begin with the familiar question of national representation, one, in this case, occasioned by the film's somewhat pioneering representation of the Scottish-Asian experience. Examining this aspect of the film involves contextualizing it in relation to the long-running and changing traditions of British representations of multiculturalism. At the textual level, the chapter also takes on the changing approaches to narrative strategy and thematic exposition that have been observed across Loach's oeuvre since the 1990s, changes that have seen the ardently political film-maker turn increasingly to the conventions of popular cinema. A central question here is the relationship of this stylistic shift to the financial realities of contemporary Scottish cinema, realities in which public funding looms large.

A fundamental assumption of this chapter is thus that *Ae Fond Kiss* is a film which can yield a great number of insights into contemporary Scottish cinema. We can begin to explore these more fully with a discussion of the authorial figure who is central to the film at all levels.

Ken Loach, policy and the importing of national cinema

Ken Loach occupies a singular place in the British film industry, where he is one of the last practitioners of overtly politically engaged social realism. He also occupies a distinct place in British cinema historiography, where his work has for some become associated with a certain ideal of national cinema production. Hill describes the director's continuing importance in the 1990s (nearly thirty years after his career was effectively launched with *Cathy Come*

Home [1965]), in the following terms during a review of his 1998 film *My Name is Joe*:

[I]n the context of contemporary British film-making a Loach film is clearly more than 'just another film'. At a time when the would-be champions of the British film industry are fixated on the need for more 'commercial' films, it is clearly important that the kind of socially questioning cinema *My Name is Joe* represents is seen and supported. (Hill, 1998, p. 21)

This passage is a very significant one for my analysis of *Ae Fond Kiss*. We can begin with what Hill describes as Loach's 'socially questioning cinema' and how this is related to the director's place in the canon of British national cinema broadly, and Scottish national cinema in particular. A cursory glance at the titles of book-length studies of Loach's oeuvre is enough to illustrate how important the politically engaged content of his films are to the ways in which his career is understood: *The Cinema of Ken Loach: Art in the Service of the People* (J. Leigh, 2002); *Agent of Challenge and Defiance: The Films of Ken Loach* (McKnight, 1997); *Which Side Are You On?: Ken Loach and His Films* (Hayward, 2004); and *Ken Loach: The Politics of Film and Television* (Hill, 2011). All four titles unambiguously signal the fact that their respective analyses is in large part dedicated to the political orientation of his work, concentrating on the capacity of those films to act as social criticism.

Hill also hints at a number of important issues when he writes that because of this aspect of Loach's work, his films should be 'seen and supported'. Attracting audiences on a large scale, especially within Britain, has been a consistent problem throughout Loach's career since it was effectively revived by the success of *Hidden Agenda* (1990) (Fuller, 1998, p. 178; Hayward, 2004, pp. 203–207). Despite this lack of success at home, his films have consistently attracted audiences in Europe. His film *The Navigators* (2001), for example, received only a television airing in Britain while it ran in cinemas across the continent. Like heritage cinema, Loach's films are thus known for being more popular abroad, but unlike heritage cinema, this is not seen by critics as a shortcoming in those making the films, but instead as a shortcoming in British audiences. For this reason many critics sympathetic to Loach have bemoaned his lack of popularity in Britain, leading one to call the under-appreciation of the director in his homeland 'scandalous' (Wayne, 2002, p. 46). While the place where each kind of film-making is thought to be popular is surely relevant to how export is understood by critics (in this case America versus Europe), the principle is nonetheless the same.

Hill is, in one sense, participating in this larger critical plea to the British public, but 'supported' can also be taken to have an institutional meaning. Elsewhere in his writing Hill has argued that 'a nationally specific cinema characterised by questioning and inquiry' – the cinema his model prefers, and which Loach's films exemplify – 'is not the kind of "national cinema" which is encouraged by the market-place', but is one that is necessary, nonetheless (1992, p. 17). The use of the word 'supported' thus takes on a special resonance in Hill's writing, one that implicitly chides government to continue to make such cinema possible, substantiating Higson's observation that Hill's historiography is often underpinned by an implicit argument about film policy (2000, p. 39).

Intertwined with the political concerns that mark his films, have been Loach's preferred aesthetic strategies – specifically his commitment to social realism of the type that was en vogue when he began his career in the mid-1960s. As Hill indicates, Loach is commonly described as adhering to this practice long after it had fallen out of favour with many other British film-makers. Loach's commitment to such politics and aesthetics has helped to cement his position in the British national cinematic canon. Higson (1986) has pointed out that the tradition of social realism has attained a hegemonic status in discussions of British cinema and has become a paradigm that is critically endorsed by many scholars as well as film-makers, showing the 'British way of life' and distinguishing the national product from that of other cinemas, particularly that of Hollywood. Moreover, critics such as Peter Wollen (1993) have identified this strand of British cinema as being the equivalent of an art cinema tradition for a national film culture, which for a great deal of its history had not embraced the aesthetics of political modernist film practice (see also Hill, 2000b, p. 18).

Loach's aesthetic commitment to realism also enhances his 'national' credentials because of the sort of representational 'authenticity' that a social realist style has allowed the director to create in his films. Many of the his most widely known practices are aimed at presenting 'real' people and places, and his critical reputation within film studies at large still rests on this aspect of his work.[41] These practices include location shooting and the casting of non-professional actors from the social and geographical milieux he portrays, practices which are continued in *Ae Fond Kiss*. By attempting to show various parts of the nation with some degree of 'authenticity', Loach's cinema helps to diversify the representations of the 'British way of life' visible on television and cinema screens and thus implicitly interrogates the image of the nation as it has become known in mainstream film and television.

Within the context of Scottish cinema, where national representation has been at the top of the critical agenda, this aspect of Loach's work takes on a very distinct resonance. Petrie (who is not only a Scottish cinema historian but was also on the Lottery Panel that approved the production funds allotted to *Ae Fond Kiss*) has cited *My Name is Joe* as being amongst a group of films of the 'new Scottish cinema' that were performing the long overdue task of representing the contemporary Scottish city, which implicitly comes as a response to decades of mainly rural visions of the nation (2000a, p. 199). As we see, *Ae Fond Kiss* takes this notion of authentic representation a bit further by attempting to depict the realities of Glasgow's changing ethnic, racial and religious landscape; an attempt which played a major part in the project receiving the endorsement of Scottish Screen.

Politics and/versus genre in Loach's oeuvre

Although Loach's films deploy a visual style and mise-en-scène that correspond with the conventions of social realism, as Jacob Leigh (2002), Hill and others have pointed out, the narratives of his films are very much indebted to the conventions of melodrama and increasingly in recent years, other popular genres such as comedy. Hill, who described *My Name is Joe* as a 'social realist male weepie' (1998, p. 21), describes the coexistence of these seemingly contradictory modes of representation in a particularly concise manner:

> [M]uch of the power to unsettle in Loach's work derives from the apparent impassivity of his cinematic style in relation to the disturbing events in front of the camera. But though his films are shot from a distanced observational standpoint, many of them rely on the dramatic machinery of melodrama: impossible choices,

misjudgements, coincidences, a foreshortened sense of cause and effect. (1998, p. 20)

Leigh, who has taken issue with what he sees as Hill's pejorative description of the use of melodrama in Loach's work, more precisely describes Loach's brand of melodrama as being that of the 'melodrama of protest' which 'attempts . . . to rouse the audience to activate a sense of outrage at the injustices or atrocities of the authorities against an innocent protagonist' (2002, p. 22). Leigh's gloss on the function of melodrama is part of his vindication of melodrama as a practice that is suitable for Loach's political purposes, and not one that undermines the messages of his films, a claim that is implicit in Hill's piece (to which *Sight and Sound* added the opening line, in large print: 'Why does Britain's most political film-maker rely on the themes and devices of melodrama?' [1998, p. 18]). I go into the melodramatic and generic aspects of *Ae Fond Kiss* in more detail later, but for now I am interested in showing that the very usage of generic conventions, especially those relating to melodrama, can be perceived as weakening political messages and thereby threatening to undermine the aspect of Loach's work that has helped to maintain his place in the British canon.

Melodramatic tendencies, as Leigh argues above, allow for a degree of accessibility to the political messages Loach hopes to convey to his audience. Differentiating his films according to their balance of politics and generic form, Leigh describes the quality of the director's films as residing in their ability to keep their political messages from disrupting the narrative flow and turning them into overt didacticism (2002, p. 22). This becomes important to my analysis of *Ae Fond Kiss* as a strong affinity can be seen between being 'accessible' and being 'commercial'. Being 'more commercial' is something that Hill, in the passage cited at the beginning of this section, derisively describes as typifying the British cinema zeitgeist of the late 1990s, which he describes Loach as acting in opposition to. Such a zeitgeist is also reflected in British film policy during the 'cultural industries' period, which has seen greater emphasis placed on being 'commercial'. It is with this policy shift and its possible ramifications for Loach's work, which has almost always depended on some form of public support, in mind that we move to an examination of Scottish Screen's participation in the making of *Ae Fond Kiss*.

Funding *Ae Fond Kiss*

Scottish Screen provided £500,000 for the making of *Ae Fond Kiss*; this amounted to about 16 per cent of the overall budget for the film and, according to the applicants, was a provision necessary in order to obtain the remainder of the funds from other backers (Scottish Screen, 2003, p. 4). The remainder of the funding came from pre-sales to distributors in Italy, Belgium and Spain as well as finance raised from a UK tax scheme (Martin-Jones, 2009, p. 181). One very prominent problem for the Scottish Screen Lottery Panel was the extent of their partnership with the film-makers, with Scottish Screen having funded the last two films made in Scotland by Sixteen Films, Loach's production company. The Lottery Panel recognized that this continued support appeared to be problematic. In their decision minutes they wrote, 'It was noted that Scottish Screen could be criticized for backing the same team, as this would be the third film the Lottery had invested in' (Scottish Screen, 2003). Implicit here perhaps is the fear that Scottish Screen would be seen as helping to support a film-maker who had access to the resources to make the film without Lottery money. The Panel's decision minutes conclude with a somewhat half-hearted seeming resolution to utilize this problem as leverage with which to bargain for a more favourable recoupment position. This was never actually agreed or even suggested to the film-makers (O'Brien, 2006), but the very suggestion of such an unorthodox strategy speaks to the depths of the Panel's insecurity over this issue.

Given these apparent problems with the application, why would Scottish Screen want to support this film and its director? Even the indigenous talents mentioned in the application – Paul Laverty and Rebecca O'Brien – were by this point very well established and not in need of support in the way that film-makers like Ramsay or Mackenzie were. Somewhat paradoxically, it was precisely the previous successes of these film-makers that made them attractive to Scottish Screen. Ken Loach's high international profile and the socially activist/realist associations that his authorial persona brings with it were apparently very much on the mind of Scottish Screen when supporting both *Sweet Sixteen* and *Ae Fond Kiss*,[42] and in the case of the latter film it played a significant part in overcoming Lottery Panel's reservations about supporting the project. Language from the decision minutes such as: 'The Committee acknowledged that this team was consistently strong and had an increasing European appeal' (Scottish Screen, 2003) suggest this and comments from one Panel member reinforced this suggestion. Petrie, who as previously mentioned was on the Panel that approved the application for *Ae Fond Kiss*, has said that, despite the misgivings about repeatedly funding an established artist such as Loach, on balance, it was more important that the project be supported because, as he put it, 'the Scottish film industry needs high profile people like Loach as much as they need the Scottish film industry (possibly more!)' (2005b). Such a mindset on the part of the Lottery Panel speaks to a power dynamic that is surprising in some ways – after all, it is supposed to be the applicants to a subsidy body that need the resources that body has on offer – but the reality in the case of a small national cinema is that imported film-makers can raise the national profile (and that of the subsidy body itself) in ways that unproven local film-makers cannot.

This seems to have been something the applicants themselves were aware of as Loach's 'high profile' surfaces at several junctures in the application form. An example of this would be a response to questions pertaining to artistic quality: 'Our projects have a proven artistic quality. The two films of our West Scotland trilogy both won prizes at the Cannes film festival and went on to reap many awards and accolades around the world' (Scottish Screen, 2003, p. 9). In addition to references to Loach's international critical reputation, the applicants also refer to the style that has won him that reputation. Realism, and the supposedly attendant authenticity of Loach's representations – in short, his authorial brand – is brought up in a response to the project's potential Scottish cultural relevance: 'this is the third of a trilogy of Scottish films that we wish to be seen as a *triptych of true life in Scotland at the turn of the millennium*' (Scottish Screen, 2003, p. 7; emphasis added).

Describing *Ae Fond Kiss* as a part of a West Scotland trilogy is a particularly interesting way of rhetorically reinforcing the authorial brand on the project, not the least because mention of such a trilogy is difficult to find before the making of the film. The idea of the three films forming a thematic trilogy was also mentioned briefly in the application to Scottish Screen for production funds for *Sweet Sixteen* (Scottish Screen, 2001a, p. 9), but it was mainly articulated during the production and promotion of *Ae Fond Kiss*. The term 'trilogy' is used somewhat loosely in the promotional discourses surrounding the film and Loach himself has admitted that the appellation 'West Scotland trilogy' may have been a created to impress funding bodies.[43] Through answers that refer to larger bodies of authorial output, mention awards and branded styles, and so forth, we see the applicants laying out their side of the bargain: supporting a Loach film, they hint strongly, means garnering international acclaim, acclaim that will likely be couched in language praising the depiction of 'true life' in contemporary Scotland.

For Scottish Screen, there was also a competitive dimension to their relationship with Loach. As Hill has argued, strictly speaking, Loach's Scottish films before the recent *The Angel's Share*, did not need to be set in Scotland. Their settings are, in some senses, incidental and their themes could have been engaged with, according to Loach himself, just as effectively had they been set in English cities such as Liverpool or Manchester (2011, p. 188). For Hill, the possible factors contributing to setting the 'West Scotland trilogy' in Scotland boil down to screenwriter Paul Laverty wanting to write about a milieu he knew very well, the political complexion of Scotland itself which has historically leaned further to the left than England, and the availability of public funding for his films (2011, pp. 182–183). While the first two reasons were important, they did not in, and of, themselves determine the settings of the films. Laverty has written very successful screenplays set in Ireland, England, the USA and Bolivia in addition to his work in Scotland. Similarly, Loach has effectively utilized other settings to deal with his favoured themes of the inequities of life under capitalism, most notably the traditionally working-class environs of London's East End and the north of England (Hill, 2011, p. 182). Taking these two reasons out of the equation leaves only public support as a determining factor for setting the films in Scotland.

If Loach had not made these films in Scotland, Scottish cinema would have been robbed of some of its most accomplished films, but what is crucial here is that in 'landing' these Loach films for Scotland, Scottish Screen and the Glasgow Film Office harnessed the forces of globalization to benefit Scottish film culture in ways that go beyond the typical 'runaway production'. As shown in Chapter 1, when it comes to cinema Scotland is usually seen as a victim of transnational forces, even though many film-makers have actually benefited greatly from these same forces. The case of Loach and Laverty in Scotland provides yet another reminder that the effects of the free movement of creative talent and capital are complex, multifarious and – to put it crudely – not all 'bad' for Scotland. Moreover, this observation is echoed by the ways in which O'Brien's complex transnational funding packages for Loach's films – which typically involve at least three distributors from continental Europe as well subsidy bodies and public service broadcasters from all parts of Britain – have given the director the creative freedom he had lacked for much of the 1980s and 1990s. Loach has said that these arrangements have ensured 'that nobody has [me] by the throat' when it comes to creative control (quoted in Hill, 2011, p. 166).

If Scottish Screen hoped to import these desirable aspects of Loach's film-making, they were also aware of some of the drawbacks attendant to his brand of cinema, namely the reputed failure of his films to find local audiences. While Loach's films have in fact been very profitable and found large audiences in Europe (Hill, 2011, p. 168), they have had more difficulty in connecting with British audiences. The worry that *Ae Fond Kiss* would be another Loach film that no one in Scotland or the UK at large goes to see can be detected in the first sentence of their approval of the project: 'On the whole the Committee were supportive of this project and agreed *it was possibly more commercial* and less grim than previous Ken Loach projects' (emphasis added). It is important to note that the Panel speaks of the project's commercial potential before any mention is made of the socio-political content of the film, which comes in the next sentence: 'It was noted that the script was very topical and covered interesting territory with the introduction of an ethnic theme.' The film-makers also realized this perceived problem and sought to address it both directly and indirectly in their responses to questions throughout the application form. When responding to questions as to the nature of the film's planned distribution strategy, for example, the applicants tellingly comment on the likely (local) commercial viability of the project vis-à-vis their previous work:

> We would very much hope to get the same sort of release (*or better as this time it's a love story!*) as we had for *Sweet Sixteen*. . . . *This is almost like a mainstream release*. Through *Sweet Sixteen* and *My Name is Joe* before it, we have begun *to build a strong Scottish audience for our work and* hopefully through the terrific Scottish support have introduced a *wider audience* to the difficult issues we

Figure 7 Ken Loach telling a love story: Casim (Atta Yaqub) and Roisin (Eva Birthistle) embrace in *Ae Fond Kiss*

explored in these two films. (Scottish Screen, 2003, p. 9; emphases added)

The hope expressed here that the deployment of genre, the love story narrative (Figure 7), could possibly lead to a 'wider audience' has very significant implications for the way in which we can view *Ae Fond Kiss* and its potential to be both politically important and palatable to wider audiences, and I will be returning to such deployment when analysing the film. But for now it is important to register the prominence of audience appeal and commercial potential in the discourse of what is implicitly described in Scottish cinema history as a culturally oriented organization. The applicants make sure to mention these commercial aspects of the project as much as possible and the decision minutes show them to be foremost in the Panel's statements.

Audiences, or the lack thereof, may have been anticipated as a major reason for possibly turning down the application. However, in keeping with the importance of authorial branding throughout the application process for the film, approving it was also justified with reference to its potential to address social problems; in short, its promise as a piece of socially engaged art that would address issues relating to multicultural Scotland: 'It was noted that the script was very topical and covered interesting territory with the introduction of an ethnic theme' (Scottish Screen, 2003). Again, the applicants themselves were clearly aware that this was one of the strengths of their proposal. To the questions on the application which specifically relate to the project's potential 'public benefit', the applicants give two answers that reference multiculturalism. The first is a reference to the audience of the film as it relates to its content. Asked: 'How many people will benefit from the project and in what ways will they benefit?', the applicants respond by citing the economic impact the project will have, including local employment and spending, but then go on to mention a different sort of public benefit: 'we would hope that the specific communities that the film deals with will benefit by seeing issues important to them played out and explored on the big screen' (Scottish Screen, 2003, p. 7). Thus, 'public benefit' is seen as addressing an audience with similar concerns to the characters in the film and helping them to come to terms with a social problem, namely ethnic and religious difference.

That this is the intended message of the film, at least at this point in its development, is reiterated by the next question and response. Replying to a query about equal opportunities policy for the production company, the applicants respond with reference to the film's content: 'The film deals overtly with cultural and religious differences within the community and the concomitant issues that arise. The message of the film is one of tolerance within our multi-cultural society. We would hope to reflect this within the way in which we make the film' (Scottish Screen, 2003, p. 7). What makes this response interesting is how indirect it is given the question itself. One would expect an applicant to respond to this question by discussing their human resources policies, not by discussing the themes of the film being produced. The applicants are clearly taking this question as an opportunity to insist on the socially relevant thrust of the film. The next question deals more directly with this aspect by asking 'How is your project culturally relevant to Scotland?' The applicants' respond: 'The film is set in Scotland and deals with issues and problems that are very relevant not only to Scotland, but also to the rest of the UK and other European countries' (Scottish Screen, 2003, p. 7). Social function, cultural relevance, local address and potential for exportability are thus conflated in a single sentence.

That these multiple goals could be perceived as conflicting can be seen by returning to the applicants' response to the distribution question. After hinting at the possibility of mainstream release in the passage previously cited, the applicants are quick to assign the blame for their past failures in reaching wider audiences on the politically engaged content of their films, effectively balancing an assertion of commercial viability with one of the need for market protection: 'The films we make are still perceived as "art-house" productions and, as such, it is difficult for us to break into the mainstream, especially as we concentrate on tough subjects' (Scottish Screen, 2003, p. 9). The question that this all begs, then, is how all this apparent conflict between communicating a political message whilst also being accessible plays out in tangible terms. Did the film end up 'selling out', being so commercial in a bid to win audiences that it failed to make a substantial 'Loachian' impact? Or was it so intent on its message that audiences will be driven away by dread of didacticism?

Ae Fond Kiss and multiculturalism: a return to 'the cinema of duty'?

Until the release of *Ae Fond Kiss*, there were not many films dealing with the immigrant experience in Scottish cinema. A few films, such as Bill Forsyth's *Comfort and Joy* (1984) and the low-budget comedy *American Cousins* (Don Coutts, 2003), dealt with the experiences of Italian immigrants to Scotland and their descendants, but since *The Gorbals Story* (David MacKane, 1950) no film had attempted to deal directly with the experience of Scottish Asians.[44] In comparison, representations of British-Asian life are well established fixtures of the British cinema canon. Two of the most high-profile British films of the 1980s were *My Beautiful Laundrette* and *Sammy and Rosie Get Laid* (Stephen Frears, 1987) both of which were critically acclaimed box-office successes. In his study of British cinema in the 1980s, Hill points to these two films as important works from the decade as they 'challenge traditional conceptions of "race" and celebrate the emergence of new kinds of hybrid identities' during one of the otherwise most politically conservative epochs in post-war British history (1999, p. xiii). The success of the films on all fronts proved to be very influential. As Christine Geraghty argues in her book on *My Beautiful Laundrette*, these films helped to create a market niche for films about the British-Asian experience and as such paved the way for the later box-office successes *East is East* (Damien O'Donnell, 1999) and *Bend it Like Beckham* (Gurinder Chadha, 2002) (2005, p. 78). Taken together, films like *My Beautiful Laundrette*, *East is East* and *Bend it Like Beckham*, as well as less high-profile films such as *Wild West* (David Attwood, 1992), *Bhaji on the Beach* (Gurinder Chadha, 1993), and *Anita and Me* (Metin Hüseyin, 2002) constitute institutional, industrial and ideological models which *Ae Fond Kiss* can be seen as reacting to in a variety of ways. Casting the net more widely, we could also point to other prominent European and American films about the multicultural condition – such a list would include Spike Lee's *Do the Right Thing* (1989) and *Jungle Fever* (1992), the German-Turkish/Turkish-German films of Fatih Akin, or French beur-themed films such as *La Haine* (Mathieu Kassovitz, 1995), to name just a few. As we have seen in the funding application and the examination of Loach's authorial persona, a discourse of social relevance – a promise of authentically representing life in contemporary Scotland – helps to justify the funding of *Ae Fond Kiss*, a discourse which brings to mind the cultural value assigned by Hill and others to the Kureishi-Frears films. As we have seen, the impulse to be 'more commercial' is also present in funding discourses and the most high-profile examples of films that have successfully attempted to be popular while also reflecting on 'serious' issues pertaining to multiculturalism were *East is East* and *Bend It Like Beckham*. For this reason, as well as others that will become apparent, these films can be seen as important intertexts for Loach's film.

Discussing differences between contemporary British-Asian films and those of the 1980s, Geraghty notes that while the earlier films felt the need to establish a separate space for British-Asian identity, one distinct from being *either* British or Asian, the later films 'take such diversity for granted' with 'the mainsprings of the plots lying elsewhere' (2005, p. 78). Is this true of *Ae Fond Kiss*? The opening scenes seem to imply a certain acceptance of diversity and a condition of multi-ethnic consensus. The film begins in a crowded nightclub in which we see a number of people of different ethnicities uninhibitedly dancing together to bhangra music. This choice of music is itself significant as bhangra is a hybrid form of club music drawing on South Asian and British musical forms. This hybrid heritage has led to the form taking on a cinematic life of its own, having featured in films such as Gurinder Chadha's acclaimed short *I'm British But . . .* (1990) as a symbol of the synthesis of western and eastern cultures and Mira Nair's *Monsoon Wedding* (2001) to similar symbolic ends. As Karen Ross, Sarita Malik and others have argued, music is one of the most prominent sites of the mixing of immigrant cultures and often plays an important textual role in representations of multiculturalism (Malik, 1996, p. 211; Ross, 1996, p. xiv).

Besides the aforementioned prominence of bhangra in Chadha's and Nair's films, music also plays notable thematic parts in: *Wild West*, where a group of British-Pakistani youths form a country and western band, with comedy deriving from this cultural juxtaposition; *Anita and Me*, in which Anita's Punjabi-born father performs a medley of Punjabi songs only to break into 'Volare' at a neighbour's wedding; and *Bend It Like Beckham*, where Italian opera (Puccini's 'Nessun dorma') is juxtaposed comically with hallucinatory images of Jess's Indian aunts when she is taking an important free kick late in the film. Writing in 1996 regarding changes in representations of people of colour in Britain, Malik described the increasing turn towards celebrations of hybridity as shift in focus 'from the political arena to the cultural arena, where "the politics of race" are interwoven with the "politics of the dancefloor", the former inextricably linked to the latter' (1996, p. 211) (Figure 8). Without wanting to suggest that Loach and Laverty are directly referencing Malik's description, the opening of *Ae Fond Kiss* is almost too perfect a reference to the trend that she identifies.

The film's images of multicultural harmony in the club are grafted onto the Scottish city through the opening montage sequence. The sequence inside the club is followed by a landscape shot of an urban space which, with its terraced architecture, is identifiably British. The film's title, taken from a Burns lyric, is printed on the screen above the cityscape, making it clear that this is a Scottish space. As Martin-Jones points out, the juxtaposition of these shots implies that the Scottish city is home to the hip, celebratory cultural diversity seen in the nightclub (2009, p. 184). Further intercutting shows a South Asian shopkeeper, who will later be revealed to be Tariq (Ahmad Riaz), the father of Casim, who is the DJ seen in the club and the film's protagonist, as he comically attempts to

Figure 8 'The politics of the dancefloor': Casim and Roisin clubbing in
Ae Fond Kiss

keep dogs from urinating on his newspaper placard. The tone
of comedy in this sequence further aligns the film with trends in
British multicultural cinema, and much European multicultural
cinema.[45] More specifically, this montage sequence recalls the
humorous content and tone of *East is East*. The contrast between
Casim and his father evokes both the gap between the two generations as well as the comic absurdity of the elder man, bringing
to mind Om Puri's character in O'Donnell's film as well as the
generation gap in that film which is, initially at least, presented
with a similar degree of humour. Also like *East is East*, *Ae Fond
Kiss* is in large part concerned with peeling back this seemingly
comic surface layer and exposing an insurmountable divide between
the generations of British Asians, but unlike *East is East*, the film
locates that divide in the present day instead of the early 1970s.

As the opening credits conclude and the film's narrative begins,
we come to a student assembly of some sort in a Catholic school.
The first shot in this sequence continues the theme of apparent
integration, as we see a Catholic priest framed in the foreground
with two school students of Asian ethnicity in the background, one

of whom is wearing a traditional headscarf, an item of clothing that accentuates her religious difference from the priest. On the soundtrack we hear Tahara (Shabana Bakhsh), who was established as the daughter of the shopkeeper in the opening montage, giving a debate club talk arguing against western essentializing of Islamic identity. This speech and the reaction it elicits from the students are very significant to the overall film and the scene is therefore worth looking at in some detail.

In the authorial context, this is one of the Loachian moments which Leigh, drawing on Judith Williamson, terms the 'keynote speech' in which a character explicitly states the point of view that Loach and his screenwriter are trying to make with the film (2002, p. 13). The context of these moments, according to Leigh, vary from film to film and can occasionally be so nakedly didactic as to alienate the audience and prevent viewers from being absorbed into the film; this then demands that Loach and his screenwriters find ways to seamlessly integrate the speech into the story so that it is not off-putting (2002, p. 22). It seems quite clever on the part of screenwriter Paul Laverty to begin the film with a debate that conveniently allows for an opportunity to set out the themes of the film, but as we will see in the reception portion of this analysis, it did not fool anyone as many reviewers thought this 'keynote speech' (a fitting term given both its diegetic and ideological context in the film) was a heavy-handed authorial intrusion.

The speech does more than introduce the themes of the film, it also introduces us to Tahara, who seems very reminiscent of another figure from contemporary British-Asian films. With her references to football (former Celtic striker Henrik Larsson is mentioned before the Rangers top is revealed) and generally spirited attitude here and throughout the film, Tahara echoes the character of Jess (Parminder Nagra), the rebellious football-obsessed British-Asian teenager from *Bend It Like Beckham*. Her fellow students, for their part, are certainly more interested in her stance on football than in the issue of Islamic identity. It is her support of Rangers, with its attendant sectarian reference,[46] not anti-Islamist sentiment, that angers Tahara's male classmates and sets the plot in motion (Martin-Jones, 2009, pp. 186–187). The faces of the other students, both white and Asian, listening to Tahara's speech are consistently bored and listless throughout the discussion of British-Asian identity and terrorism; they also remain quiet even when she appears to be undressing on the stage, something that seems implausible in a room full of young adolescents.

As soon as the Rangers top is revealed, however, a murmur goes through the crowd and mixed booing and clapping begins among the students. We see students clapping, mainly the girls in the crowd who seem to be most affected by Tahara's defiant yell of 'Bring it on'. Boys in the crowd begin heckling Tahara, but the shouts of derision stem from their support of Celtic and not racism or xenophobia. A confrontation ensues between Tahara and the other students after school. This being a Loach film, we would expect something of an ugly racist incident to occur, but this is not exactly what the film gives us. There are racial taunts, some of which are combined with sectarian insults ('Paki-Hun' one student yells, 'hun' being a derogatory word for a Protestant), but the tone of the scene is not as dark and disturbing as it, perhaps, could have been. Throughout the incident, Tahara is anything but a helpless victim as she first rebukes the boys, telling them to 'grow up', and subsequently kicks and chases the would-be tormentors. Finally, there is additional tomboy comedy in the final inversion during which the boys run in fear of Tahara. This is not to say there is no a dark undertone to the boys' taunts, but there is still a feeling that this could have been worse.[47]

Surprisingly, given how much Tahara has been developed by this point, we have been misled somewhat with this introduction if we think that she will be the film's main character. The whole sequence was actually an elaborate way of introducing themes and setting the stage for the meeting between Casim and Roisin. Their romance will, from here on, become the centre of the film as well as the primary narrative vehicle for forwarding the film's socially critical agenda. Love stories of some sort or another, especially interracial ones, have figured prominently in nearly every film about the British-Asian experience, and are also among the plot devices featured in many European and American multicultural films.[48] The pressures on the couple in any given film can be said to be representative of the larger socio-cultural problems that film-makers are hoping to critique. The major pressures on Roisin and Casim in *Ae Fond Kiss* are familiar from other films: Casim's arranged marriage (a plot device that Geraghty describes as a cliché in British-Asian films when used with female British-Asian characters [2005, p. 67]) brings to the fore his conflict with his parents' traditions. Roisin's problem resides with her parish priest whose bigotry will lead him to abuse his power and deprive Roisin of her job. Finally, the two must face up to their inability to understand or sympathize with one another in the face of their respective pressures.

Of these conflicts, the final one turns out the best for Roisin and Casim. The couple ultimately survives the strain and Roisin and Casim continue loving each other. The underlying cultural conflicts, however, are not resolved so optimistically. Despite early scenes showing the elder Khan seemingly happily integrated with Scottish society – he is seen at one point bantering with the white working-class builders who he has hired to build the extension to his house – the film comes to insist on the fundamental non-assimilation of the older generation of Scottish-Asians. This is another aspect of the film which initially, at least, recalls *Bend It Like Beckham*, in which, as Paul Dave points out, Jess's father carries 'the burden of racial misery as a memory' (2006, p. 16) and because of such memories is reluctant to let his daughters fully integrate into British society. Also like *Bend It*, the film shows very little racial abuse taking place. Apart from the chasing of Tahara described above, racism in the film takes place indirectly as characters of the same ethnicity discuss those of the other, for example when Hammid (Shy Ramsan) tells Casim that Rosin is just some 'goree', or the priest (Gerard Kelly) admonishes Roisin for thinking she can sleep with 'any Tom, Dick or Mohammed' and still be approved to teach in Catholic schools. To this end, a number of scenes depicting explicit racial abuse of the couple and the parents were deleted from the finished film.[49] Racism in *Ae Fond Kiss* thus becomes a social force that lurks behind the veneer of polite society but which is nonetheless pervasive.

Though we do not see it, again and again we are reminded that Casim's parents have suffered racism and discrimination and partly because of this will never accept Roisin as his partner. Neither will Catholicism ever tolerate their relationship. The representatives of both sets of values act in increasingly appalling ways, including the memorably malevolent parish priest's tirade at Roisin which concludes with his advice to 'go teach the Protestants'. In terms of heavy-handed presentation, this is matched only by the Khan family's equally mean-spirited charade in which they attempt to make Roisin think that Casim will be going through with the marriage that they have arranged for him in an attempt to split

the couple up. By the end we are left with a sense of the hopeless-
ness of trying to change the minds and attitudes of most of the
older generation.

This is one aspect that fundamentally distinguishes the film from
its contemporaries: though it begins with humour and high spirits,
its narrative arc is one that reverses that of a film like *Bend It Like
Beckham*. This is encapsulated by the ways in which the two films
parallel the Irish experience in Britain with that of Asian immigrants.
In Chadha's film the two groups can each relate to the other's
experience of discrimination and ethnic prejudice. This is encapsulated in one particularly saccharin moment after Jess has been called
a 'Paki' during a football match and been sent off for lashing out
at the girl who used the slur. She complains to her coach and love
interest (Jonathan Rhys-Meyers) that he does not understand what
it feels like to be racially abused in such a manner and he responds:
'Of course I do, I'm Irish.' Loach and Laverty's treatment, on the
other hand, has the two groups seeming to peacefully coexist only
to reveal them to be as intolerant of one another as the host culture
is. Writing about the narrative arc of the romance genre, Geraghty
writes that in such stories, 'while there are problems on the way,
the narrative drives to the resolution in which the integration of
the couple into society provides a happy ending' (2005, p. 42).
Though Casim and Roisin do stay together, their arc is actually
one of dis-integration from their respective societies, a pattern that
distinguishes the film from many of its counterparts.

This can be seen by comparing the ways in which the Asian
fathers are depicted at the ends of *Bend It* and *Ae Fond Kiss*. The
final image of *Bend It* has the coach playing cricket with Jess's
father, a scene that Dave describes as resembling the village green,
which in iconic terms is 'a nostalgic benchmark of Englishness'
(2006, p. 16). In contrast, one of the final images of the Khan
patriarch in *Ae Fond Kiss* shows him destroying the extension he
built for Casim in a fit of despairing rage. The film's concluding
reconciliation between Casim and Roisin is upbeat in tone, but
remains somewhat unresolved and ambivalent. The happiness of
the ending is a private one, set within the lovers' flat. Public space,
however, remains hostile to the couple, as seen by the lack of
resolution of the motif in which Casim continually asks Roisin to
duck her head down so that his cousins do not see them together.
In a more optimistic film, this motif would be concluded with

Roisin bravely holding her head up no matter where the couple were. Thus, while unlike many of Loach's films up to this point, there is some hope expressed by virtue of Casim and Roisin's relationship surviving the stresses of these conflicts, their love still comes with the likely consequence that Casim will never speak to his parents again and Roisin will be alienated from the traditional institutions of her culture and will indeed have to teach the Protestants. The Khan family will also suffer greatly. The last time we see him, Tariq cannot bear to make eye contact with Tahara when she tells her parents that she plans to attend Edinburgh University against their wishes, a scene which offers little hope for the future of the family. This is on top of the high probability that, as Blandford points out, the wedding of Casim's older sister will have to be called off owing to his relationship with Roisin (2007, p. 77). Calling the ending of *Ae Fond Kiss* a happy one, as several critics do (e.g. Martin-Jones, 2009, p. 181), would thus be something of an overstatement and the Lottery Panel's description of it as 'less grim than other Ken Loach films' is perhaps more fitting.

In keeping with Hill's description of his oeuvre generally, with *Ae Fond Kiss* Loach unfashionably insists on a bleaker view of multiculturalism, even if he utilizes the conventions of more mainstream commercial cinema in order to do so. By doing this, *Ae Fond Kiss* represents a return to what Malik, using the work of Cameron Bailey to discuss changes in black-themed British films, describes as the 'cinema of duty'. Such films, according to Bailey and Malik were 'social issue in content, documentary realist in style, firmly *responsible* in intention' and present the tradition which subsequent British films beginning with *My Beautiful Laundrette* sought to break from (1996, pp. 203–204). Rather than simply providing another instance of Loach being an old-fashioned filmmaker in this regard, we can look at films contemporary to *Ae Fond Kiss*, such as *A Way of Life* (Amma Asante, 2004) and *Yasmin* (Kenny Glenaan, 2004) which also, and with more intense pessimism, insist that British-Asians are not accepted or assimilated into mainstream British culture, a pessimism that is echoed in the less social realist-minded hit comedy *Four Lions* (Christopher Morris, 2010). In light of these films, we could perhaps see *Ae Fond Kiss* as being part a new trend towards grim views of multicultural British society.[50]

Loach and cross-over cinema

Even if *Ae Fond Kiss*'s precise permutation of the popular elements drawn from the British-Asian cinema of the 1990s and early 2000s is not fully in keeping with the 'feel good' tone of that period, the fact that those elements are incorporated into the film at all is significant. As seen above, Loach's authorial persona is closely tied to his politically didactic themes and social critique is in many ways the *raison d'être* of his work. As Hill's work on the director details (1997, 1998, 2009, 2011), over the course of his long career, which now spans nearly fifty years, Loach has experimented greatly with forms and aesthetics suitable to his ideological project. This quest for an appropriate form has seen him move from documentary realism in his early television dramas to Brechtian modernism in his first feature films, to documentary and art cinema in the 1970s and 1980s, followed by a turn to popular genre film-making beginning approximately with films such as *Hidden Agenda* (1990), which utilized the political thriller as a vehicle for his views on British human rights abuses in Northern Ireland. This trajectory towards greater use of popular cinema conventions, according to Hill, reflects a desire on Loach's part to get his message to larger audiences. It also contrasts somewhat ironically with the ways in which the films themselves circulate, which are largely in keeping with the industrial practices associated with auteur art cinema (2011, p. 171).

Crucially for Hill, this trajectory within Loach's cinema is not unique. The generic hybridity in the director's oeuvre can 'be seen to correspond to a growing generic hybridity with British cinema more generally' (2011, p. 169). This hybridity is seen throughout contemporary Scottish cinema, as has been seen throughout this book, and *Ae Fond Kiss* is no exception to this trend and may, despite its many unique qualities, indeed be one of the most typical Scottish films of the 2000s. Hill suggests that the reasons for this hybridity in *Ae Fond Kiss* in particular, especially its relatively upbeat tone, can be traced to the reputation he had accrued as a purveyor of bleak melodramas, with one critic even calling him the 'visiting professor of doom' (2011, p. 190). Breaking from these negative expectations of his film-making was thus a priority for Loach, as can be seen in the application itself with all of the promises of commercial viability and love story genre 'hooks'. The necessity of these promises, though, hints at the role that funding bodies had come to play in propelling Scottish and British film-makers towards the hybridity that Hill and others such as Caughie and Geraghty have seen as typifying contemporary British cinema. After all, without promises that the film would be both 'serious' and 'less grim than previous projects', *Ae Fond Kiss* may not have been made in Scotland. As shown in previous chapters, similar promises were expected of other Lottery funded films, raising important historical questions about the industrial contexts of this larger shift in British film-making.

The perils of crossing over: the promotion, reception and distribution of *Ae Fond Kiss*

One of the key problems for the film-makers at a number of levels was thus balancing accessibility and politics, commerce and culture, begging the question of whether or not the film was perceived to have done so with any degree of success. In this section I look more closely at the terms on which the film circulated in British and European film cultures,[51] beginning with the film's UK trailer and what that tells us about the ways in which its distributors sought to frame the film. In keeping with what I have described as the film's intertextual referencing of *Bend It Like Beckham* and other more upbeat British-Asian films, the UK trailer features bhangra music, images taken from the nightclub sequence, Tariq comically stumbling through the garden, and most tellingly, Tahara's 'keynote speech' which culminates in her undressing to reveal her football top. All of these images appear together in a montage preceding an overview of the film's plot, which forms the main body of the trailer and which ends with Casim's father destroying the extension. Such an arrangement of images presents a concise overview of the film as a whole, replicating its arc from Tahara's mild act of rebellion, through the moments of comedy that recall similar moments in *East is East*, focusing heavily on the romance which is the main audience 'hook', and touching only obliquely on the film's ambivalent conclusion. When it does so, the sense one gets from seeing it in the trailer is that this is not the film's denouement but one of the complications that will be overcome by the couple; after all trailers tend not to reveal the film's ending. By so doing, the trailer presents the film as more or less the same film as these predecessors, packaging it as a film that tackles social issues but which is still entertaining and upbeat.

The balance between the film's socially critical content and its mainstream appeal are also the main objects of much of the journalistic reception of the film, as is the relationship between these elements and the persona of the film's director. Judging by some of the journalistic reviews, the film's relatively upbeat ending was unexpected. Instead of being seen simply as something that is good about the film, many reviewers responded to the conflict between such an ending and what has come to be expected from Loach. The love story as a whole prompted the *Guardian*'s reviewer Geoffrey MacNab to ask: 'Has Ken Loach gone soft?' (2004, p. 10). Another reviewer's headline proclaims: 'We Need More Punch from this Glasgow Kiss' (*Daily Mail*, 2004). The promotional piece for the film in *Sight and Sound* likewise implicitly raises this question with reference to commercial appeal, comparing the film to other popular treatments of British multiculturalism:

> Loach hints – as producer Rebecca O'Brien has already suggested to me – that the project is a mite more 'commercial' than some of his previous outings. The recent successes of Anglo-Asian films such as *Bend It Like Beckham* certainly makes the production timely, though Loach is quick to dismiss the notion that he's jumping on the bandwagon. (Mottram, 2004, p. 22)

Conversely, other reviewers felt *Ae Fond Kiss* to be too much of a Loach film, seeing this branding as a negative quality. The *Daily Telegraph*'s review, for example, features the self-explanatory headline: 'Tell us something we don't know, Ken. Ken Loach's Glaswegian cross-race love story is passionate and sexy but lacking in subtlety' (Robey, 2004, p. 20) and takes issue specifically with the didacticism of Tahara's speech at the beginning of the film. At this point in their collaboration, in trying to balance their twin obligations of being commercially accessible and providing the serious thematic content that is expected of a Loach and Laverty film, the film-makers ended up displeasing their core supporters whilst also failing to convince their detractors. This would not be true of later films, such as *The Wind That Shakes the Barley* (2006) or *Looking for Eric* (2009), but in 2004 we can still see Loach attempting to strike the balance that many British film-makers try to strike – a balance, it is worth reiterating, that is required by all backers for British films, including subsidy bodies.

In terms of reaching audiences, overall figures for the film were roughly as predicted in the application, with nearly 1.3 million admissions recorded across Europe (Lumiere Database, 2013), with the significant exception, however, of local viewing of the film. Total admissions within the UK were 102,000 (Lumiere Database, 2013). This number is not broken down by region, but Rebecca O'Brien has said that approximately half of the audiences for Loach's films come from the regions where they are set (O'Brien, 2006). If that were to hold true for *Ae Fond Kiss*, this would represent significant market penetration for a nation the size of Scotland, but on the whole the film's impact within the UK was still dwarfed by its impact abroad. Furthermore, Loach and Laverty's other Scottish films all had greater impact on the UK box office, with *Sweet Sixteen* drawing 180,000 admissions and *My Name is Joe* drawing 240,000 (Lumiere Database, 2013). The film was, however, more commercially successful overall than other Loach films such as *Sweet Sixteen* (approximately one million total admissions) and *The Navigators* (600,000 total admissions) (Lumiere Database, 2013). But the audience figures for *Ae Fond Kiss* were affected by the actions of one of the film's UK exhibitors, Cityscreen, which curtailed its run in some theatres after audiences complained about the film's love story content. This, according to O'Brien, was thought by the chain to clash with their art-house niche (2006).[52] In other words, the very thing that led the film-makers to hope that the film had mainstream appeal ended up undermining its ability to reach audiences in the UK, an irony that poignantly demonstrates the contradictions at the heart of Loach's cinema, which Hill describes as circulating as 'auteur art cinema' while textually closely resembling popular genre cinema (2011, p. 171).

Conclusion

I have hoped in this chapter to highlight some of the key insights that *Ae Fond Kiss* offers for Loach's work in Scotland and Scottish cinema more generally in the contemporary period. As we have seen, the film and its contexts of production and circulation can tell us a great deal about the role that policy has played in shaping the film and the period as a whole. The film is also a significant text within a larger British tradition of representing the nation in multicultural terms and performs the vital function of localizing those traditions within a specifically Scottish milieu. In all of these contexts, the role played by transnational forces is important. Not only is the tradition of British-Asian cinema a distinctly post-imperial phenomenon, but the ways in which Loach ended up making this vital contribution to Scottish cinema is itself also underpinned by transnational movement – in this case a film-maker – and transnational capital – here being European financial resources. Above all else, the film represents yet another instance of cross-over film-making, the form that dominates Scottish cinema as a whole during this period. As we will see all of these different commercial and artistic trends will also be important to the book's last case study, to which we can now turn.

6

Not British, Scottish?:
The Last King of Scotland and
post-imperial Scottish cinema

Idi Amin (Forest Whitaker): You are British?
James Garrigan (James McAvoy): Well, I'm Scottish ... Scottish ...
Idi Amin: Scottish? Why didn't you say so?
(Dialogue exchange from *The Last King of Scotland*)

With a number of major awards to its name – including an Oscar
and a Golden Globe – and an international box office return second
only to *Trainspotting*, *The Last King of Scotland* is one of the most
high-profile films that Scotland has seen. Despite this, it has only
received the most cursory of discussions within Scottish film history,
with brief mentions being found in the leading works in the field
(e.g. Martin-Jones, 2009, p. 63). In years past, the lack of engagement between national cinema scholars and a film like *Last King*
could perhaps be explained by the challenges the film presents to
normative definitions of national cinema; it is, after all, a film
funded by sources from several different nations, features a multi-
national cast and is set and shot outside Scotland. But given the
transnational turn in film studies generally and Scottish cinema
studies particularly (as seen in works by Martin-Jones [2009], Street
[2009], Hjort [2010b] etc.), the failure to engage with this film
is curious and problematic. This chapter seeks to fill this gap and
in so doing, attempts to foreground the film's transnational aspects
at all levels of its existence while also resolutely insisting on its
thematic engagement with Scottishness. As we will see, the ways
in which the film was born out of a sophisticated multinational
production network – one that is in many ways linked to the imperial history of Scotland and Britain – coincides in very interesting
ways with the film's themes, which centre around Scottish involvement in post-imperial neo-colonialism.

The chapter concludes with some discussion of the film's reception which is shown to overlook the film's Scottish content and themes in favour of critical plaudits for Forest Whitaker's performance as Idi Amin and an ongoing fascination with Amin himself. Given such a reception context – one which has arguably contributed to the neglect of the film itself within Scottish cinema circles – this chapter is concerned with re-emphasizing the Scottishness of *The Last King of Scotland*. This is a critical act which is important from historical and national points of view, but also reveals the film as an even more complex text and artefact of contemporary transnational Scottish cinema than current understanding would have it. Moreover, we see by the end of this chapter that, despite its many superficial differences from this book's other case studies, *Last King* is in many ways one of the most typical Scottish films of the 2000s. This realization then allows us to make a number of conclusions for this study as a whole.

Making *The Last King*: co-production, runaway production and the networks of Scottish cinema

Funding for *Last King* came from several different sources, including investment from the speciality division of a major Hollywood studio – Fox Searchlight – a division of a London-based public-service broadcaster – Film4 – and the UK Film Council through DNA Films, a part of the short-lived Lottery franchise scheme. The film also received funding from Scottish Screen and was made in co-production with the German firm Tatfilm. As is often the case with co-productions, all of the partners came with their own agendas, demands and contributions. In keeping with their branding as the prestige wing of a Hollywood conglomerate, Fox Searchlight was seeking a film that would garner critical acclaim and win major awards (Meir, 2012, p. 57). Ironically, given Forest Whitaker's subsequent success, Fox Searchlight initially opposed his casting as well as that of James McAvoy, hoping for bigger name actors in those roles (Meir, 2012, p. 58).

Film4 had played a major role in developing the project from its earliest stages and particularly wanted to continue working with screenwriter Peter Morgan and director Kevin Macdonald, the latter coming directly following the critical success of his documentary *Touching the Void* (2003). Scottish Screen, according to Andrea Calderwood, were interested in being part in a high-profile film that had discernibly Scottish elements to it – as Calderwood puts it – a film 'that was somehow connected to Scotland; a Scottish film with Scottish talent in it' (Meir, 2012, p. 57). This relatively small investment from Scottish Screen (approximately £350,000 or 7 per cent of the overall budget [Scottish Screen, 2006, p. 2]) was, according to Calderwood, instrumental in protecting the Scottish content of the film in light of pressures to make a 'more studio-type film'. Tatfilm was engaged to provide equipment as well as post-production services, but the reasons behind the co-production also included ensuring that the film would qualify as British under UK policy guidelines (Calderwood, 2012). Though seemingly small and from a creative point of view inconsequential, this deal does, iron-ically, speak to the film's post-imperial contexts, a point to which I will return shortly.

In addition to these co-production arrangements, the film-makers also decided to shoot the film on location in Uganda after initially considering South Africa. This was a decision with several ideological and aesthetic ramifications. South Africa has long been a major hub for film production in Africa, particularly for 'runaway productions', that is to say films shot outside the home nations of the film-makers. These productions have seen the nation regularly stand in for an assortment of foreign countries and particularly for African countries. With relatively low costs and an established production infrastructure, South Africa would have been the safer choice for the shoot, but out of a desire for authenticity and real-ism, the film-makers insisted on shooting in Uganda. Speaking of this decision, Macdonald said,

> There is a very limited structure of any kind in Uganda. But what you do have is this extraordinary sort of place, with extraordinary architecture, with a texture, a flavour, a smell that's never really been captured before. That's quite exciting as a filmmaker. My priority was to go and do it in Uganda. (Munro, 2007)

In so doing, the film-makers followed in the footsteps of, and in some cases drew direct inspiration from, contemporary British projects such as *The Constant Gardner* (Fernando Meirelles, 2005) (Meir, 2012, p. 61). A distinct strand of the film's promotion and reception centred on portraying the film as one had a positive impact on Uganda in a number of ways. But we should not wholly overlook nor shed too cynical a light on the positive impact that the decision to film in Uganda had for the country itself, which benefited from internal investments that simply would not have been made had the film been shot in somewhere like South Africa. Within the larger context of globalized film practices, the film-makers opted against an 'economic' runaway production, which at the very least separates the film from the most exploitative practices employed by travelling first-world film crews.[53]

Obtaining permission to film in Uganda added another level of transnational cooperation, this one involving the Ugandan government. As Calderwood explains, this largely involved getting the support of President Yoweri Museveni, who had his own agenda for supporting the production:

> We went to see him with Kevin [Macdonald] and some of the other producers and he was very smart and very astute about it. He knew that it was a good idea to remind people how bad Idi Amin as a former dictator had been; he wanted to be viewed as a more demo-cratic President. That was one thing. He wanted to promote inter-national investment and industry in Uganda and he wanted to put Uganda on the map as a tourist destination. (Meir, 2012, p. 62)

Though there was no creative interference from Museveni on the film, the authority that the Ugandan government wielded over the production, with their own set of demands and expectations for the project, made them tantamount to de facto co-producers, adding to the complexity of the film's production. This arrangement was not without its own ideological problems. As Lesley Marx (2011, p. 58) has argued, and Kevin Macdonald himself has admit-ted ('Director's Commentary', 2007), the film-makers were them-selves – in ways that eerily mirror the situation that the film's Garrigan (James McAvoy) finds himself in – unwittingly complicit with a political regime that was engaged in violence against its own people, in this case an ongoing civil war in northern Uganda.

The unsavoury aspects of the film crew's stay in Uganda aside, there are other important questions to examine in relation to the funding and production package as a whole. Such a complex multi-lateral co-production and runaway production context naturally gives rise to questions regarding the creative freedom of the film-making team. As has been seen throughout this book, and indeed much writing about co-production generally, conventional wis-dom is that the practice inhibits creative freedom and undermines artistically cohesive film-making. In the case of *Last King*, however, the opposite seems to have been the case. Co-production here actually *increased* the film-makers' creative freedom, and did so precisely because of the number of partners involved. Discussing the aforementioned disputes over the film's casting, Calderwood explains that since so many partners were involved in the making of the film, the influence of Fox Searchlight was limited and they were therefore not in a position to veto the film-makers' casting choices. She says of this experience: 'that's the advantage of co-production, it can allow film-makers more independence because they don't have the direct studio pressures to deal with' (Meir, 2012, p. 57). Once again, just as we did with Loach's film and *Morvern Callar*, we see here evidence that assumptions within Scottish cinema studies about money and creative control are not in keeping with the historical realities of Scottish film-making, at least not to the extent that some accounts would suggest.

Transnational networks thus played a vital role in the making of a Scottish film, but again, scrutinizing the specific contours of that network reveals some interesting insights into Scottish cinema's place in global cinema. It now hardly needs pointing that Scottish cinema depended on English capital as, once again, London-based institutions – this time Film4 and DNA/the Film Council – were essential to the making of a Scottish film. This involvement need not be seen as that exploitative, though. Film4 after all insisted on the involvement of a Scottish director, while also helping to push for a Scottish actor in the lead role. As was the case with *Mrs Brown*, an American company was also central to the project and was the single biggest beneficiary of the international success of a Scottish film. Even though their creative input was limited, it was Fox Searchlight as the film's distributor in several key territories that ultimately took the bulk of the profits from the film (Meir, 2012, p. 58).

European dynamics are also apparent through the partnership with Tatfilm, but as intimated previously, this particular partnership is not as straightforward as it may initially seem. The services of Tatfilm, which primarily makes films in European languages, were sought in order to circumvent the UK Film Council's cultural test for qualifying a film as 'British'. As an official British co-production, made under the auspices of the UK-German treaty, the film was automatically deemed 'British'. This was required in order to access the subsidies from both the UKFC and Scottish Screen. Under the provisions of this treaty, the film had to have a significant amount of labour that qualified legally as European or British. Significantly, this particular treaty had language that allows labour from nationals of Commonwealth nations to be counted as British. The film-makers were then able to count the Ugandan nationals employed on the film as 'British', allowing them to meet the legal requirements needed to define the film as British and thus obtain the necessary subsidies (Calderwood, 2012).

There is a great deal to note in this particular arrangement. At one level, we can marvel at the intricacy of this financing package, which cleverly exploits a number of loopholes in international trade law and subsidy regulations. This speaks to the skill and creativity of the film's producers, all of whom had, by this point in their careers, become adept at navigating the terrain of the global film industry. Another crucial observation to make here is the importance of post-imperial networks to the making of the film. Not only was the film's narrative rooted in a distinctly post-imperial situation involving the British in eastern Africa – a theme to which I will return shortly – but its production context was also shaped by similar dynamics. The post-imperial idea of Commonwealth played a vital role in helping to secure funding, including finance from the British state. At the heart of this loophole in co-production policy is a definition of Britishness on the part of policy-makers that included the former Empire. While this may seem an antiquated idea now – the treaty itself was signed in 1975 – it is worth noting that British co-production policy in recent years has shifted towards reinforcing industrial ties with parts of the former Empire as treaties have been signed with Jamaica (2007), South Africa (2006) and India (2008), treaties which supplement long-standing pacts with Australia, Canada and New Zealand. While the Department for Culture, Media & Sport has also pursued treaties with countries such as Morocco and China, and has long held treaties with the EU, this push at the international level has created a network that in some ways eerily recalls the contours of the Empire itself.

Scottish cinema has thus been shaped by the legacy of Empire, and in this sense it is a very British cinema. As discussed in Chapter 5, British-Asian cinema constitutes a vital context for historicizing and interpreting *Ae Fond Kiss*, and as Martin-Jones has shown, similar things can be said about Hindi films made in Scotland and their counterparts made in England (2005b). *Last King* should also be understood in relation to the larger British cinema, more specifically in this case, the long tradition of films about the British in Africa, films which also often have had production stories that echo their thematic and representational content in interesting and revealing ways. With this in mind, we can now turn to the film itself.

Intercultural representation in *The Last King of Scotland*: looking through a 'young imperialist's' eyes

I always saw Nicholas as the British imperialist, he might have been young and it might have been the 70's and he might have been a bit left wing, but he was still a young imperialist. In that he's selfish, he corrupts and destroys. – James McAvoy (Munro, 2006)

The Last King of Scotland raises important questions about intercultural representation, particularly in relation to issues of political economy – issues which have fostered a long tradition of bigoted representations of Africa and the peoples of Africa. Any exploration of *The Last King of Scotland* in this regard does well to start with Leslie Marx's scathing critique (2011). Her polemic against the film is complex and nuanced and involves specific attention to the ways in which the screenwriters (Peter Morgan and Jeremy Brock) and director Kevin Macdonald handled the adaptation of Giles Foden's source novel as well as the ways in which both book and film dealt with history. More specifically, her critique of the film takes particular umbrage with the foregrounding of Garrigan over Amin himself, the distortions to history made by the film-makers and the 'ameliorative' representation of Amin (p. 58). For Marx, these changes have the net effect of aligning the film with cinematic traditions representing Africa as 'the dark continent' that hark back to the days of European empires in Africa and continue to this very day in the form of 'Afro-pessimist films made by western directors', such as *Blood Diamond* (Edward Zwick, 2006) and the apartheid-set thriller *Catch a Fire* (Philip Noyce, 2006) (p. 73). Central to this negative representation of Africa, according to Marx, are narrative and generic strategies that have distorted both Foden's novel and the historical events of Amin's reign in favour of the demands of popular genre cinema, namely those of the political thriller and melodrama. This section seeks to take on these claims and relate these arguments to the production contexts discussed above.

At first glance, there is much to support Marx's claims about the film's cultural politics. Most of the Ugandans who act in the film perform background roles; the people themselves are shown as having implicitly backward, superstitious beliefs (e.g. we see witch doctors very early in the film) and are easily swayed by the charismatic Amin. In addition, Ugandan women are depicted almost exclusively as sexual objects either for Amin or Nicholas. The historical events that form the basis of the film are also problematic from the point of view of African representation. Choosing to make a film about Amin's rule is in and of itself a decision to focus on one of the worst moments in the post-independence era for Uganda and Africa at large. He is, of course, one of the most extreme examples of a brutal, strong-arm dictator that the continent has seen. Also, his bizarre and sometimes grotesque antics – such as his habit of sending nonsensical, insulting and sometimes obscene telegrams to world leaders including the Queen – and alleged (though never proven) cannibalism, combined with charming and sometimes buffoonish way of ingratiating himself to foreign journalists made him an object of perverse fascination in the West. When this is considered alongside his rotund frame, dark complexion and stereotypical east African accent, it is easy to sympathize with journalist Jon Snow's claims, in a BBC special on Amin that accompanies the film's DVD release, that Amin presented the West with a grotesque stereotype on which it could heap racist scorn ('Capturing Idi Amin').

Despite the film-makers', and Whitaker's, project of bringing human dimensions to Amin, and despite the many claims that the film does not show directly many of the worst atrocities committed by the dictator, the film's version of Amin is nonetheless one that perpetuates many of the most negative views of the man and his rule. Even if the film stops short of giving a definitive statement on Amin's supposed cannibalism, it does dwell a great deal on the atrocities committed during his regime as well as his expulsion of Asian Ugandans and his selfish grandstanding during the Entebbe hijacking crisis. In fact, as Marx details (p. 67), the film-makers actually go beyond the constraints of history and knowingly fabricate a particularly horrific atrocity to attribute to Amin: the dismembering of his wife Kay and the sewing of her limbs back on to her body in a grotesque manner so that her legs were attached to the arm sockets and her arms were attached to her pelvis.

While it has long been rumoured that Amin did indeed have his second wife killed and dismembered the subsequent act is completely fictitious (though also rumoured), a historical distortion which, as Marx points out, is explicitly acknowledged by the film-makers in the film's promotional materials (p. 67). This addition – along with others, such as the compression of Amin's rule from eight years to, seemingly, a couple of weeks, or even just the basic invention of Garrigan and other characters – makes the film all the more misleading in view of the strategies adopted to lend it authenticity. These include the use of Ugandan locations and actors, the generally realist/documentary approach to camera style and mise-en-scène as well as the film's closing credits which feature archival footage of Amin's rule – footage that underscores the film's simulacra of Amin himself and Uganda as a whole during the period. Such techniques imply a historical verisimilitude that the film ultimately fails to deliver, at least at the narrative level.

The film is thus problematic as a work of historiography. Marx blames these supposed failings on the film's need for 'narrative thrill' and 'generic sensationalism' (p. 54). But in her desire to castigate the film-makers for their 'betrayal' of Foden's novel and Ugandan history at large, Marx minimizes and sometimes completely overlooks significant aspects of the film that make a very complex work, in both historiographical and ideological terms. The most important of these is point of view, both on the part of the film-makers themselves as well as within the film's narrative. Marx acknowledges this issue in relation to Macdonald's many explicit remarks about the film being a Scottish/British story and not a Ugandan one, but quickly glosses over these, asserting that they undermine the film's capacity to act as a representation of history (pp. 56–58). She then goes on to argue that Macdonald should have made the film as a documentary if he had wanted to take this point of view (p. 59). This is an astonishingly frank example of prescriptive historiography on Marx's part, essentially dismissing commercial fiction film-making as a medium capable of making valuable contributions to our understanding of history.

Whatever its flaws may be in historical terms, *Last King* does at least draw attention to British (though unlike the novel, not American or Israeli) involvement in the Amin regime and by extension the post-colonial world at large. By most historical accounts this was the reality in the case of Amin's ascent to power (see for instance Snow's mainstream account in *Capturing Idi Amin*) but this remains little discussed. The film achieves this largely by means of the political thriller, a generic dimension that Marx objects to, but her critique of the film overlooks debates about genre and politics that have been found in Film Studies since the 1960s, in the form of the so-called 'Costa Gavras debates' which pitted the political thrillers of Costa Gavras against the modernist work of Jean-Luc Godard in a debate over the proper form that political film-making should take. Such a debate need not be rehashed here as it is essentially the same controversy that underpinned debates about Loach's film-making (Hill, 1997), which, as seen in Chapter 5 has struggled mightily with the balance between genre and ideology. Marx's position that a genre film is inherently unfit for the exposition of progressive political sentiments closely parallels claims made by Loach's or even Costa-Gavras's detractors. Likewise is her wish that Macdonald had made a documentary very reminiscent of those who felt that only Brechtian, modernist and/or documentary film-making could articulate progressive positions. The benefits and drawbacks of generic approaches to politics and history can be somewhat crudely described thus: the fictional, generic film will lose subtlety and nuance relative to its counterparts in other modes of cinema, but will nevertheless reach larger audiences and make complex issues both accessible and palatable to those audiences. While such a trade-off is distasteful to some, the larger context of film-making in the cultural industries era means genre film-making will most likely continue to be more prevalent than its more esoteric counterparts. The task of the historian in this case is not to scorn the film for what it is not, but instead to account for the ways in which it attempts to make the most of the circumstances that affect the film.

Similarly, it is ultimately not altogether useful to continue to criticize the film for not presenting an African view of events. While many would agree with Marx (and indeed Macdonald) that indigenous views are needed on African history, this simply is not the project that *Last King* seeks to undertake. Instead of again admonishing the film for what it is not, a more productive approach would be to follow the example of Nigel Penn in his study of European and American films made about east Africa (2007). This approach openly acknowledges that these films do not represent the history of east Africa per se, but instead are documents of the history of outsiders in east Africa. Writing about films such as the British film *White Mischief* (Michael Radford, 1987) and the German film *Nowhere in Africa* (Caroline Link, 2001), Penn argues that 'rather than judging the historical veracity of the films by their sensitivity to the experience of Africans, it is more fruitful to ask whether they are accurate portrayals of the experience and sensitivities of European colonists' (2007, p. 167). It is within a similar context that we can properly appreciate *Last King*. Not only does this approach allow us to better understand the film's complex views on history, but it also allows us to appreciate the innovations the film makes within a decidedly Anglocentric tradition of British film-making.

British film-making about Africa dates back to 1909 when film-makers began recording exotic travelogues that depicted events such as lion and falcon hunts.[54] Films made by the colonists grew in complexity and quickly took on a significant role in imperial ideology. Marcia Landy has detailed the ways in which the Empire served as a source of jingoistic pride in fiction films of the 1930s, with white protagonists fighting against the 'savages' of Africa in ways that recall the conflicts between white cowboys and the Indians of the American Western (1991, pp. 97–110). Though this tendency did not disappear after the war – indeed it reached is apex in terms of popularity in *Zulu* (Cy Endfield, 1964) – both Landy (1991, pp. 110–120) and Christine Geraghty (2000, pp. 112–132) have shown how this generic formula underwent a degree of change in the 1950s and 1960s as a relatively liberal sensibility became apparent and white protagonists now sought to protect the native peoples of whatever specific colony from either other anti-modern natives or other, exploitative whites.

Despite their good intentions, these films, which include such titles as *Simba* (Brian Hurst, 1955) and *Where No Vultures Fly* (Harry Wyatt, 1951), were often patronizing and condescending in the extreme, with the (somewhat oxymoronic) liberal imperialist acting as the force of good that 'protects' and seeks to modernize colonized peoples. The 1980s saw an upsurge in the popularity of imperial films in Britain, most notably those of the so-called 'Raj revival' which dealt with the British in India, including films such as *Heat and Dust* (James Ivory, 1983) and the television series *The Jewel in the Crown*. Surveying this cycle, Hill has shown how these films often outwardly profess an extremely critical view of the Empire on the one hand, but at the same time often feature a nostalgic tone, an ideological paradox that recalls the paradoxes at the heart of the heritage film, from which the 'Raj revival' originate in many ways (1999, pp. 99–123).

While British India may have been the focus of the most famous imperially themed films of the 1980s and 1990s, there were also several African-set British films. Most notable among these is *White Mischief*, but one can also consider *The Sheltering Sky* (Bernardo Bertolucci, 1990) among others in this category. Such films are beset by nearly identical problems as their Raj-themed counterparts. Though they often express liberal, anti-imperialist sentiments vis-à-vis African nations and even overtly criticize the decadence and moral bankruptcy of the English occupiers, they nevertheless maintain a visual nostalgia for the imperial past as well as a quasi-orientalist fascination with African peoples. *White Mischief*, for example, deals at great length with the moral turpitude of the British in Kenya where sexual experimentation and casual infidelity among the British leads to the murder of one of their own by a jealous husband. Running parallel to the film's love triangle storyline is a simultaneous fascination with the Maasai, whose simple life of cattle-herding and subsistence farming stands in marked contrast to the complex and morally dubious entanglements of the colonists. Significantly, the Maasai themselves speak very little in the film and are instead spoken for by Gilbert (John Hurt) a white settler who has 'gone native' and lives among them. More recent examples of depictions of the British in Africa include the 2005 film *Wah Wah* (Richard E. Grant) – a remarkable example of the continuation of the critical yet nostalgic tradition. In addition to its representational politics, which fit easily into this pattern, *Wah Wah* also featured a marketing campaign based around writer-director Richard E. Grant's bittersweet, nostalgic memories of life growing up in Swaziland where his father worked as an educator.[55]

Most other films from the 2000s that depict the British in Africa stay away from nostalgia and instead focus directly on problems caused by British and European neo-colonialism. *The Constant Gardner* and *Shooting Dogs* (Michael Caton-Jones, 2005) are vivid examples of this tendency. Both films continue the tradition of projecting African suffering onto white characters, but in each film the protagonists' dilemmas revolve around efforts to stop injustices in Africa and the narrative arc of each moves those protagonists from naivety to knowledge about the realities of life on the continent.

In the case of *The Constant Gardner*, Justin Quayle (Ralph Fiennes) and his wife Tessa (Rachel Weisz) both come to discover the atrocities being committed by large pharmaceutical companies in Kenya with the blessings of the British government. After Tessa is murdered to silence her, Justin journeys further into the world of the poor that Tessa was trying to help and learns (along with the audience) the true extent of the suffering of the people of Kenya and the Sudan (where Justin briefly travels to interview a doctor involved in the experiments which his wife was trying to stop) while also learning of the vast corporate and governmental conspiracy underpinning the atrocities. The film then ends pessimistically as Quayle, powerless to stop the corporations which are working with the protection of the British and Kenyan governments, virtually commits suicide while his accounts of what is going on in Kenya are smuggled to his wife's cousin who melodramatically reads them out at Justin's funeral, symbolically communicating the truth to the West.

Shooting Dogs deals with the genocide of ethnic Tutsis in Rwanda in 1994, centring on a school run by a British expatriates Christopher (John Hurt), who is a priest and headmaster, and English teacher Joe (Hugh Dancy). The two get drawn into the ethnic violence and attempt to shelter Tutsis from the surrounding villages. Their efforts lead to Christopher's death protecting a group of escaping Tutsis while Joe accepts the offer from UN troops to escape the massacre. As is indicated by the film's title – which refers to the absurd bureaucratic rules that allowed the UN's peacekeepers to fire at dogs eating Tutsi corpses but not on the rampaging Hutu militias – the film is largely an indictment of Western reluctance to get involved in the conflict. In a coda that drives home British culpability, Joe, who has moved back to England and taken a position at an elite private school, is confronted by one of his surviving ex-pupils from Rwanda who asks him why he did nothing to stop the genocide. Besides their critical and expository stance on European influence in Africa, these films are linked by genre, each packaging their historical themes as melodramatic thrillers. In fact, the thriller has become a frequently utilized mode of representing recent African history in British cinema, as seen in these two films as well as South African-set films such as *Catch a Fire* and *Endgame* (Pete Travis, 2009), while melodrama is foregrounded alongside some elements of the thriller in *Red Dust* (Tom Hooper,

2004), *The World Unseen* (Shamim Sarif, 2007) and, most famously, *Hotel Rwanda* (Terry George, 2004), all of which were British co-productions.

It is within this cycle of British *mea culpa* African-themed films that we can locate *Last King* and note two particularly significant differences on the part of Macdonald's film. The first is a merging of the self-lacerating theme with the tendency towards historical representation that borders on – but never crosses into – imperial nostalgia. Though *Shooting Dogs* is set in the historical past, it is not so distant a past as *Last King*, neither is its setting one that is either explicitly colonial (like *Wah Wah* or *White Mischief*) nor neo-colonial like *Last King*. *The Constant Gardner* on the other hand does deal with corporate and political neo-colonialism but does so in a particularly activist manner that presents the events of the films in the present tense, a strategy largely in keeping with what was going on in Britain during the mid-2000s, a time which saw a vogue for campaigning for helping Africa, a vogue typified by the Bob Geldof-led Live 8 campaign in 2005.

Last King combines elements of all of these tendencies, effectively presenting a sort of activist version of history, using melodrama and the thriller genre to expose British culpability for the atrocities of the Amin years and, implicitly, the political instability of Africa since decolonization. To accomplish this, the film uses the imperial nostalgia pose seen in films like *White Mischief* and *Wah Wah*, but crucially distances itself from that tradition by rooting the film's narration in the flawed subjectivity of Nicholas Garrigan. It is this character, not the film per se, who sees Uganda in imperialist and orientalist ways, who sees Ugandan women as little more than sexual objects and who sees Amin as, by turns, both fascinating and repulsive. Marx's conflation of Garrigan's point of view with that of the film itself confuses the issue and loses sight of what makes the film so interesting in light of post-imperial discourses. For a film largely marketed and promoted as being about Amin, Garrigan is virtually omnipresent as there are no scenes in which he does not appear and the film-makers actually removed scenes from earlier cuts that did not feature Garrigan, reinforcing his position at the centre of the film.[56] Indeed, some of the film's most hallucinatory sequences, such as the breakdown that leads to his seduction of Kay (Kerry Washington) are explicitly aligned with his agitated consciousness.

Even in more subtle, seemingly straightforward moments we are always seeing and hearing from Nicholas's point of view and the film hinges on the spectator's identification with his initial fascination with Uganda, which he sees as a playground, only to feel the horror as it becomes apparent that all is not as it seems. This is a major departure from the novel, which Nicholas narrates, a decision that doubly foregrounds his limited subjectivity as he narrates from after the fact and often editorializes about his own naivety at the time that the events took place. Not only does the film abolish the first-person narrator but it also removes that frame within a frame, leaving the audience to do the work of recognizing the distance between character and film-maker, meaning they will follow Garrigan's trajectory, effectively becoming complicit in that journey. This particular trajectory does have ramifications for the film's ability to deal with the extent of Amin's atrocities, but in other senses it is one of the film's strengths. This paradox is succinctly described by one African reviewer who writes of the point of view in the film that, 'what makes [*Last King*] excellent is also one of its shortcomings' (Clark, 2006).

Though Marx acknowledges Garrigan's distastefulness as a character (she quotes one reviewer to describe him as a 'classic gap-year tosser' [p. 64]), she falls short of recognizing the ramifications of this perspective for how we understand the ideology of the film. Such can be seen in her reading of the film's politics based on an argument that Garrigan has with Stone (Simon McBurney), an oily English diplomat who later turns out to be working for MI6. Here, while the two are sunning themselves poolside, Stone points out to Nicholas the reports of violence in the countryside against supporters of the deposed Milton Obote and the disappearance of an anti-Amin judge. Nicholas, almost as a reflex, defends Amin, saying that Stone, and by extension Britain, is unhappy at the principle that an African leader would have the temerity to act independently of European wishes. He then goes on to tell Stone: 'This is Africa. You meet violence with violence. Anything else and you're dead' (quoted in Marx, p. 70). Marx calls this exchange 'a particularly embarrassing example of the film's ideological confusion' (p. 70) as Nicholas's liberal, anti-colonialist stance gives way in mere seconds to a stereotypical view of Africa in the most crudely barbaric terms. This reading, though, misses the complexity of the scene and by extension the film as a whole, when it takes as its premise that 'we are meant to read Stone as the antagonist and, for the moment, Nicholas as the politically correct protagonist' (p. 70). Garrigan's trajectory in the film is precisely that he realizes he is more like Stone than he initially believes, and perhaps worse (Stone at least is well informed and without illusions about his role in the world), while he simultaneously realizes the full implications of his naivety about Amin himself. Within the overall arc of his character, this scene illustrates his confused logic and state of denial about how to understand Africa, but this should not be mistaken for the film's logic.

Central to Garrigan's delusion that he is somehow better than Stone and therefore a good person who is helping an independent Uganda is the role played in his mind by national identity. Identification with Scotland is clearly a key issue in the film, both for Garrigan and Amin, and this brings us to the second innovation *Last King* makes within a tradition of British cinema that has been dominated by English characters. Examining the film's use of Scottishness can help to unpack the film's nuanced usage of the theme as part of its larger ideological project. What Marx dismissively refers to as Garrigan's 'overplayed Scots' antipathy' towards the Englishman Stone (p. 68), is actually a way into the film's political statement on Britishness in the post-imperial era. Garrigan's relationship with Stone foregrounds this antipathy and also showcases Nicholas's complacent assumption that being a Scot precludes him from being involved in the larger British machinations in Uganda. This disavowal of British/Englishness takes several forms, including explicit assertions of Scottishness as well as less direct digs at Stone's class and language ('Is there some special school where you can learn to talk that bollocks?' Garrigan mockingly asks Stone when asked to help spy on Amin) and his subtle cringe at Stone's use of a cricketing metaphor – 'he plays with a straight bat' – to describe Amin early in the film. As one reviewer put it, Garrigan believes that 'as a Scot, he can merrily criticize the English/British for their neo-imperialist meddling' (Smyth), but the narrative arc reverses that assumption and implicates the Scottish character in that neo-colonialist project.

This is a crucial historical theme in the film (Figure 9). As Calderwood succinctly notes, Scotland and Scottish people have played a central part in the imperial project:

[Scotland is] a great country with a lot to answer for and that is one of the things that drew me to [the film]. It's a real theme in [the film], the legacy of colonialism and the impact of dictatorship, all that stuff that a lot of countries in the world are still dealing with. It's a fundamentally Scottish story I would say. (Meir, 2012, p. 59)

In this sense, the film is perhaps taking a greater interest in its views on Scottish national identity than its source novel. Marx – who holds the opposite viewpoint – describes the novel's usage of Scotland as one which posits a kinship between the nation and Uganda itself. She says of the novel's narrative arc, which sees Garrigan return to the Highlands instead of London where he is bound at the end of the film, that it has Garrigan returning to 'a marginalized world with its own history of brutal oppression and

Figure 9 Reminders of Scottish imperial complicity: Idi Amin (Forest Whitaker) and his fascination with Scottishness in *The Last King of Scotland*

dispossession' (p. 62). In Marx's view this kinship between the two lands allows the cold world of the Highlands to act as a corrective to the tropical world of moral corruption in Uganda (p. 62). But the usage of Scottishness, which is essentially a pose that allows Garrigan to delude himself about the true nature of his activities in Uganda, actually reveals a more critical view of Scotland's relationship to the Empire and implicitly critiques the stance of victimhood at the hands of the English that underpins some manifestations of Scottish identity.[57]

This theme is also apparent in Amin's fascination with Scottishness. This has long been treated as one of the dictator's many absurd eccentricities, but if we look a bit more closely at this imagined affinity on Amin's part, we can see links that once again reiterate Scottish complicity in the imperial project, though we also see here a missed opportunity on the part of the film. As the film briefly explains, Amin's fascination with Scottishness was rooted in his experiences as a soldier in the King's African Rifles, a colonial regiment that was the Empire's major military presence in eastern Africa and which barbarically helped to quell the Mau Mau uprising in Kenya in the Empire's last days. While serving in this regiment, Amin was impressed by his commanding officers, many of whom were Scottish, and his love for all things Scottish was born. This anecdote once again speaks to the Scottish involvement in the Empire. Moreover, given the reputed atrocities committed in the suppression of the Mau Mau and the widespread assumption that it was during his service in Kenya that Amin learned at first hand the sort of ruthless tactics that he would later visit on his own people this seemingly small detail in Amin's life can help to establish a bloody legacy for Scottish imperial influence in eastern Africa. The film ultimately stops short of exploring this dimension of Amin's love for all things Scottish and instead presents this character trait as one of the dictator's many seemingly meaningless caprices, missing an opportunity for an even more critical exploration of history.

History, representation and the reception of *The Last King of Scotland*

Perhaps unsurprisingly, the questions surrounding African history and representation were very much present in the film's critical reception. As mentioned at the beginning of this chapter, Whitaker's performance as Amin was the most talked about aspect of the film, with the actor receiving numerous critical plaudits and awards, including the Oscar for Best Actor. McAvoy and Macdonald were given more attention in British media coverage and the film's promotional materials, but even in these spheres Whitaker loomed large. Press attention focused particularly on his method acting techniques as a now very familiar way of promoting both the artistry of an actor as well as the historical verisimilitude of the film itself. The film's marketing campaign also focused on this particular 'hook' with a featurette concerned exclusively with Whitaker and another dealing with the casting of the film, a featurette that is largely concerned with the casting of Whitaker as Amin. In their interviews promoting the film, McAvoy and Macdonald spent much of their time praising their colleague, with the former relating stories about particular scenes and the latter often repeating the same anecdotes about casting Whitaker as Amin despite the director's initial reluctance.

This fascination with Whitaker's performance was part of a larger interest in Amin himself, who features largely in the film's reception and often does so in ways that recall the previously dis-cussed problems of African historical representation. Innumerable stories dealt with the dictator himself, rehashing some of his worst atrocities and bizarre acts as well as long-standing rumours such as Amin's cannibalism and his supposed battle with syphilis, which may or may not have been the root cause of his erratic behaviour. Another related and troubling aspect of the film's reception is the tendency to focus on Amin with a similarly racist view as the media had viewed the real Amin during his rule. This is to say that Amin who was the embodiment of all of the (white) West's worst fears about an independent Africa falling prey to the rule of ruthless tyrants, is precisely the one found in the reviews, magazine features, DVD extras and even interviews with the film-makers that sur-rounded the film. A review in the *Daily Mail* ran with the headline 'Cannibal, Tortured and Crazed Tyrant' (Hudson, 2006), while *The Times* ran a piece entitled 'Terrific Portrayal of Tartan Tyrant in His Crackpot Kingdom' (Christopher, 2006). Even African reviewers were quick to take this view of the film, though with less histrionic rhetoric than their western counterparts (e.g., 'A Review of Amin's Reign', 2006). Macdonald himself promoted the film in this way.

Speaking in a BBC documentary he described Amin as representing 'all that is brutal and savage about the dark continent'.

This is not to say, though, that there were no attempts on the part of the film-makers to assert the film's British/Scottish themes. As Marx points out, McAvoy himself called his character a 'young imperialist' (p. 65) and Macdonald has argued that the film was not about Uganda per se but, instead, 'the relationship between Britain and Uganda' (p. 56). Other marketing materials, such as the film's trailers and many of its poster images also attempted to foreground these themes, but it was Amin who nonetheless dominated the film's reception.

The progressive and critical aspects of the film's historical project were thus largely overlooked in the film's reception, a fact that lends credence to those who argue that the film perpetuates the worst kind of African stereotypes. Another worrying aspect of the film's reception was that at least one reviewer, writing for the *Daily Mail* (Hudson, 2006) includes the film's version of Kay's death, dismemberment and post-mortem reassembly among the list of actual deeds committed by the dictator. Such confusion within a widely read newspaper suggests that Marx's misgivings about the film's manipulation of history could be well founded. But other critics were more circumspect about the film's fidelity to historical reality. Pieces in newspapers such as the *Guardian* and the *Seattle Post-Intelligencer* took on the film's fidelity, or lack thereof. Grading the film's version of history, a writer in the *Guardian* gave the film a C– (Von Tunzelmann, 2009), while the reviewer for the American newspaper noted with irony that the film was 'a wee bit of a cheat' in historical terms (Arnold, 2006). Other reviewers were also far from naive about this issue, openly acknowledging its failure to adhere to the literal facts of history but in doing so they also, significantly, took this lack of accuracy as a given in fiction film-making. A reviewer in *The Times*, for example, acknowledged that the film 'departs from reality' at many points but also praised the film as 'nerve-shredding' and 'thoroughly enjoyable' (Christopher, 2006).

Another prominent theme in the film's reception is concerned with the selfsame issues of African representation that have been discussed throughout this chapter. Across reviews of the film, one finds again and again recognition of the now familiar pattern of foregrounding white characters and their perspectives even while trying to represent African problems. An article in an American paper described the film as the latest in a long line of films (which are listed in the piece) foregrounding white characters in 'African' stories (Williams, 2006), while a piece in the *Independent* similarly considered the film along with contemporaries such as *Blood Diamond* and *Catch a Fire*, and pondering how long this fad for film-making in Africa would last (Gumbel, 2006). As if anticipating comparisons such as these – and largely in keeping with the tendencies of other African-themed, ostensibly liberal and compassionate films of the time – the film-makers were also keen to emphasize the responsibility they felt towards the people of Uganda before, during and after the making of the film. Throughout his interviews promoting the film and his DVD commentary on its making, Macdonald repeatedly emphasizes all he and the producers did to hire local Ugandans (though he does not mention the co-production treaty, its stipulations and the benefits that the film reaped from hiring local people). Here too we can see the importance of the precedent set during the making of *The Constant Gardner*, when producer Simon Channing-Williams set up a charitable foundation in Kenya to help those living in the impoverished areas where the film was shot. A similar attempt was made in the case of *Last King* (Crilly, 2006) and such attempts are in one sense ways in which the respective film-makers assert their liberal politics, assuring their audiences that they practise what they preach through their film-making while tacitly reinforcing the idea of a paternalist European culture acting benevolently in east Africa. This is not to say that these charitable acts were cynical marketing ploys, but we should at least be aware of the ways in which these acts were likely to be interpreted by the media and the public.

Last King's promotional materials spotlighting Whitaker's performance all take great pains to point out Whitaker's fear that the role would encourage racialized stereotypes and depict the actor as trying to make his character into something more complex than the bloodthirsty monster that the West has long thought Amin to be. Perhaps anticipating objections in principle to their making a Ugandan-themed film, the film-makers were also very vocal in claiming that the film had been well received in Uganda itself. Calderwood (Meir, 2012), Macdonald ('Director's Commentary') and Whitaker ('Forest Whitaker') have also spoken of the on-set Ugandan crowds' belief that Whitaker actually was Amin. Such anecdotes are highlighted by the film-makers as evidence that the film is an accurate representation of Uganda itself.

This rhetorical strategy along with the film-makers' speed in pointing out their hiring of local people to make the film, can be seen as attempts to brand the film as a cinematic example of 'fair trade', a context that was necessary to balance some of the concerns that were likely to arise in debates about a European film being made in an African country. While it may be tempting to conclude that this was a way of obscuring some exploitative film-making practices, it is worth remembering that the film did bring economic activity to Uganda and also assisted in the project of exposing neo-colonialism in post-independence Africa. The exact power dynamics underpinning the film's production and reception are thus complex and multifaceted and it is with this realization in mind that we can now draw some conclusions about *Last King* and its place in the context of Scottish cinema in the 2000s.

Conclusions

Despite being almost wholly absent from accounts of Scottish cinema, what we have seen in this chapter is that this film is resolutely Scottish and uses its Ugandan setting to project an image of Scottishness that challenges our understandings of that nation's role in the Empire. *Last King* also juggles history, representation, point of view and genre in complex ways. For some, this complexity has led to complaints about the film's representational politics. What I have hoped to show, though, is that this is a mistaken apprehension because it overlooks the film's manipulation of point of view to make a critical statement on Scottish post-imperial politics. Still, it must be remembered that this nuance was also lost on many critics during the film's reception, meaning that the film did, despite what may have been liberal intentions, go some ways towards reinforcing stereotypes about Africa.

These extremely important debates about the representational politics of the film aside, we can also at this point observe some aspects of the film that make it very typical of Scottish cinema in the period under scrutiny. These aspects include, once again, the seemingly endless debate about genre and cultural content – in this case the politics of Scottish-African relations – that has characterized much Scottish and British cinema in the 'cultural industries' epoch. Such can be seen in Marx's complaints about the emphasis placed on generic concerns which supposedly prevents the film-makers from realizing the critical potential of the source novel or Amin's story as a whole. As we saw in Chapters 1 and 5, in the cases of *Local Hero* and *Ae Fond Kiss* respectively, generic discourses need not undermine political themes and such an observation is once again germane in the case of *Last King* where the thriller can help to broaden the appeal of a politically-minded film.

A further parallel between *Last King* and many of this book's case studies lies in its sophisticated usage of transnational production networks to create a film that is resolutely 'Scottish' despite, and arguably because of, its 'global' nature. Like all of the films studied in this book, *Last King* drew on significant sources of funding from outside Scotland but unlike the European nature of the production of *Young Adam* and *Ae Fond Kiss* or the British-North American films like *Local Hero*, *Morvern Callar* and *Mrs Brown*, *Last King* displays a particularly adept hand when it comes to manipulating post-imperial networks. I say this even though the film-makers' two major non-British backers were German and American. There was indeed a significant element of American involvement, but as Calderwood has explained, the creative participation of Fox Searchlight was limited by the active involvement of both Film4 and Scottish Screen – and the latter must be acknowledged in this case for its protective stance in favour of Scottish artists and insistence on Scottish themes. In a particularly shrewd and ironic manoeuvre, the film-makers used a European partner to enable them to use their Ugandan production base as leverage to make the film legally qualify as British, thereby ensuring British financial involvement, which in turn provided the freedom from American control that the film-makers required. When one considers this production context alongside the location shooting in Uganda and the thematic decision to focus on Scottish-Ugandan relations in the post-imperial era, a picture emerges of a film that is itself dependent on post-imperial networks.

Structuring this complex financial and logistical undertaking (the difficulties of bringing an international cast and crew to shoot in Uganda did not, of course, end once the permissions were granted), fell to the film's producers, Andrea Calderwood, Lisa Bryer and Charles Steel. Herein we see evidence of the film's typicality within the context of contemporary Scottish cinema, which has relied increasingly upon the efforts of producers as film production becomes a much more complex enterprise. As we have seen throughout this book, and indeed in other writing on Scottish cinema (e.g. Hjort 2010b, Street 2009), such ingenuity is particularly important for a country as small, and with as limited resources as Scotland. The creativity of producers was apparent not only in the intricate funding package assembled for the film, but also in the drive to assemble other creative talent and to give them the freedom to work. In the case of *Last King*, as with all the films in this book, we can see Scottish cinema, like its larger British counterpart, is in many ways a cinema of producers. With such a realization in mind, we can now turn to some concluding thoughts for the book and the period as a whole.

Conclusions

Having now traversed thirty years of film-making in Scotland and explored six very different films in depth, utilizing a range of approaches, we can now make some observations and conclusions regarding Scottish cinema in a period of unmatched productivity and popularity at home and abroad. Primary among these are observations related to the making of Scottish films. As has been thoroughly documented throughout this book, changes in the industrial landscape of Scottish cinema have been vital to the upsurge of film-making, but it is vital to note that these changes have been much more profound than the simple establishment of culturally oriented devolved funding bodies. As significant as Scottish Screen, the Glasgow Film Office, BBC Scotland, Channel 4 and others have been in supporting Scottish film-makers, their agendas have never been as noble or indeed clear as other writers have implied. Indeed, when comparing the actions of these institutions to private sector companies discussed in these pages, including financiers such as Goldcrest Pictures, Alliance Atlantis or Bianca Films (an Italian distribution/production partner on *Ae Fond Kiss*) there has not been a great deal that sets the private sector apart from the public. This is not to say that the institutions have not done a great deal of good for Scottish film-makers and artists. Channel 4 and Scottish Screen went out of their way to support James McAvoy and Kevin Macdonald, for instance, in the case of *The Last King of Scotland*. But for every good deed done by public funders, an equal number were done by private backers, a case in point being the artistic freedom extended to Bill Forsyth by David Puttnam or the 'hands-off' attitude of the Irish and American backers of *Mrs Brown*. Moreover, it has not just been the private backers who have constrained Scottish artists. Private financiers may have forced 'marquee casting' on Lynne Ramsay, but Scottish Screen was also very vocal in seeking changes to *Young Adam* and Loach's *Sweet Sixteen*, a film that has not been discussed in length here but which was, nevertheless, subject to similar pressures as *Young Adam*.[58] Moreover, the cases of Mackenzie and Ramsay suggest that the development of individual artistic approaches to film-making cannot be sustained by institutional support and that the film-makers must ultimately bend to the marketplace if they are to have extended careers.

This book has thus shown that the relationship between Scottish film-making and the industrial institutions that surround it is much more complex than other accounts suggest, but further issues have arisen in the course of the research that are significant for our understanding of Scottish cinema as a whole. Across this book's diverse case studies were a number of patterns which became apparent. Primary among these was a particular industrial model which dominates this period. In all of the films studied here, explicit and implicit pressures from funders steered the films towards an industrial and aesthetic ideal that combined 'serious' artistic content with elements of popular genre film-making. This mould is one that all Scottish films were at one point or another were squeezed into, either by financiers or marketers, and as such is extremely important for understanding Scottish cinema as a whole during this period. Whether we call this form of cinema 'quality cinema' (Caughie, 2007, p. 104), 'generic hybridity' (Hill, 2011, p. 169), or 'cross over cinema' as I have chosen to do following the examples of Christine Geraghty (2005) and Andrew Higson (2003, pp. 91–92), it is the most typical form of Scottish cinema. Significantly, it is also the form of cinema most typically found in British cinema generally. Scottish cinema as seen in this book fits very easily into this mould, a realization which is at odds with the reputation the nation has accrued in British cinema studies circles as being home to an art cinema that distinguishes it from its English counterpart.

A further pattern that we see across this book is related to this question of the Britishness of Scottish cinema. As shown, English capital is still extremely important to Scottish film-making. Not only does every case study in this book feature production finance from bodies such as Channel 4, the UK Film Council and private companies based in London, but other landmark films such as

Trainspotting, *Ratcatcher* and *Orphans* were likewise dependent on such sources of finance. Though Martin-Jones has found this to be problematic in the case of Mullan's film (2005a, p. 227), as shown particularly in Chapter 1, this need not mean a weakening of the films' Scottish content. In fact, if anything, one could argue that Scottish films unfairly benefit from British backing, as many of the films analysed in this book and throughout the history of Scottish cinema over the last thirty years have been able to 'double dip' when it came to production subsidies, receiving awards from devolved institutions as well as from central institutions in London. Other British regional film-makers have also been able to do this, but with the resurgence of Scottish nationalism in recent years, largely in response to the Conservative-led coalition government in Whitehall, the future sustainability of Scottish cinema could be perceived to be in danger. If the SNP is successful in gaining Scottish independence, the pool of resources for Scottish film-makers will be significantly lessened, undermining, perhaps fatally, the efforts to maintain the unprecedented levels of production seen in Scotland since the late 1970s.

Whatever the future may hold for Scottish cinema, historiography must account for the Britishness of Scottish cinema, a realization which in part bears out Petrie's argument (2000a, p. 186; 2009, p. 154) that Scottish cinema must be understood as a devolved British cinema. To this argument, I would also pose the question of just how 'devolved' Scottish cinema actually is from the rest of British cinema. Another aspect of Scottish cinema seen across this book that speaks to its Britishness has been the importance of producers in its development. Writing in the seminal collection *All Our Yesterdays*, Caughie called British cinema 'a cinema of producers' dependent on these figures to navigate an otherwise disjointed and unpredictable industrial landscape and to standardize products to meet the demands of distributors (1986, p. 200). Such a description is very apropos of contemporary Scottish cinema, a period which owes its great productivity and achievements to producers like Andrea Calderwood, Rebecca O'Brien, David Puttnam and Jeremy Thomas as much, if not more, than it does to the efforts of directors like Forsyth, Ramsay, Loach or Mackenzie. Stepping beyond the confines of this book's case studies, we can also add the names of producers such as Gillian Berrie, Paddy Higson and Andrew Macdonald to this list. The efforts of producers in negotiating complex transnational financing arrangements was seen in every one of this book's chapters as were their efforts in getting films out to audiences while balancing the concern for artistic expression with the demands of the marketplace. While they were not always successful in this latter capacity, without their efforts it is unlikely we would have had any films at all.

That the producer would be essential to the development of Scottish cinema was initially predicted by Petrie in *Screening Scotland* (2000a, p. 178) and the subsequent years, which featured a marketplace and financing terrain that grew increasingly fragmented and unstable, have proved him right. This is not to denigrate the importance of directors, stars or screenwriters – whose efforts have also been documented here – but it is simply to stress the importance of a figure that is often overlooked in film studies generally despite their creative contributions to film-making. Crucially, producers are especially important in small, developing industries where the working conditions require greater resourcefulness and organizational prowess than may be needed in richer, more established environments. As the industrial landscape of Scottish cinema grows more unpredictable in this era of austerity and possible independence, the producer will only become more important to Scottish film-making as the need to broker multilateral, most likely transnationally oriented, financial deals will become more and more pressing.

Whatever the future may hold for Scottish film-making and whatever problems and complexities have characterized Scottish cinema during this period, we cannot overlook the significant achievements that have also marked the period. As shown, Scottish films have challenged our understanding of Scottish national identity and representation, engaged with national history and the national literature; in short, they have constituted a body of work that deserves and rewards attention as a national cinema. Scottish films have also made waves internationally, which is itself important for a national cinema to achieve. The international market will always loom large in Scottish cinema, just as it must with all small national cinemas whose economies of scale require export if they are to survive and provide employment and opportunities for artistic expression for indigenous film-makers. Such things are inevitable in this age of economic neo-liberalism and it unlikely that policy instruments will fundamentally change this basic power dynamic. Indeed, based on what is seen here, if anything, they are likely to encourage dependence on international distribution. As shown throughout this book, this will necessarily mean some adaptation by Scottish film-makers but it need not mean a wholesale discarding of Scottishness nor will it necessarily mean resorting to stereotypical representational discourses.

If, as Petrie argues, Scottish cinema historiography was once too optimistic in its hopes that the burst of film-making in the late 1990s would continue and grow uninterrupted (2009, p. 155), there is also a danger that we can now be too pessimistic about the inconsistent production of aesthetically interesting, commercially high-profile films. After all, the realities of scale will mean that Scottish film-making will be sporadic and of an inconsistent quality, but this need not mean that we should then throw dirt on the hopes for Scottish national cinema. Instead, Scottish cinema, with the rich history and artistic traditions of the nation and complex industrial and political situation that nation finds itself in, will always remain a cinema worth watching if for no other reason than the unique brand of cinema created by such complexity.

Notes

Introduction: surveying Scottish cinema, 1979–present

1 *Trainspotting* was the subject of a book by Murray Smith (2002) while Annette Kuhn has written one on *Ratcatcher* (2008). Martin-Jones (2005a) has written the definitive study of *Orphans* while numerous writers including Mette Hjort (2010b) and Jonathan Murray (2007) have discussed *Red Road* at length.

1 'Raking over' *Local Hero* again: national cinema, indigenous creativity and the international market

2 Interestingly, the film's political satire did not go unnoticed by the Soviet government, which stopped the film from being screened by the British consulate in Moscow. For accounts of this diplomatic incident, see for example newspaper articles by Peary Jones (1983) and Robin Stringer (1983).

3 See Michie for one explicit comparative remark (1986, p. 261).

4 See McArthur's account of the anecdote for just one version (2003b, p. 6).

5 The joke then recurs late in the film when the villagers anxiously await Ben's decision. As a group of men wait grimly in Gordon's kitchen, they hold the model in their hands and one tries to sell his model house to another.

6 See, for instance, recent special issues on the producer in journals such as *Wide Screen* (2.2) and *The Journal of British Cinema and Television* (9.1). See also the forthcoming anthology *Beyond the Bottom Line* (eds) Andrew Spicer, Anthony McKenna and Christopher Meir (Bloomsbury, 2014).

7 Suggestion number 8; page 23 in the screenplay.

8 Suggestion number 22.

9 Suggestion number 14, p. 3.

10 Puttnam memo, item number 27, p. 4.

11 This part of the trailer, in which the audience is presented with the implication of a narrative twist that does not occur in the actual film, can be seen as an example of what Kernan describes as a deceptive use of the Kuleshov effect, a practice she finds to be fairly common in her survey of Hollywood trailers (2004, pp. 10–11).

12 The alternate poster images, as well as the illustrator's memo can be found in the David Puttnam collection housed at the BFI, box no. 7, item no. 36.

13 John Caughie, in a brief discussion of the promotion of Forsyth himself within Scotland, says that this promotion specified that winners would stay in the same rooms that the crew stayed in while they were filming the movie (1983, p. 45).

14 Documents relating to these screenings as well as an entry form for the John Menzies Outfitters contest can be found in the BFI David Puttnam collection, box no. 7 item no. 35.

15 The name and date of this publication has not been recorded by David Puttnam's archivist. A clipping of the article itself can be found in the BFI David Puttnam collection, box no. 9 item 41.

16 See a memo found in the David Puttnam collection, box no. 6, item no. 34.

17 For more on this sort of strategy, see Tiiu Lukk's description of marketing and distribution practices for independent and 'foreign' films (1997, pp. 120–143). In the course of analysing the release patterns of many British heritage films, Andrew Higson expands upon Lukk's description (2003, pp. 98–100).

2 *Mrs Brown*: Scottish cinema in an age of devolved public service broadcasting

18 These are *Trainspotting*, *Shallow Grave* and *Carla's Song* (Ken Loach, 1995), which were funded in part or wholly by Channel 4, and *Small Faces*, which was made by BBC Scotland.

19 Another co-producing partner on the film, who is not discussed here at length, was Irish Screen. This firm acted as equity investors in the film and did not make any significant creative contributions to the project (Meir, 2012, p. 57). In light of the controversies which plague American involvement in British television, I confine my analysis, for the most part, to the involvement of American public television institutions.

20 To reach this conclusion, Steemers draws on a piece by Manuel Alvarado (2000) which lists a number of poorly received works such as *Our Mutual Friend* (1998) and *Middlemarch* (1994), but which also conspicuously excludes the extremely successful adaptation of *Pride and Prejudice* (1995).

21 Here one can look, for example, at the ironic usage of the Highland mists in *Local Hero* or the Highland ball in *Shallow Grave* which the housemates snigger their way through, and where Alex (Ewan McGregor) is involved in a punch-up with kilt-clad Cameron (Colin McCredie), a former candidate to let a room in Alex's flat.

22 Christine Geraghty also discusses the aspect of British costume drama acting that demands actors convey emotional repression, noting that such performances often command critical esteem and recognition through awards (2002, p. 47). Dench is among the actors mentioned by Geraghty in this regard, though Gwyneth Paltrow and Kate Winslet are the main objects of her analysis.

23 This context was not completely lost among the film's journalistic reviewers. Alexander Walker (1997), for one, noted in the *Evening Standard*, that, despite impending devolution 'here you have the future of the British crown dependent on a Scotsman' (p. 27).

24 In the years following *Mrs Brown*'s release Channel 4 produced a documentary on Victoria – *Queen Victoria's Men* – which dealt with Brown as well as numerous other reputed lovers that the Queen had. The more popular mainstream representation, *The Young Victoria* (Jean-Marc Vallée, 2009), however, focuses on the monarch's romances with Melbourne and Albert and thus continues the tradition of marginalizing Brown.

25 See, for example, Joshua Mooney's profile of Judi Dench in the *Chicago Sun-Times* (1997), in which Dench talks of some of the discussions about Victoria and Brown with Connolly: '"Their relationship has always been speculated about as long as I've known," says Dench, who was born and raised in England. Well, did they or didn't they? "Billy Connolly will tell you yes", Dench says, chuckling, "because the Scots like to think somebody got their leg over the queen. And everybody in England will tell you, "I don't think so"" (p. 20).

26 See, for instance, his account of Channel 4's mid-1990s 'move towards the US market and a form of relatively 'safe filmmaking' typified by films such as *The Madness of King George* (n.d., p. 169). This part of Hill's overview presents this shift in strategy as something to be lamented.

3 Lynne Ramsay, cross-over cinema and *Morvern Callar*

27 These included objections as to the size of the cast (Warner had apparently included many of the novel's peripheral figures) and the decision to have Morvern narrating the film, among other things.

28 Scottish Screen has not paginated the application package for *Morvern Callar* and I have therefore not included page numbers in my citations from that package.

4 The many authors of *Young Adam*

29 *Red Road* generated 163,000 admissions in Europe compared to 360,000 for *Young Adam*. Both films received a similarly positive critical reception in the press. Martin-Jones seems to take the academic interest in *Red Road* – which, as discussed in the introduction of this book, has been widely written about – as evidence of its greater success as an art film, but that reception is largely based on optimism expressed particularly by Mette Hjort (2010b) over the transnational collaboration between Danish and Scottish film-makers that underpinned the film rather than its aesthetic achievements per se.

30 In a piece in the *The Times*, the head of Council's Premiere Fund, Robert Jones, claims that the Council was not in fact lobbied by McGregor or anyone else, but does say that the Council was reluctant to invest in the film, saying: 'We do not live in a subsidy culture where we can afford to put money into films without the chance of making it back' (Alberge, 2003, p. 11). For his part, Stephan Mallman, associate producer on the film, has downplayed this aspect of the film's production history saying that the Council did suggest ways of lowering costs but that they were merely hypothetical and not quite as pressurizing as McGregor's comments may imply (Mallman, 2006).

31 For a general discussion of pastiche and how it is deployed in relation to genre and history, see Richard Dyer's *Pastiche* (2007). Relevant portions of Dyer's book for this section include his discussion of critical discrepancy in pastiched representations (2007, pp. 58–63), as well as the discussion of pastiche in neo-noir films (2007, pp. 120–125).

32 *Young Adam* would turn out not to be Mackenzie's debut feature. His first feature was in fact *The Last Great Wilderness*, a film that is referenced in the decision minutes. But the application was accurate when it was submitted; owing to the numerous delays in completing *Young Adam*, Mackenzie was able to complete *Wilderness* while waiting for financing for *Young Adam*.

33 Before Joe attempts to seduce Ella he reminisces: 'And I remembered Cathie, whom I had lived with for two years before I ever came to the barge . . .' (Trocchi, 1983, p. 36).

34 For a survey of the erotic thriller genre, see Linda Ruth Williams's *The Erotic Thriller in Contemporary Cinema* (2005). Her account of the relationship between the genre and the conventions of film noir (pp. 1–76) are especially pertinent to films such as *Young Adam*.

35 For a more detailed account of audience reactions to the sex scenes in *Crash* and the controversies that arose following the film's release in Britain, see Martin Barker, Jane Arthurs, Ramaswami Harindranath, *The Crash Controversies* (2001).

36 See Peter Lev's *The Euro American Cinema* for an account of the controversies surrounding the release of *Last Tango*, as well as a convincing argument that this was part of producer Alberto Grimaldi's strategy for raising the profile of his projects (1993, pp. 52–53).

37 The scene is also referenced in headlines for Romney (2003) and Sandhu (2003a), in addition to innumerable mentions within individual reviews.

38 For just a few examples of such mentions, see Macleod (2004), Hodgkinson (2002) and Sandhu (2003a).

39 For just a few examples of such mentions, see Brooks (2003), Scott (2003) and Romney (2003).

40 See Barker et al. for a discussion of how *Crash*'s erotic content and the controversy which accompanied its release led to the film being exhibited at both art-house cinemas and multiplexes, as well as an account of how audiences at both types of venues understood the film (2001, pp. 48–61).

5 Importing national cinema: Ken Loach, *Ae Fond Kiss* and multicultural Scottish cinema

41 See for instance James F. English's overview of Loach's career since *Hidden Agenda* in which 'seemingly modest provincial dramas' such as *Raining Stones* (1993) and *Riff Raff* (1991) are argued to be more important achievements than 'internationally-oriented' films like *Hidden Agenda* and *Land and Freedom* (1995), which according to English lack the 'sense of place' of the other films (2006, p. 279). Interestingly, English's dichotomous reading of Loach's late career, which runs up to *The Wind that Shakes the Barley* (2006) omits *Ae Fond Kiss*, which could be said to fit into both of the categories he outlines.

42 Information on the exact make-up of the funding package for *My Name is Joe* and *Carla's Song* could not be obtained.

43 Loach made these comments in an interview at the Edinburgh Film Festival contained on the DVD release of *Ae Fond Kiss*. In the DVD commentary for *Ae Fond Kiss*, Laverty also mentions that they had only conceived of the films as a trilogy during the writing of the film.

44 At least not within the context of the British/Scottish film industry. For a discussion of how Hindi-language films such as *Pyaar Ishq Aur Mohabet* (Rajiv Rai, 2001) have represented the Scottish Asian experience, see Martin-Jones's chapter in *Scotland: Global Cinema* (2009, pp. 67–88). This chapter also engages with the Scottish produced film *Nina's Heavenly Delights* (Pratibha Parmar) which was released in 2006, and which did not make enough of a critical or commercial impact on the domestic or international film scene to warrant lengthy discussion here.

45 As Deniz Göktürk notes, humour is one of the distinguishing charac-
   teristics of Turkish-German films which have sought to counterpoint
   older social-realist, miserablist representations of the Turkish-German
   experience (2002, p. 248). Such a trend echoes the trend within black
   British cinema described by Malik and cited above.

46 The rivalry between Glasgow football clubs Rangers and Celtic has
   long been underpinned by sectarian tension between the city's Protestants, who traditionally support Rangers, and Catholics, who traditionally support Celtic. This ostensibly sporting rivalry has been the excuse
   for countless acts of sectarian violence in Glasgow. For an academic
   study of the history of this rivalry and its relationship to Irish immigra-
   tion, see W. J. Murray's study *The Old Firm: Sectarianism, Sport and
   Society in Scotland* (1984).

47 This could have been a product of Loach's preference to allow his
   non-professional actors to improvise their own dialogue. The film's
   script does include much more overtly racist things for the boys to
   shout, including 'Jihad' as they chase Tahara (Laverty, 2003, p. 4), but
   such lines are not included in the finished film.

48 See Sherzer (1999) for an account of the bi-racial love story in French
   post-colonial cinema. See Göktürk (2002) for the usage of the plot
   device in German-Turkish films. Lee's *Jungle Fever*, with the bi-racial
   love affair at the heart of its narrative, would also be a key film in
   this context.

49 See for instance a racist incident at a Glasgow wine bar which is found
   in the film's original script (Laverty, 2003, p. 23), and the stabbing of
   Casim's father by racist thugs, which is described in the film and
   included among the deleted scenes on the DVD release of the film.

50 Such a zeitgeist can be seen as part of the reason that *Nina's Heavenly
   Delights*, a much more conventionally upbeat view of Scottish multiculturalism, failed to get much of an audience at home or abroad.

51 Unlike most of the films examined in this book, *Ae Fond Kiss* had very
   little success in reaching North American audiences. According to
   Variety.com (2013), the film grossed approximately $30,000 at the US
   box office. Additionally, the film was only reviewed in one newspaper
   in North America, *The New York Times* (Holden, 2004).

52 Wayne reports a similar situation occurring with Artificial Eye's distribution of *Land and Freedom*, in which the distributor would not allow
   the film to be shown in multiplexes, even though there were requests
   for prints from a number of exhibitors (2002, p. 21).

6 Not British, Scottish?: *The Last King of Scotland* and post-imperial Scottish cinema

53 The term 'economic runaway production' is used by Greg Elmer (2002) to describe productions which choose their locations for filming based solely on cost savings. He opposes this type of production with 'creative runaway productions' which select their locations based on script demands. For an overview of the ways in which 'economic runaway productions' in particular have contributed to a global 'new international division of cultural labour' which exploits host countries, see Toby Miller et al.'s *Global Hollywood* (2001).

54 Here I am indebted to the comprehensive survey of British colonial films found on the website *Colonial Film: Moving Images of the British Empire*. This catalogue lists titles such as *Falcon Hunting in Africa* (1910) and *Native Lion Hunt* (1909) as being among the first British films shot on the continent.

55 Grant took centre stage in the marketing and promotion of the film as an autobiographical work. Part of this campaign included a memoir of his time writing the screenplay and directing the film, an account which was interspersed with memories from his childhood in Swaziland (2006).

56 The film-makers had originally intended to open the film with a scene depicting Amin's career as a boxer while serving in the King's African Rifles. According to Macdonald's commentary on the film's DVD release, this scene was cut in order to more closely focus on Nicholas.

57 The novel goes further in paralleling the postcolonial situations of Scotland and Uganda, for example, in the character of Major Weir, who betrays MI6 in Uganda by informing Amin of their activities and deserts the service only to resurface in Scotland as a nationalist terrorist. The film deletes this character entirely and thus pointedly polarizes Nicholas as a Scot and the agents of the British state as English.

Conclusions

58 The decision minutes recording the *Sweet Sixteen* award read, in part: '[T]he Panel agreed that the relationship between Liam and Pinball should be strengthened early on and the character of Suzanne should be developed further. The Panel supported this project but indicated that funds should be withheld until the script has been redrafted to incorporate the above points' (Scottish Screen, 2001a).

Based my perusal of the version of *Sweet Sixteen*'s screenplay which was submitted along with the film's Lottery application (Laverty, 2001), no changes were made by the film-makers.

References

Adler, T. (2003) 'Scottish Lottery Bodies Only Recoup 15% of Investment', *Screen Finance*, 16 (19), 22 October, p. 6.

Adler, T. (2004) *The Producers: Money, Movies and Who Really Calls the Shots*. London: Methuen.

Ae Fond Kiss (2005) Directed by Ken Loach [DVD]. London: Icon Entertainment and Warner Brothers.

Alberge, D. (1997) 'Today's Young Comedians are a Joke, Says Connolly', *The Times*, 13 May. No pagination, accessed using the Factiva database.

Alberge, D. (2003) 'McGregor in Attack on "Betrayal" of British Films', *The Times*, 19 May, p. 11.

Alvarado, M. (2000) 'The "Value" of TV Drama: Why Bother to Produce It?' *Television and New Media* 1 (3), pp. 307–319.

Andrew, D. (2000) 'The Unauthorized Auteur Today', in R. Stam and T. Miller (ed.) *Film and Theory: An Anthology*, Malden, MA and Oxford: Blackwell Publishers, pp. 20–29.

Andrews, N. (2003) 'Custard, Ketchup and Sugar Leave a Bad Taste', *The Financial Times*, 25 September. No pagination, consulted using the Factiva Database.

Arnold, W. (2006) '*The Last King of Scotland* is a Fanciful Take on a Ruthless Tyrant', *Seattle Post-Intelligencer*, 6 October 2006, p. 5.

Ashdown, D. (1975) *Queen Victoria's Family*, London: Hale.

Bamigboye, B. (2003) 'Sorry Ewan, You'll be Having the Snip', *Daily Mail*, 5 November. No pagination, consulted using the Factiva Database.

Barker, M., J. Arthur and R. Harindranath (2001) *The Crash Controversy: Censorship Campaigns and Film Reception*. London and New York: Wallflower Press.

Bear, L. (2004) 'Tough Talk with *Young Adam* Director David Mackenzie' [online]. Available at: www.indiewire.com/people/people_040416young.html (accessed 22 November 2006).

Bickelhaupt, S. and M. Dezell (1997) 'Scottish Actor Likes Boston Better the Second Time Around', *The Boston Globe*, 24 July, p. E2.

Blandford, S. (2007) *Film, Drama and the Break-Up of Britain*. Bristol and Chicago: Intellect.

Bordwell, D. (1986) *Narration in the Fiction Film*. London: Methuen.

Bradshaw, P. (1997) 'At Least Billy's Got a Bit of Fight Left', *Evening Standard*, 18 August, p. 13.

Brooks, R. (2003) 'No More Nice Guy as McGregor Bares All', *The Sunday Times*, 25 May. No pagination, consulted using the Factiva Database.

Brooks, Xan (1999) 'The Mouse that Roared', *Independent*, 12 November, p. 12.

Brown, J. (1983) 'A Suitable Job for a Scot', *Sight and Sound*, 52 (3), pp. 157–162.

Brown, J. (1984) 'The Land Beyond Brigadoon', *Sight and Sound*, 53 (1), pp. 40–46.

Brunsdon, C. (1990) 'Problems With Quality', *Screen*, 31 (1), pp. 67–90.

Bruzzi, S. (1997) *Undressing Cinema: Clothing and Identity in Movies*. London: Routledge.

Burnside, A. (2002) 'Sex, Drugs and Murder, He Wrote', *The Sunday Times*. 3 February. No pagination, consulted using the Factiva Database.

Calderwood, A. (n.d.) 'Film and Television Policy in Scotland', in J. Hill and M. McLoone (ed.) *Big Picture, Small Screen: The Relations Between Film and Television*. Luton: University of Luton Press, pp. 188–195.

Calderwood, A. (2012) Email to Christopher Meir. 18 January 2012.

Caldwell, J. T. (2008) *Production Culture: Industrial Reflexivity and Critical Practice in Film and Television*. Durham: Duke University Press.

Campbell, A. and T. Niel (eds.) (1997) *A Life in Pieces: Reflections on Alexander Trocchi*. London: Rebel Inc.

Caughie, J. (1982) 'Scottish Television: What Would it Look Like?', in C. McArthur (ed.) *Scotch Reels: Scotland in Cinema and Television*. London: BFI, pp. 112–122.

Caughie, J. (1983) 'Support Whose Local Hero?', *Cencrastus*, 14, 44–46.

Caughie, J. (1986) 'Broadcasting Cinema 1: Converging Histories', in C. Barr (ed.) *All Our Yesterdays: 90 Years of British Cinema*. London: BFI, pp. 189–205.

Caughie, J. (2000) *Television Drama: Realism, Modernism and British Culture*. Oxford: Oxford University Press.

Caughie, J. (2007) 'Morvern Callar, Art Cinema and the "Monstrous Archive"', *Scottish Studies Review*, 8 (1), pp. 101–115.

Chapman, J. (2005) *Past and Present: National Identity and the British Historical Film*. London: I. B. Tauris.

Christopher, J. (2003) 'A Marvel from the Mean Streets', *The Times*, 14 August, *Times2*, p. 11.

Christopher, J. (2006) 'Terrific Portrayal of Tartan Tyrant in His Crackpot Kingdom', *The Times*, 19 October, p. 8.

Clark, M. K. (2006) '*The Last King of Scotland*', *All Africa Global Media*, 16 October. No pagination, consulted using the Factiva Database.

Cook, P. (1996) *Fashioning the Nation: Costume and Identity in British Cinema*. London: BFI.

Crilly, R. (2006) 'Touched by Africa, Hollywood Gives a Little Back', *The Christian Science Monitor*, 21 December, p. 1.

Cumming, T. (2003) 'Mean Streets', *Guardian*, 8 August. No pagination, consulted using the Factiva Database.

Daily Mail (2004) 'We Need More Punch from this Glasgow Kiss', 17 September. No pagination, consulted using the Factiva database.

Dale, S. (2002) *Alan Warner's Morvern Callar: A Reader's Guide*. New York and London: Continuum.

Dave, P. (2006) *Visions of England: Class and Culture in Contemporary Cinema*. Oxford and New York: Berg.

Del Belso, R. (1982) Reports from test screenings of *Local Hero* in Seattle and Toronto, dated 18 October. Memo available from the BFI David Puttnam Collection.

Donaldson, S. (2002) 'Film-Makers on Film: Lynne Ramsay on John Cassavetes's *A Woman Under the Influence*', *The Daily Telegraph*, 2 November, p. 12.

Dyer, R. (1995) 'Heritage Cinema in Europe', in G. Vincendeau (ed.) *Encyclopedia of European Cinema*. London: BFI, pp. 204–205.

Dyer, R. (2007) *Pastiche*. London and New York: Routledge.

Ebert, R. (2003) '*Morvern Callar* Proves Life is What You Make It', *The Chicago Sun-Times*, 21 January, p. 27.

Elmer, Greg (2002) 'The Trouble with the Canadian "Body Double": Runaway Productions and Foreign Location Shooting', *Screen*, 43: 4, pp. 423–431.

Elsaesser, T. (2005) *European Cinema: Face to Face with Hollywood*. Amsterdam: Amsterdam University Press.

English, J. F. (2006) 'Local Focus, Global Frame: Ken Loach and the Cinema of Dispossession', in L. Friedman (ed.) *Fires Were Started: British Cinema and Thatcherism*, 2nd edn. London and New York: Wallflower Press, pp. 259–281.

Flynn, B. (1997) 'Victoria's Bit of Rough', *Guardian*, 3 May, p. 24.

Foden, G. (1998) *The Last King of Scotland*. London: Faber & Faber.

Forde, L. (2002) 'Case Study: *Morvern Callar*', *Screen International*, 1345, 22 February, p. 21.

Forsyth, B. (1981) *Local Hero: Screenplay*. Second draft of the film's screenplay dated November 1981. Available in the BFI Library, London, UK.

Franklin, B. (2001) 'Section Introductions', in B. Franklin (ed.) *British Television Policy: A Reader*. London and New York: Routledge.

Fuller, G. (ed.) (1998) *Loach on Loach*. London: Faber & Faber.

Geraghty, C. (2000) *British Cinema in the 1950s: Gender, Genre and the 'New Look'*, London: Routledge.

Geraghty, C. (2002) 'Crossing Over: Performing as a Lady and a Dame', *Screen*, 43 (2), pp. 41–56.

Geraghty, C. (2005) *My Beautiful Laundrette*. London: I. B. Tauris.

Gibbons, F. (2003) 'McGregor Rages at Film Fund's Agenda', *Guardian*, 19 May, p. 7.

Gilbey, R. (2003) 'Written on the Body', *Sight and Sound*, 13 (9), pp. 16–19.

Glover, G. (1997) 'Top of the Scots', *The Scotsman*, 12 December, p. 17.

Göktürk, D. (2002) 'Beyond Paternalism: Turkish German Traffic in Cinema', in T. Bergfelder, E. Carter and D. Göktürk (eds) *The German Cinema Book*. London: BFI, pp. 248–256.

Goode, I. (2007) 'Different Trajectories: Europe and Scotland in Recent Film and Television', in *Portal*, 4 (2), pp. 1–11.

Goode, I. (2008) 'Mediating the Rural: *Local Hero* and the Location of Scottish Cinema', in R. Fish (ed.) *Cinematic Countrysides*, Manchester, Manchester University Press, pp. 109–126.

Grant, C. (2000) 'www.auteur.com?', *Screen*, 41 (1), pp. 101–108.

Grant, R. E. (2006) *The Wah Wah Diaries: The Making of a Film*. London: Macmillan.

Gumbel, Andrew (2006) 'Africa Provides Storylines for Next Generation of Hollywood Blockbusters', *Independent*, 28 October, p. 35.

Hayward, A. (2004) *Which Side Are You On?: Ken Loach and His Films*. London: Bloomsbury.

The Herald (1983) 'Local Successes', 11 July, p. 3.

Higson, A. (1986) '"Britain's Outstanding Contribution to the Film": The Documentary-Realist Tradition', in C. Barr (ed.) *All Our Yesterdays: 90 Years of British Cinema*. London: BFI, pp. 72–97.

Higson, A. (1989) 'The Concept of National Cinema', *Screen*, 30 (4), pp. 34–46.

Higson, A. (1993) 'Re-presenting the National Past: Nostalgia and Pastiche in the Heritage Film', in L. Friedman (ed.) *British Cinema and Thatcherism: Fires Were Started*. London: UCL Press, pp. 109–129.

Higson, A. (1995) *Waving the Flag: Constructing a National Cinema in Britain*. Oxford: Clarendon Press.

Higson, A. (1996) 'The Heritage Film and British Cinema', in A. Higson (ed.) *Dissolving Views: Key Writings on British Cinema*. London: Cassell, pp. 232–248.

Higson, A. (2000) 'The Instability of the National', in J. Ashby and A. Higson (eds) *British Cinema, Past and Present*. London and New York: Routledge, pp. 35–48.

Higson, A. (2003) *English Heritage, English Cinema: Costume Drama Since 1980*. Oxford: Oxford University Press.

Hill, J. (n.d.) 'British Television and Film: The Making of a Relationship', in J. Hill and M. McLoone (eds) *Big Picture, Small Screen: The Relations Between Film and Television*. Luton: University of Luton Press, pp. 151–176.

Hill, J. (1986) *Sex, Class and Realism: British Cinema, 1956–1963*. London: BFI.

Hill, J. (1992) 'The Issue of National Cinema and British Film Production', in D. Petrie (ed.) *New Questions of British Cinema*. London: BFI, pp. 10–21.

Hill, J. (1996) 'British Film Policy', in A. Moran (ed.) *Film Policy: International, National and Regional Perspectives*. London: Routledge.

Hill, J. (1997) 'Finding a Form: Politics and Aesthetics in *Fatherland, Hidden Agenda* and *Riff-Raff*', in George McKnight (ed.) *Agent of Challenge and Defiance: The Films of Ken Loach*. Trowbridge: Flicks Books, pp. 125–143.

Hill, J. (1998) 'Every Fuckin' Choice Stinks', *Sight and Sound*, 8 (11), pp. 18–21.

Hill, J. (1999) *British Cinema in the 1980s*. Oxford: Clarendon Press.

Hill, J. (2000a) 'From New Wave to "Brit-grit": Continuity and Difference in Working-Class Realism', in J. Ashby and A. Higson (eds) *British Cinema, Past and Present*. London and New York: Routledge, pp. 249–260.

Hill, J. (2000b) 'The Rise and Fall of British Art Cinema: A Short History of the 1980s and 1990s', *Aura*, 6 (3), pp. 18–32.

Hill, J. (2009) '"Bonnie Scotland, eh?: Scottish Cinema, the Working Class and the Films of Ken Loach' in J. Murray, F. Farley and R. Stoneman (eds) *Scottish Cinema Now*. Newcastle: Cambridge Scholars Publishing, pp. 88–104.

Hill, J. (2011) *Ken Loach: The Politics of Film and Television*, London: BFI.

Hjort, M. (2010a) 'On the Plurality of Cinematic Transnationalism', in N. Ďuričová and K. Newman (eds) *World Cinemas, Transnational Perspectives*, London: Taylor & Francis, pp. 12–33.

Hjort, M. (2010b) 'Affinitive and Milieu-building Transnationalism: The *Advance Party* Initiative', in D. Iordanova, D. Martin-Jones and B. Vidal (eds) *Cinema at the Periphery*, Detroit: Wayne State University Press, pp. 46–66.

Hodgkinson, W. (2002) 'Menace a Trois', *Guardian*, 17 May. No pagination, consulted using the Factiva Database.

Holden, S. (2004) 'Defiance Cuts Two Ways in a Tempestuous Catholic-Muslim Romance Set in Scotland', *The New York Times*, 26 November. No pagination, consulted using the Factiva Database.

Horovitz, M. (1997) 'Wasted Genius', *The Sunday Times*, 7 September. No pagination, consulted using the Factiva Database.

Hudson, C. (2006) 'Cannibal, Torturer and Crazed Tyrant. But the Bitter Irony is that the British Created Idi Amin', *Daily Mail*, 21 October, pp. 46–47.

Hume, R. D. (1999) *Reconstructing Contexts: The Aims and Principles of Archaeo-Historicism*. Oxford: Oxford University Press.

Hunter, A. (1990) 'Bill Forsyth: The Imperfect Anarchist', in E. Dick (ed.) *From Limelight to Satellite: A Scottish Film Book*. BFI and Scottish Film Council, pp. 151–162.

Janusonis, M. (1997) 'Lukewarm Scandal, but a Fascinating Look at Court Life', *The Providence Journal*, 15 August, p. E–06.

Jones, P. (1983) 'Soviet Ban on *Local Hero*', *The Scotsman*, 18 November, p. 15.

Kael, P. (1983) '*Local Hero*', *The New Yorker*, 21 March, pp. 115–118.

Kernan, L. (2004) *Coming Attractions: Reading American Movie Trailers*. Austin: University of Texas Press.

Klinger, B. (1997) 'Film History Terminable and Interminable: Recovering the Past in Reception Studies', *Screen*, 38 (2), pp. 107–128.

Landy, M. (1991) *British Genres: Cinema and Society, 1930–1960*, Princeton: Princeton University Press.

The Last King of Scotland (2007) Directed by Kevin Macdonald [DVD]. London: Fox Searchlight. DVD contains the following extras: 'Director's Commentary Track'; 'Capturing Idi Amin', 'Forest Whitaker: Idi Amin'; 'Fox Movie Channel Presents: Casting Session: *The Last King of Scotland*'; 'Deleted Scenes'.

Laverty, P. (2001) *Sweet Sixteen: Screenplay*. Submitted to Scottish Screen, dated 4 September. Obtained courtesy of Scottish Screen.

Laverty, P. (2003) *Ae Fond Kiss: Screenplay*. Submitted to Scottish Screen, dated 6 February. Obtained courtesy of Scottish Screen.

Leigh, D. (2002) 'About a Girl', *Guardian Weekend*, 5 October, pp. 26, 28, 30, 32.

Leigh, J. (2002) *The Cinema of Ken Loach: Art in the Service of the People*. London and New York: Wallflower Press.

Lev, P. (1993) *The Euro-American Cinema*. Austin: University of Texas.

Local Hero (1999) Directed by Bill Forsyth [DVD]. Burbank, CA: Warner Brothers.

Lukk, T. (1997) *Movie Marketing: Opening the Picture and Giving it Legs*. Los Angeles: Silman-James Press.

Lumiere Database (2011) *Lumiere Database on Admissions of Films Released in Europe* [online]. Available at: http://lumiere.obs.coe.int/web/sources/histo.html (last accessed 28 August).

Lyon, V. (1982a) Test screening report, dated 22 October. Report available in the BFI David Puttnam Collection.

Lyon, V. (1982b) Second test screening report from London audiences, dated 6 November. Report available in the BFI David Puttnam Collection.

MacDonald, F. (2002) 'Interview with Alwin Kuchler, Jane Morton, Lynne Ramsay and Lucia Zucchetti', in J. Boorman, F. MacDonald and W. Donohue (eds) *Projections 12: Film-Makers on Film Schools*. London: Faber & Faber, pp. 101–123.

Mackenzie, D. (2002) *Young Adam: Screenplay*. Submitted to Scottish Screen, dated 25 January. Obtained courtesy of Scottish Screen.

Macleod, H. (2004) '*Young Adam*: E-mail From Tilda Swinton', 14 April [online]. Available at: www.gapingvoid.com/Moveable_Type/archives/000695.html. (accessed 22 November 2006).

MacNab, G. (2003a) 'Body Politics', *Independent*, 16 May. No pagination, consulted using the Factiva Database.

MacNab, G. (2003b) 'The Force in Me', *Independent*, 1 August. No pagination, consulted using the Factiva Database.

MacNab, G. (2004) 'This is Not a Love Story: Has Ken Loach Gone Soft?', *Guardian*, 20 August, p. 10.

Malik, S. (1996) 'Beyond "The Cinema of Duty"?: The Pleasures of Hybridity: Black British Films of the 1980s and 1990s', in A. Higson (ed.) *Dissolving Views: Key Writings on British Cinema*. London: Cassell, pp. 202–215.

Mallman, S. (2006) Interview with Christopher Meir, 6 June.

Martin-Jones, D. (2005a) '*Orphans*, a Work of Minor Cinema from Post-Devolutionary Scotland', *Journal of British Cinema and Television*, 1 (2), pp. 226–241.

Martin-Jones, D. (2005b) 'Sexual Healing: Representations of the English in Post-Devolutionary Scotland', *Screen*, 46 (2), pp. 227–233.

Martin-Jones, D. (2006a) 'Kabhi India Kabhie Scotland: Recent Indian Films Shot on Location in Scotland', *South Asian Popular Culture*, 4 (1), pp. 49–60.

Martin-Jones, D. (2006b) 'Cinema in a Small Nation/Small National Cinemas in the World: the New Scottish Cinema Conference, Huston School of Film and Digital Media, National University of Ireland, Galway, 4–5 November 2005', *Journal of British Cinema and Television*, 3 (1), pp. 151–155.

Martin-Jones, D. (2009) *Scotland: Global Cinema: Genres, Modes and Identities*. Edinburgh: Edinburgh University Press.

References 195

Marx, L. (2011) 'The Last King of Scotland and the Politics of Adaptation', Black Camera, An International Film Journal, 3(1), pp. 54–74.
Mathieson, K. (2005) 'Embracing the Chaos: Interview with Tilda Swinton', Arts Journal [online]. Available at: www.hiarts.co.uk/jun05_interview_tilda_swinton.html (accessed 22 November 2006).
McArthur, C. (1982a) 'Introduction', in C. McArthur (ed.) Scotch Reels: Scotland in Cinema and Television. London: BFI, pp. 1–6.
McArthur, C. (1982b) 'Scotland and Cinema: The Iniquity of the Fathers', in C. McArthur (ed.) Scotch Reels: Scotland in Cinema and Television. London: BFI, pp. 40–69.
McArthur, C. (1993) 'In Praise of a Poor Cinema', Sight and Sound, 3 (8), pp. 30–32.
McArthur, C. (1994) 'The Cultural Necessity of a Poor Celtic Cinema', in J. Hill, M. McLoone and P. Hainsworth (eds) Border Crossing: Film in Ireland, Britain, and Europe. Belfast: The Institute of Irish Studies, pp. 112–125.
McArthur, C. (2001) 'Mrs Brown', in G. Vincendeau (ed.) Film/Literature/Heritage: A Sight and Sound Reader. London: BFI Publishing, pp. 184–186.
McArthur, C. (2003a) Whisky Galore! and The Maggie. London: I. B. Tauris.
McArthur, C. (2003b) Brigadoon, Braveheart and the Scots: Distortions of Scotland in Hollywood Cinema. London and New York: I. B. Tauris.
McCance, R. (1996) BBC Scotland Script report, dated 12 August, on Alan Warner's screenplay for Morvern Callar.
McCrone, D., Morris A. and Kiely, R. (1995) Scotland – The Brand: The Making of Scottish Heritage. Edinburgh: Edinburgh University Press.
McKechnie, K. (2001) 'Mrs Brown's Mourning and Mr King's Madness: Royal Crisis on Screen', in D. Cartmell, I. Q. Hunter and I. Wheleman (eds) Retrovisions: Reinventing the Past in Film and Fiction. London: Pluto Press, pp. 102–119.
McKechnie, K. (2002) 'Taking Liberties with the Monarch: The Royal Bio-pic in the 1990s', in C. Monk and A. Sargeant (eds) British Historical Cinema. London and New York: Routledge, pp. 217–236.
McKnight, G. (ed.) (1997) Agent of Challenge and Defiance: The Films of Ken Loach. Trowbridge: Flicks Books.
Meir, C. (2004) 'Bill Forsyth'. Senses of cinema [online]. Available at: http://sensesofcinema.com/2004/great-directors/forsyth/
Meir, C. (2009) 'The Producer as Salesman: Jeremy Thomas, Film Promotion and Contemporary Transnational Independent Cinema', The Historical Journal of Film, Radio and Television, 29 (4), pp. 467–481.
Meir, C. (2009) 'Chasing "Cross-Over": Selling Scottish Cinema Abroad', in J. Murray, F. Farley and R. Stoneman (eds) Scottish Cinema Now. Cambridge: Cambridge Scholars Press, pp. 188–205.

Meir, C. (2010) '"The Heads and Tails of the Kingdom": *Mrs. Brown* and Devolutionary Scotland', *The International Review of Scottish Studies* 35, pp. 123–148.

Meir, C. (2012) 'On the Art of "Making Movies Happen": An Interview with Andrea Calderwood', *The International Journal of Scottish Film and Television*, 4 (2), pp. 51–65.

Michael, D. (2003) '*Young Adam*: Interview with Tilda Swinton' [online]. Available at www.bbc.co.uk/films/2003/09/23/tilda_swinton_young_adam_interview.shtml (accessed 22 November 2006).

Michie, A. (1986) 'Scotland: Strategies of Centralisation', in C. Barr (ed.) *All Our Yesterdays: 90 Years of British Cinema.* London: BFI, pp. 252–271.

Miller, T., N. Govil, J. McMurria and R. Maxwell (2001) *Global Hollywood.* London: BFI Publishing.

Minns, A. (2003) 'A Very Public Affair', *Screen International*, 1415, 8 August, pp. 10–11.

Monk, C. (2002) 'The British Heritage Debate Revisited', in C. Monk and A. Sargeant (eds) *British Historical Cinema.* London and New York: Routledge, pp. 176–198.

Mooney, J. (1997) 'Judi Dench Rules as Queen Victoria', *Chicago Sun-Times*, 25 July, p. 20.

Morvern Callar (2003) Directed by Lynne Ramsay [DVD]. New York: Lionsgate Films.

Mottram, J. (2004) 'In the Mood for Love', *Sight and Sound*, 14 (3), pp. 22–23.

Murray, J. (2004) 'Convents or Cowboys?: Millennial Scottish and Irish Film Industries and Imaginaries in *The Magdalene Sisters*', in K. Rockett and J. Hill (eds) *National Cinema and Beyond: Studies in Irish Film I.* Dublin: Four Courts Press, pp. 149–160.

Murray, J. (2005a) *That Thinking Feeling: A Research Guide to Scottish Cinema 1938–2004.* Edinburgh: Edinburgh College of Art and Scottish Screen.

Murray, J. (2005b) 'Kids in America? Narratives of Transatlantic Influence in 1990s Scottish Cinema', *Screen*, 46 (2), pp. 217–225.

Murray, J. (2007) 'Scotland', in M. Hjort and D. Petrie (eds) *The Cinema of Small Nations*, Bloomington and Indianapolis: Indiana University Press, pp. 76–92.

Murray, J. (2011) *Discomfort and Joy: The Cinema of Bill Forsyth.* Berlin: Peter Lang.

Murray, T. G. (2006) 'Small Voices in the Big Picture', in T. Hubbard and R. D. S. Jack (eds) *Scotland in Europe.* Amsterdam: Rodolpi, pp. 265–280.

Murray, W. J. (1984) *The Old Firm: Sectarianism, Sport and Society in Scotland.* Edinburgh: Donald.

Nairn, T. (1981) *The Break-Up of Britain: Crisis and Neo-Nationalism*, 2nd edn. London: Verso.

Nairn, T. (2000) *After Britain: New Labour and the Return of Scotland*. London: Granta.

Nash, A. (1998) 'Kailyard, Scottish Literary Criticism and the Fiction of J. M. Barrie'. Unpublished PhD Thesis, University of St Andrews.

Neely, S. (2003) 'Adapting to Change in Contemporary Scottish and Irish Culture: Fiction to Film'. Unpublished PhD Thesis, University of Glasgow.

Neely, S. (2005) 'Scotland, Heritage and Devolving British Cinema', *Screen*, 46 (2), pp. 241–245.

Neely, S. (2008) 'Contemporary Scottish Cinema', in N. Blain and D. Hutchison (eds) *The Media in Scotland*. Edinburgh: Edinburgh University Press, pp. 151–165.

O'Brien, R. (2006) Interview with Christopher Meir, 26 August.

Ogborn, K. (2000) 'Pathways into the Industry', in R. Murphy (ed.) *British Cinema in the 1990s*. London: BFI, pp. 60–67.

O'Regan, T. (1996) *Australian National Cinema*. London: Routledge.

Orr, D. (1999) 'Young, Gifted and Scottish', *Independent*, 31 October, Features section, p. 2.

Pearce, G. (2002) 'The Naked Truth', *The Sunday Times*, 30 June. No pagination, consulted using the Factiva Database.

Pearce, G. (2003) 'She's Gone from Jarman's Art-House Muse to Hollywood Heroine', *The Sunday Times*, 17 August, Culture section, p. 4.

Penn, N. (2007) 'Whites in Africa: Kenya's Colonists in the Films *Out of Africa, Nowhere in Africa* and *White Mischief*', in V. Bickford-Smith and R. Mendelsohn (eds) *Black and White in Colour: African History on Screen*. Cape Town: Double Storey Books, pp. 167–184.

Petrie, D. (1991) *Creativity and Constraint in the British Film Industry*. Hong Kong: Macmillan.

Petrie, D. (1996) 'Peripheral Visions: Film-Making in Scotland', in W. Everett (ed.) *European Identity in Cinema*. Exeter: Intellect, pp. 93–102.

Petrie, D. (2000a) *Screening Scotland*. London: BFI.

Petrie, D. (2000b) 'The New Scottish Cinema', in M. Hjort and S. MacKenzie (eds) *Cinema and Nation*. London and New York: Routledge, pp. 153–170.

Petrie, D. (2001) 'Devolving British Cinema: The New Scottish Cinema and The European Art Film', *Cineaste*, 26 (4), pp. 55–57.

Petrie, D. (2004) *Contemporary Scottish Fictions: Film, Television and the Novel*. Edinburgh: University of Edinburgh Press.

Petrie, D. (2005a) 'Scottish Cinema: Introduction', *Screen*, 46 (2), pp. 213–216.

Petrie, D. (2005b) Email sent to Christopher Meir, 14 November.

Petrie, D. (2009) '*Screening Scotland*: A Reassessment', in Fidelma Farley, Jonathan Murray and Rod Stoneman (eds) *Scottish Cinema Now*. Newcastle: Cambridge Scholar's Press, pp. 153–170.

Pidduck, J. (2004) *Contemporary Costume Film: Space, Pace and the Past*. London: BFI.

Puttnam, D. (1997) *The Undeclared War: The Struggle for Control of the World's Film Industry*. London: HarperCollins.

Ramsay, L. and Leigh, M. (2005) 'Lynne: People Quote Your Movies at Parties. Mike: Those are Lousy Parties', *Guardian*, 4 February [online]. Available at: http://film.guardian.co.uk/interview/interviewpages/0,, 1405345,00.html (accessed 15 April 2011).

Recorded Picture Company (2003) *Young Adam* press pack. Housed at the BFI Library, London, UK.

Rees, J. (2002) 'Local Hero: An Interview with Alan Warner', *The Times*, 2 November. No pagination, consulted using the Factiva Database.

'A Review of Amin's Reign' (2006) *All Africa Global Media*, 17 November 2006. No pagination, consulted using the Factiva database.

Richards, J. (1997) *Films and British National Identity: From Dickens to Dad's Army*. Manchester and New York: Manchester University Press.

Robey, T. (2004) 'Tell Us Something We Don't Know, Ken Loach's Glaswegian Cross-Race Love Story is Passionate and Sexy but Lacking in Subtlety', *Daily Telegraph*, 17 September, p. 20.

Romney, J. (2002) 'Numb? Crazy? After Revenge? Well, it all Depends on Where You're Coming From', *Independent on Sunday*, 3 November, p. 9.

Romney, J. (2003) 'Dirty, Damp and Bone-Chilling. And Let Us Not Forget the Bowl of Custard', *Independent on Sunday*, 28 September, p. 9.

Ross, K. (1996) *Black and White Media: Black Images in Popular Film and Television*. Cambridge: Polity Press.

Sandu, S. (2003a) 'Existentialism and Messy Sex', *Daily Telegraph*, 26 September. No pagination, consulted using the Factiva Database.

Sandu, S. (2003b) 'Going Out', *The Daily Telegraph*, 27 September. No pagination, consulted using the Factiva Database.

Sarris, A. (1983) '*Local Hero*', *The Village Voice*, 22 February, p. 55.

Scannell, P. (2000) 'Public Service Broadcasting: The History of a Concept', in E. Buscombe (ed.) *British Television: A Reader*. Oxford: Oxford University Press, pp. 45–62.

The Scotsman (2007) 'What's Happened to Lynne Ramsay?', 3 February [online]. Available at: http://news.scotsman.com/topics.cfm?tid=36&id =178612007 (accessed 25 May 2007).

Scott, A. O. (2003) 'Dour Postwar Scotland Breeds a Sexy Antihero', *The New York Times*, 8 October. No pagination, consulted using the Factiva Database.

Scottish Screen (2000) National Lottery Application for *Morvern Callar*. Submitted 10 April.

Scottish Screen (2001a) National Lottery Application for *Sweet Sixteen*. Submitted 10 April.

Scottish Screen (2001b) National Lottery Application for *Young Adam*. Submitted 14 March.

Scottish Screen (2002) National Lottery Application for *Natural History* (a.k.a. *Dear Frankie*). Submitted 10 May.

Scottish Screen (2003) National Lottery Application for *Ae Fond Kiss*. Submitted 7 July.

Scottish Screen (2005) Database of Films Receiving Lottery Funds, 2000–5 [online]. Available at: www.scottishscreen.com/ (accessed 25 May 2005).

Scottish Screen (2006) *Annual Report 2005/06*. Edinburgh: The Stationery Office.

Sherzer, D. (1999) 'Race Matters and Matters of Race: Interracial Relationships and Postcolonial Films', in D. Sherzer (ed.) *Cinema, Colonialism, Postcolonialism: Perspectives from the French and Francophone Worlds*. Austin, TX: University of Texas at Austin Press, pp. 229–248.

Sillars, J. (1999) 'Drama, Devolution and Dominant Representations', in J. Stokes and A. Reading (eds) *The Media in Britain: The Current Debates and Developments*. London: Macmillan Press, pp. 246–254.

Sloman, T. (1998) 'Interview with John Madden: Shakespeare and Mrs. Brown', *British Film & TV Facilities Journal*, 11, pp. 9–12.

Slovo, R. (2012) Interview with Christopher Meir, 27 February.

Smith, M. (2002) *Trainspotting*. London: BFI.

Spicer, A. (2004) 'The Production Line: Reflections on the Role of the Film Producer in British Cinema', *The Journal of British Cinema and Television*, 1 (1), pp. 33–50.

Spicer, A., KcKenna, A. and Meir, C. (2014) *Beyond the Bottom Line*. New York: Bloomsbury, 2014.

Staiger, J. (1992) *Interpreting Films: Studies in the Historical Reception of American Cinema*. Princeton, NJ: Princeton University Press.

Steemers, J. (2004) *Selling Television: British Television in the Global Marketplace*. BFI: London.

Street, S. (2000) *British Cinema in Documents*. London: Routledge.

Street, S. (2001) *Costume and Cinema: Dress Codes in Popular Film*. London: Wallflower.

Street, S. (2002) *Transatlantic Crossings: British Feature Films in the USA*. New York and London: Continuum.

Street, S. (2009) 'New Scottish Cinema as Trans-national Cinema', in J. Murray, F. Farley and R. Stoneman (eds) *Scottish Cinema Now*. Newcastle: Cambridge Scholars Publishing, pp. 139–152.

Stringer, R. (1983) 'Soviet Ban on British Film Entry', *Daily Telegraph*, 28 June, p. 1.

Trocchi, A. (1983) *Young Adam*. London: John Calder.

Turok, I. (2003) 'Cities, Clusters and Creative Industries: The Case of Film and Television in Scotland.' *European Planning Studies*, 11 (5), pp. 549–565.

UK Film Council (n.d.) *Success Through Diversity and Inclusion*. Available online at: www.ukfilmcouncil.org.uk/usr/ukfcdownloads/37/Diversity%20Report%20FinA.pdf. (accessed 16 March 2007).

Variety.com, Box Office Database (2007) *Variety.com* [online]. Available at www.variety.com/index.asp?layout=b_o_weekend&dept=Film (last accessed 28 August 2007).

Vidal, B. (2012) *Heritage Film: Nation, Genre and Representation*, London: Wallflower Press.

Von Tunzelmann, A. (2009) 'The Last King of Scotland: Getting Away Scot-Free with Genocide', *The Guardian*, 11 June. Available online at www.theguardian.com/film/2009/jun/10/last-king-of-scotland-history (consulted 21 May 2011).

Wakefield, P. (1997) 'Here's to You, Mrs Brown', *Evening Post*, 25 September, p. 26.

Walker, Alexander (1997) 'Mrs. Brown Review', *The Evening Standard*, 13 May, p. 27.

Warner, A. (1995) *Morvern Callar*. London: Vintage.

Warner, A. (1997) *These Demented Lands*. London: Vintage.

Wayne, M. (2002) *The Politics of Contemporary European Cinema: Histories, Borders, Diasporas*. Bristol: Intellect Books.

Williams, J. (2006) 'Africa in Black and White: *The Last King of Scotland* Renews Debate about Racial Point of View', *St Louis Post-Dispatch*, 15 October 2006, p. F1.

Williams, L. R. (2002) 'Escape Artist', *Sight and Sound*, 12 (10), pp. 23–25.

Williams, L. R. (2005) *The Erotic Thriller in Contemporary Cinema*. Edinburgh: Edinburgh University Press.

Wollen, P. (1993) 'The Last New Wave: Modernism in the British Films of the Thatcher Era', in Friedman, L. (ed.) *Fires Were Started: British Cinema and Thatcherism*. London: UCL Press, pp. 35–51.

Wyatt, J. (1994) *High Concept: Movies and Marketing in Hollywood*, Austin: University of Texas Press.

Young Adam (2004) Directed by David Mackenzie [DVD]. London: Warner Brothers.

Index